World Peace in Our Time

The Logic behind Universal Creation

A novel by
Howard Dimond

Copyright © 2022 by Howard Dimond

All rights to this material work are reserved. No unauthorized reproduction or copying of this work whether in part or in full by any means may be undertaken without the express written permission and consent of the author. Reproduction of this work in any medium rests solely with the author.

Howard Dimond lives with his family in Sydney, Australia.

Publisher:
Inspiring Publishers
P.O. Box 159, Calwell, ACT Australia 2905
Email: publishaspg@gmail.com
http://www.inspiringpublishers.com

National Library of Australia Cataloguing-in-Publication entry

Author: Dimond, Howard

Title: **World Peace in Our Time:** The Logic behind Universal Creation/
   Howard Dimond

ISBN: 978-1-922792-79-2 (Print)
ISBN: 978-1-922792-80-8 (eBook)

In memory of Nicolaus Copernicus (1473–1543),
the father of modern astronomy and Galileo Galilei (1564–1642),
the father of observational astronomy among others,
who began the search for global enlightenment,
to more correctly interpret the positioning
of our planet, among Universal Forces.

In the vast heavenly, cosmological expanse,
how was our planet, originally formed?

Do we exist on a world as imagined in earlier times,
created by ancient mythology?

Or in a universe, governed by natural forces and
environmental laws?

Consider the logical evidence,
revealed inside by our researchers.

Then ask yourself if this illumination,
enriches your own view.

The longer we accept the many culturally diverse
ancient beliefs about our origins, society will remain ill-
informed and this will only continue, to divide us all.

This quest, begun by Copernicus for global enlightenment,
must continue.

In so many ways, we need to correctly interpret Nature's reality,

To heal the many divisions, created within our communities.

"The future, depends on what we do in the present."

Mahatma Gandhi

The Path to Global Peace, Happens One Step at a Time

Other books by the same author, on the continuing search for enlightenment with the adventures of Michael include:

I. Return of the Light Prince.
II. The Ascension of Mharn.
III. A Convention of Elders – A Dream Comes True.
IV. By Accident or Design – Unscrambling Newton's Code.
V. What Lies Beyond – The Quest for the Original Truth.
VI. World Peace in Our Time - The Logic behind Universal Creation

Living Trees and the Nature of Rain Forests

*They've grown tall, surviving with stamina,
since the dawning of their times.
Standing silent and resilient, weathering numerous
storms, as they climb.
Yet their future is uncertain, as their timber is often
harvested and sought.
Still, they survive enlightened from the pettiness,
of trifling human thought.*

*In giant forests, they search for sunlight,
reaching out in each other's way.
Often covered by creeping vines,
clinging to supporting branches, as they play.
Like an enormous family of natural species,
living in colors of various shades.
Yet, no smears or slurs are uttered,
as they scramble freely in the fray.*

*No spiteful cruelty or hatred among them,
about their color, race or creed.
In woodlands across the planet, they live
in unity, with character as they breed.
Never a critical word between them,
apart from the clatter, of a passing breeze.*

World Peace in Our Time: *The Logic behind Universal Creation*

*This is Nature, living in silence, with a culture of
composure and harmony.*

*For millions of years before mankind, flora and fauna,
have adorned this Earth.
Yet no naming, blaming or shaming, in our forests,
since the origin of their birth.
A staunch and unfaltering paradigm,
from the deeper waters, of our shallows.
That nations from around the world, failed
to heed this clue and lead or follow.*

*There's an unpretentious spirit, of warm personalities,
hidden in Nature's charms.
An enchantment of playful critters and fascinating
characters, having fun.
Creature's great and small, in this fertile splendor,
seeking energy heaven sent.
Ancient forests, inspiring us all, with another way to live,
to love and not to vent.*

*The meek and mild still live in hope, that one day
peace on Earth will be found.
And reasons for global hostility will be uncovered,
by searching with an open mind.
It is Nature, which fosters love and peace,
building cheerful friendships over time.
And one day Nature's inspirational visions,
will be discovered by all of human kind.*

Howard Dimond

Foreword

Embracing Natural discovery.

Ever wish you could take a major leap forward into the future and discover what the universe is really like? Nicolaus Copernicus {1473-1543} did, and yet much of the logic from his earlier discoveries, has never been revealed. Since his time, a new age of reason has begun to unfold, exposing other forces, throughout the universe.

His discoveries, showed that he was right to question ancient belief and his findings changed many of our views. Educating ourselves to better understand universal origin is not a contest between science and ancient belief. It is a struggle for open minds, to more correctly interpret cosmological reality, through research and reasoned debate.

So why did Copernicus, question ancient belief?

Many ancient civilizations, believed existence began through an imaginative creation, where after a lifetime of mixed experiences, the souls of humanity could rise up and return to an angelic utopia. This heavenly existence, on the near Earth planets, named after their ancient gods, became a celebrated mythical vision, promising an eternal afterlife, for all those followers, who kept the faith and held this belief.

Today, there still remain countless followers, dedicated to many themes, of these same ancient spiritual beliefs. The motivation for researchers like Copernicus, was to more accurately interpret, the motion and positioning of heavenly bodies.

In more modern times, the combined forces impacting on elementary matter, have given cause to question, if a unique and remarkable intelligence, did actually exist at the time of elementary origin.

There is evidence to suggest that the creation of elementary particle matter, is part of the greater universe's intelligent design.

Whatever you accept, humanity has been at war with itself, for thousands of years over many interpretations of belief and this divisiveness, is all so completely unnecessary.

In the following pages, we will share compelling new evidence, to help unravel previously held misconceptions and then you can decide, what to believe for yourself.

It is Nature's time, to be heard?

From your very first breath, to your last dying gasp of fresh air, the experience of existence, on Earth has been a natural one. Nature has laws, giving humanity a mind, which inspires us to think. Nature, does not impose its will on us. Instead, humanity has been skilled with the ability of logical reasoning, to help influence a greater insight.

For thousands of years, scholars have been searching for enlightenment, to solve the great enigmas of our times. The following answers have been found by knowing, where to look, how to look and what to look for. Above all else, please remember this, whatever your background and position in life, your choices or place of existence, we are part of an incredibly diverse living force, within a vast universal expanse.

More than ever before, it is time for humanity to be inspired with a sense of courage, to focus on future discoveries. For only a short time really, being alive, captures our uniquely shared ability, to discover, this greater enduring reality. We will always have the past, however all of humanity needs to come together now, to find a united future.

Nature's gift at birth, is one of fundamental innocence. Life begins with an innate sense of moral virtue, with a searching inquisitiveness and an enthusiasm to survive. Each newborn embarks with courage, on a path of inspired character values, sharing harmony, decency and civility. This search for answers, among the minds of all gifted creatures still endures, giving us all everlasting hope.

The true spirit, of Nature's force, inspires resolve with self-discipline to live with hope, to love and to find peace. This revered concept, hidden within the foundations of Nature's calm and peaceful existence, can help civilizations, come together once more.

What has been holding, enlightenment back?

Only an open mind can reason with itself. For centuries, questioning heavenly reality has been discouraged, as researchers faced inquisitions, with claims of heresy from Biblical scholars, protecting historical beliefs.

That was the brilliance of a doctrine of faith or principle of belief, handed down throughout the ages. Belief was given by instruction at an early age, during periods of primary, elementary and adaptive learning, when our cultural youth are taught to accept, to trust, to believe and to have faith.

From AD325, the Roman Empire inspired a united belief and faith, to influence an advancing change, while exercising control over human behavior. With sound intent, they changed the course of the preexisting brutality, into an inspiring vision for cultural civilizations, across their empire. The evidence for this is overwhelming.

In some respects, it is amazing, humanity has progressed at all. Without discoveries by Copernicus, Galileo and others, we would never have seen beyond this earlier imaginative and controlling ancient strategy. Once taught from childhood, it is almost impossible to change a made up mind. Children are being programed and conditioned to accept and believe, before they are even given a chance, to think, question and reason for themselves.

Now, a new age of reason begins.

If you were able to bring an end, to all cultural conflict and hostilities, with well-reasoned logic, **would you do it?**

If you had uncovered new research, which would enlighten humanity, with these new celestial insights, **would you share it?**

We have uncovered this new research by reexamining century's old, scientific evidence, which questions the accuracy of our established planetary beliefs on Origin. This new evidence is compelling and gives, a different view of Universal Origin. Also, please remember that elementary matter in the universe, was, originally created. What we see in the universe, what we hold, touch, taste and smell has been created.

'World Peace in Our Time' continues this exploration, to search beyond our past, of mythical beliefs. We start now with a different view, a new vision if you like, where evidence clearly shows that Nature is a silent force, throughout the universal expanse.

If it is peace you want, compassion you cherish and hope still lives in your heart, then take a moment to hear the silent mentoring and whispering sounds, found in Nature.

Enlightenment for our children, is at a cross roads.

The planetary harmony we all seek, will never be found, if our existing views remain separated, with heated and divisive disputes, over each other's ancient cultural beliefs. How are people on our planet, ever going to become enlightened or find unity as a race, when mere debate, is shut down?

A time will come when society chooses to question once more, rather than just repeat what we have been taught and told as children to believe, in one culture or another over thousands of years.

Is there anything, more important now, than a unified planetary future, bringing humanity together, which all of decency seeks?

If we can openly question this new vision, then all of our children will see, humanity advancing together. It begins though with finding unity of purpose, in the present. This sense of balance, is better understood with a logical interpretation of events.

For enlightenment to be understood, it needs to be shared, with the many levels of existing belief. So please bear with us, in our efforts to reveal this greater vision.

So to be very clear.

We believe that there are glaring inconsistencies, in the chronicled records, embedded in our ancient history. Enlightenment is not something which happened hundreds of years ago and now sits on a shelf, in a reference book library. Insight is a continuous and thought-provoking struggle, to find credible answers, for our many remaining, greater unknowns. To look at conceptual ideas differently and to discover the simplicity of existence. Not to prejudge, misconstrue or to have blind faith, in any number of tutored and instructed ancient beliefs.

The road to a greater insight, begins with an open mind, heart and soul, searching for answers to other Natural forces in the universe, which have until now remained within the realms, of the yet to be discovered.

Now is the time to reveal the original messaging, from the most fundamental and creative of all primary forces. Where inspiration is found in the most elementary of questions, as to why it is so and to better understand, how life really began on Earth?

Michael's early years

Michael's quest to explore our human origins began in earnest as a student while studying science with his lifelong friend John Bran (Oats, to his friends). Oats and Michael enjoyed a very close and enduring friendship, built around this fascination they both had, for searching through the depths of our mysterious unknowns.

Both men approached these mysteries from vastly different perspectives. Michael often thought that the only way Oats' mind was going to reach escape velocity, on the issues surrounding the cosmos, was for Oats to be more flexibly open-minded.

Oats had accepted the more traditionalist views whereas Michael had a burning desire to go beyond what we know. To explore a vision his reality could logically accept. Michael's quest became an elusive crusade, because the real answers on Earth, were harder to find.

Michael's first mission (Return of the Light Prince)

Michael, when meeting Janet was able to open up about his hopes and dreams. He discovered they both shared many common pursuits. Janet saw romance in the stars where Michael was fascinated by the complexity of the cosmos.

Janet and Michael were quickly drawn to each other and captured by the same quest. Many happy and romantic experiences, rapidly grew between them. In unusual circumstances, Michael met an elderly man named WIL who was much more than he seemed at the time.

WIL offered Michael an opportunity to follow his quest, and then Michael went back to get Janet so they could follow this quest together. Michael was soon to have a number of missions, each one more adventurous and revealing than the last.

Michael's first mission, tested his character and resolve, while proving an inspiration to an important young man named Mharn.

It was much later in life, while reminiscing about his past adventures that Michael received another visit from WIL and a chance to be of service once more. Most importantly for Michael, he found the answer to his initial quest in this first mission, that Darwin's theory was completely incorrect; that there was indeed another, less obvious and much simpler answer to the origins of mankind on Earth.

Now Michaels mind became rich with more queries, where each answer gained, gave him an infinite number of further questions to follow. After his first mission the excitement for him continued.

Michael's second mission (The Ascension of Mharn)

Michael's second mission quest, spread beyond planetary evolution. The basis of his passion and desire to return was this. Knowing how life started on Earth was one thing, but how did it start in the galaxy? The more Michael thought about it, the more urgent this ongoing quest became, because for him, what we have in the cosmos doesn't seem to be an accident. Michael's second mission brought him even closer to these answers. The 'Big Bang' Theory for Michael lacked plausibility and became discredited. While his amazement at the complicated universal architecture of the cosmos continued, Michael found that in science, there was never just one 'Big Bang'.

Those who understand gravity and have experience of explosive matter in a vacuum can work this out. The pattern structure of the cosmos for those who study it closely, know that the complex composition of particle matter is symptomatic of a much more orchestrated beginning. While the universe for Michael did not appear to be an accident and did not result from one 'Big Bang' it is equally of a design, expanse and magnitude, Michael did not fully understand, or comprehend yet.

Michael's third mission
(A Convention of Elders - A Dream Comes True)

Having rescued his old friend Oats, Michael's new mission was to examine the comprehensive dynamics of this galaxy, to a greater degree; not only the structure but its cultural diversity. For Michael and Oats particularly, this was just fascinating as they struggled for clarification and their own enlightenment.

On the outer reaches of the Kindred Spirits system, existed the most distant planet of Troth. Forgotten by many and neglected by most these clans peoples time for cultural reform, had finally come. This was when Michael, Janet and Oats met with Aiden again.

Aiden was an elder from the poorer clan classes, who with limited opportunity, could see a vision of unity for his people bigger than his own, which almost everyone could accept. The heartbroken and exploited among Aiden's poorer clan's peoples, had many shattered dreams.

Michael found that they needed guidance to understand their choices, as the ruling classes had a vested interest, to do everything they could to dumb down, this poorer society. These weaker clans, had battled and struggled throughout history, facing a wall of exploitation as a result of their ignorance.

This then became the foundation of Michael's new mission. To help bring a society back from the abyss, which they had all been allowed to fall into. Despite this, the citizens on Troth were an intellectually gifted race. To understand how superior intellects fashion mind sharing was important for Michael's future missions.

With the aid of Janet, the ancients through Pim and Mharn's network of friends Michael strived to see if this civilization could face the never-ending challenge, to find a harmonious existence.

A growing part of this process was the closer involvement of Michael's great friend Oats. As a rejuvenated romantic, Oats found passion and companionship with Aiden's tantalizingly beautiful niece, Marmuron. This provided many happy moments with continuing revelations as a new love blossomed and flourished between the two of them.

This developing romance afforded a lighter note, to the more serious plight, that many of Marmuron's clans' people had found themselves in. While there have been many early successes, Michael's mission challenges now continued.

Michael's fourth mission (By Accident or Design – Unscrambling Newton's Code)

This mission is one of Michael's most enlightening experiences yet encountered. Sometimes a view from afar, looking back at our history gives us a better perspective. Evidence would soon show that our evolutionary theories on Earth are parochial, ill-conceived and flawed. However their mission began a little earlier.

Michael was still celebrating the 'Union of Companionship' between his great friend Oats and the beautiful and remarkably gifted Marmuron. During the closing stages of their celebration, both Michael and Oats discovered further insights into the secrets about the complex issues of gravity and motion. Munkhan, an intellectually gifted and brilliant galaxy historian, helped Oats and Michael revisit the early study of the simplicity of these two great forces and in doing so they discovered a third.

Following a private briefing from the ancient Council of First Kings, Michael finds himself confronted with a reality of the dynamics, within the universe. This briefing exposes a previously unforeseen and now more serious side, to their mission.

World Peace in Our Time: *The Logic behind Universal Creation*

Evolutionary research from Charles Darwin was pioneering in his time. However his flawed theories have led to some serious and unintended consequences. Michael and Oats discovered that racial intolerance was a regrettable outcome from this theory. The theory created groundless speculation which continues to hamper world peace today.

Armed with this knowledge of racisms origins, Michael's new mission objectives became clear. During this mission, Munkhan a galaxy historian, helped to peel back even more of our planet's early history, including reviewing the early times of Isaac Newton.

Michael and Oats also discovered that some implications, from Copernicus's discoveries were casually overlooked. Important findings have been obscured and concealed throughout history ever since. Michael became even more motivated to return home to Earth. They believed that by helping humanities enlightenment, a rebalancing of thought would lead to finding eternal peace. With a critical analysis from Oats, they both came closer to finding more compelling answers about our origins.

The progress of the new animal sanctuary on the planet of Pimeron is one of their major mission objectives. It will lead to a better understanding of the other forces in the universe. Uri, the exquisitely gorgeous and sensitive keeper of the picturesque animal welfare shelter, on the planet of Candon, leads this effort.

Michael's developing quest takes him into Earth's past Renaissance period. The deeper they searched, the more fascinating our history became and together, their adventures and challenges continued.

Michael's fifth mission
(What lies Beyond – The Quest for Original Truth)

Michael and Oats' continued search for original truth began, at the turning point in our history when Nicolaus Copernicus discovered that we are a solar system rather than what was previously believed as Earth being at the center of the Heavens.

However, the power to suppress original thought was not new. Opposing any changes in belief, using the influences of ridicule, scorn, and derision still exists today. Michael and Oats were determined to get genuine answers they could trust because attempting to understand our greater universal expanse has been confined to parochial debates for centuries.

They wanted reliable and decisive explanations that would help them understand why people on Earth were not living in peace. A skillfully reconstructed existence regression unearthed the innocence of what an educated society has been taught for centuries, while faith in the future of mankind's age of inspiration and enlightenment is restored and returned to humanity once more.

The more they learned, the more intense their quest became, for more answers.

Michael's sixth mission (World Peace in Our Time. – The Logic behind Universal Creation)

Michael and Oats have uncovered a slightly different interpretation of Origin. Are there still many remaining unknowns? Of course there are, however this is a puzzle with many doors to unlock. The first keys were found by Copernicus and Galileo among others. Our researchers have uncovered, some more of these critical keys.

Nature has deemed that eternal hope, can never be beaten, crushed or taken away and that a legacy of character strengths, outlives the most combative of empires.

Humanities, given intellectual resourcefulness, shows we are not born to believe. We are born to think and to question, to observe and discover, to investigate and explore and to find answers, giving humanity enlightenment. It is time to re-engage with the perceptiveness of reality, to build for global peace and to find what unites us, rather than focusing on the anxieties which divide us. Life, as seen through the eyes of Nature, is a much happier place, if we just search for it. **Yes, our recorded history has been embellished and does not make logical sense.**

Let us now rejoin our researchers Michael and Oats, in their thrilling quest, to unlock this new visionary evidence, which has been concealed, for thousands of years, since our earliest of ancient times. Come with us once more, as our researchers uncover more answers to questions, of how did life begin and are we alone in the universe?

System of Kindred Spirits

The system of Kindred Spirits (K.S.) is the home of the galaxy's ancient world. WIL is the spirit leader of this system. From the plane of galaxy rotation with an elevated side view, K.S. can be found at galaxy level 1546, quadrant 2, System 523, Planet 0. What this means is that K.S. is almost unique in that it does not have its own central star.

Our adventures with Michael and Oats have so far taken us to Kendagon, the sixth planet of eleven orbiting bodies around K.S. Michael's missions have also visited the outer planets of Candon and Pimeron (formerly Troth). Other nearby system planets that have added to Michael's adventures include the planets of Gena and Giant Vines in the nearby Lodan System.

Pim

Pim is a gorgeous historic ancient spiritual creature and remains Michael's guiding counsel on WIL's ship, the Corillion. Pim first appeared to Michael as a beautiful feminine, glistening image. In earlier times, our researchers had no idea about ancients (those with a past life) and they found Pim, as an ancient was able to form both as an image and sometimes as a mortal physical presence. Pim has phenomenal warmth and sensitivity which became more evident as she gradually let our adventurers into the closeness, of her past life. Each moment of their missions, which Janet and Michael shared with Pim, gave them an infinitely better understanding of their challenges.

No concept was too difficult and no question was left unanswered. Pim was filled with an enriching diversity of character values and a compassionate understanding for life's complexity, which is essential in the universe of evolving and developing life forms.

The Corillion

The Corillion is WIL's intergalactic ship. In every respect it was magnificent. Michael's favorite place was the Map Room which contained a mind reading image. It functioned from your thought processes, to find the answers to all of your questions.

In each suite there was the Image of resolution (I.R.). A medium formed as a disc which when stood on, lit up like a glistening transparent image, before it transported you to your next destination. The most magnificent of all was the Clean Beam. It was here you could simply clean and change or renew to your previously recorded physical life force, from an earlier age.

The Candon Group of Six Friends

Mharn, Herron and Kendu are three recent graduates from the Music Academy of Higher Learning on Kendagon, where they studied the four truths of self-interest. They are also extremely capable and successful sportsmen.

Their three companion friends add warmth and diversity. Karina comes from the largest province known as the Kingdom of the Voices. Arkina comes from the fascinating province of Desolate Plains and Mountain Caves while Urundayy (Uri) comes from the most beautiful of all, the Ancient Forests province. The three girls are the first born, hereditary members of their clans, trained from infancy and had been chosen for the timely duty and obligation of clan leadership.

All six became close friends while learning to confide in each other as their responsibilities and obligations grew. They would form the future leadership group of these three massive provinces on Candon. Their help to Michael, Oats, Janet and Marmuron would be invaluable.

Table of Content

1. Karina's Emerging Dilemma..23
2. Some Limitations of Parochial Beliefs...................................30
3. Fond Memories for Absent Friends......................................35
4. Natural Forces, Influencing Marmuron..................................43
5. An Impossible Dream..48
6. The Eternal Compassion Found in Motherhood....................52
7. Uri's Tender Encounter with the Natural Force....................61
8. Help From another Close Friend...69
9. Our Evolving Plans..72
10. Memories from Shi's Past..76
11. A Meeting with WIL..82
12. A Nervous Start to a Dream..88
13. Understanding the Clean Beam..94
14. A Galvanizing Change in Plans...100
15. Early History between Karina and Mharn..........................104
16. So, what's our Quest, Oatsy?..109
17. Understanding the Natural Force.....................................113
18. Key to Unraveling, Earth's Recorded History....................119
19. How did Mythology, become Established on Earth?...........128
20. Why was Copernicus, a Wasted Opportunity?...................134
21. The Continuation of Greatness, in Rome's Empire.............140
22. The Preservation of Rome's Greatness.............................147
23. Mythology of Biblical Proportions....................................152
24. The Narrative of 'The One True God'................................159
25. The Creation of Institutionalized Belief............................163
26. Because, 'It Is Written'..176
27. The Return of Enlightenment...187

World Peace in Our Time: *The Logic behind Universal Creation*

28. Why Earth's Parochialism, isn't Logical? 196
29. How does Tamaryn's Society, see Natural Law? 204
30. Early Reunion with Mharn. 211
31. What is Nature Trying to Teach Us? 218
32. The Inspiration, in Nature's Silent Messaging? 227
33. Begin with an Uncluttered Mind. 232
34. The Reappearance of Tamaryn's Aide. 236
35. Nature's Illuminating Laws, on Order and Morality. 240
36. Prisium, a Land of Botanical Treasures. 247
37. Velia, a Maiden in Nature's Forest. 254
38. Mharn's Evolving Mission, Unfolds. 260
39. Marmuron's Moment of Illumination. 268
40. The Frontiers of Enlightenment. 276
41. Questions for the Future. 282
42. Nature's Four Truths of Self-Interest. 287
43. Visions of Natural Serenity. 292
44. Natures Illuminating Vulnerabilities. 296
45. Long Voyage Home for Karina. 302
46. The Universe of Silent Forces. 306
47. A Welcome Surprise for Karina. 311
48. Revelations from Munkhan. 317
49. Student Program to be Trialed in our Galaxy. 323
50. Discovering, World Peace in Our Time. 327

References

I. Origins of Manuscripts, Compiled in the Holy Bible. 337
II. The History of Religious Inquisitions. 343
III. What else was discovered from Galileo's time? 346
IV. The Lasting Influences of the Roman Empire. 347
V. True Insanity of War and Persecution, over Centuries. 348
VI. Mythologies and Legends, in the Search for Truth. 349
VII. Please consider the following logic, for a moment. 353
VIII. Some Challenges to Aspects of Religious History. 354
IX. The Origin of the Species, in the Universe. 357

1
Karina's Emerging Dilemma.

Planet of Pimeron, System of Kindred Spirits.

Almost lost among the aged trees and autumn colors, Michael and his great friend Oats remained hidden, within these stunning natural surroundings, from the distant mountain ranges beyond. They could feel a gently building warm summer breeze, coming through the forest which bordered Oats's hidden alpine cabin. Oats loved this view from his back veranda, under the stars. The evening skyline stood, as a timeless and peaceful panorama. The heavens were an eternity, filled with the mystery and promise, of millions of yet to be discovered, intriguing destinations.

In this wonderful natural ambiance, Oats had been reflecting on the excitement of their continuing discoveries and those, yet to come. Their good friend Munkhan had recently left to go on the first thrilling mission to Tamaryn's galaxy and Michael and Oats were making plans to follow, soon after. As a galaxy historian, Munkhan had previously challenged Oats to reevaluate his planetary past and now the friends, were both reconsidering this earlier meeting.

Oats remembered. 'It was Munkhan who first motivated us to reassess our understanding of Natural Forces on Earth and challenged us, to review the unfolding logic, of our planets past history.'

Michael smiled 'Yes, Newton's apple falling from a tree. I remember, it was at your union of companionship with Marmuron. What made you think about this, Oats?'

Oats seemed much more convinced now, as new pieces of the puzzle began to fall into place for him. 'Much of the discoveries surrounding Natural Forces were hidden in Newton's time, because of the repressive jurisdictions, protecting ancient mythology.'

Michael was intrigued. 'So where do we go from here, Oats?'

Oats was overcome. 'This is our final frontier Michael. A chance to see for ourselves the architecture and complexity of the universes, natural forces. We are on a mission, searching for evidence to find answers, which make logical sense.'

Michael asked. 'Yes, how is it possible for the hundreds of thousands of species we have on Earth, to have evolved from one cell, when evolution of the species, gives back a blended inheritance? The single celled organism hypotheses, advanced by Darwin, doesn't make logical sense. Also there's little evidence of existence on Earth, beyond several million years ago, apart from fossilized skeletal remains. With all the species we have on our planet, I still believe this question, is yet to be fully answered or resolved.'

Oats had a beaming smile. 'Yes, we are going to find out these answers. We live at a time when an open mind, wants logical answers. This is our chance to find new evidence, behind origin and evolution, within our universe. A time, when all of humanity, will be able to move forward and find global peace and unity together, once more.'

As Oats paused, Michael grinned. Before coming on these quests, the closest romance in Oats life, had been a box of old rock samples, he kept in his study. Oh, and he use to get all excited, about some old fossils placed carefully, on one of the display cabinets in his home.

In more recent times, Oats was swept off his feet when he discovered the mesmerizing charms, of his beautiful Marmuron. It was easy to see, how he became so completely distracted. For as clever and quick witted as Oats was, he just softened in the adoring arms of his beautiful Marmuron. She brought a new sense of cheer, into his life.

Marmuron transformed Oats' social outlook, from the more analytical and logical, to a personality full of social inclusiveness and he loved her for it. Oats was becoming amused. He was still reflecting on Marmuron's inspired sense of belonging. Her happy disposition grew, when she recently claimed that this was her quest as well. Marmuron was thrilled for this chance, to go and visit Tamaryn's home galaxy.

Oats suddenly grinned and Michael asked. 'What are you so cheery about Oats?'

Oats's sense of calm turned to excitement. 'We are on the threshold of something really big, I can feel it.' Oats, became philosophically engaged. 'It might sound silly, but have you ever noticed out here, how some natural environments, don't quarrel with themselves? Trees don't argue with each other, over anything at all.'

Michael agreed. 'Yes, it is very pleasant and peaceful out here, just like a chirping melody, of musical sounds.'

Oats' attention, was temporarily refocused on their companions inside. 'We need to involve Janet and Marmuron more and the sooner the better.'

Janet and Marmuron were in high spirits as they sprinted around inside, from one room to the next, chatting happily to each other. It was as though they were packing to go away somewhere. Marmuron was overjoyed for this chance to be more closely involved and Oats just melted like a warming marshmallow, as he folded and agreed to her request to work more closely.

Janet came out through the back door. 'Something has enlivened Marmuron, Oats. She just can't wait to get going.'

Oats glanced at Marmuron and suddenly their eyes met through a large picture window. Marmuron could see Oats's childlike, sheepish eyes, smiling fondly at her. She rushed out to hug him lovingly, once more. Marmuron was gorgeous and she lifted Oats' spirits enormously. Janet heard an incoming image transfer and left them to go back inside and soon Marmuron followed Janet, with a fleeting. 'I love you, Oatsy.'

Marmuron blew Oats another kiss through the window as she followed the voices of a building conversation inside. It was Karina from the nearby planet of Candon.

Karina's smaller, three dimensional image had formed quickly, in front of Janet and as Marmuron entered, she overheard Janet already engaged, in a friendly chat.

Janet queried. 'Are you sure Karina?'

Karina seemed happy and a little uncertain. 'Yes, I guess so.'

Janet began probing a little further. 'When did you find out?'

'Just recently. I didn't know who else to talk to. I'm just not sure what to do next.'

Janet seemed puzzled. 'So, Uri and Arkina don't know yet?'

'No, I was worried it might get back to Mharn, before I had a chance to tell him.'

Janet mumbled in surprise. 'So Mharn doesn't know either?'

'No' and then 'I'm not sure whether to tell him so soon into his mission.' As Karina paused she had noticed Marmuron coming in next to Janet. She waved as they exchanged greetings and then Karina asked. 'Janet, can you both keep this between the three of us until I know what to do next?'

'Yes, yes of course.' Janet agreed and then. 'Maybe Mharn's mother San would be able to give you a more experienced perspective, with some of her kindhearted support. It could be helpful, contacting her first.'

Karina's face lit up instantly, at this suggestion. 'Yes, that's a brilliant idea. Thank you Janet.' After a considered pause. 'I'll arrange to see her next. She'll know what to do.' Karina seemed genuinely confused and then said. 'It's just that I know Mharn has been looking forward to this mission to Tamaryn's Galaxy, so much and it is such an honor for him. I don't want to spoil it for him just now, before they've even arrived.'

Janet was reassuring. 'You're going to have to tell him at some stage.' Then more caringly. 'See what San has to say first and then you can decide.'

Karina was still in deep thought. 'Yes, thank you for your support Janet. You are a good friend.'

Janet added. 'Don't forget, although not planned, this is still good news.'

Karina smiled back warmly. 'Yes, yes of course it is. We'll talk again soon.'

'Bye Karina.' And as Karina's three dimensional image vanished, Janet and Marmuron went into a closer huddle to discuss the impact of these changing events and how this could influence, Mharn's mission.

Karina was very fortunate to have a bevy of close friends in Uri (Urundayy) and Arkina, who all grew up together. Karina's companion Mharn, began playing Ice Ball, a long time ago with Herron and Kendy (Kendu) when they were all younger students, beginning their scholarships. Since those earlier times Herron and Uri had become companions as had Arkina and Kendy. Janet suddenly remembered a talk with Mharn's father Shi and his warning about time measurement. The two friends then decided to go back outside and talk to Oats and Michael on the back veranda.

Marmuron quickly followed Janet through the back door. Oats and Michael were still chatting about Tamaryn's invitation to go and visit her immense galactic formation. Janet could tell that Oats was very excited and ready to leave at any moment.

However there were so many other sensitive considerations to reflect on.

Oats quietened as Janet approached. 'I've just had Karina on an image transfer asking about Mharn and if we'd heard anything yet.' Then, another thought occurred to Janet. 'Why don't we ask her if she would like to come on our next mission? Karina could see firsthand what it is like there and they could share, some of this experience together.'

Michael seemed perplexed. 'I wish it was that simple Janet, but the distances are immense and once arriving, well there's so much to take in and see.'

'We also have to consider how long we would be away. We all need some advice ourselves on these plans.'

This sounded too complicated for Janet who was just mulling over the compassionate considerations. 'What else, is there to plan?'

Oats then suggested. 'Some of the reasons for our own excitement are all the different life forms and elementary matter compositions. The issues are enormous. Consider also, their time-honored traditions, history and languages, their customs and routines, rules of law, their many different views on survival and existence.' Oats was winding himself up but stopped momentarily as he drew breath and returned the loving glance, coming from his beloved Marmuron.

Michael could see that Oats was just as excited, as he was nervous. 'It's true Janet. We may only get one chance at this and we need to plan and prepare for the many unforeseen possibilities.'

Oats then conceded. 'You are right Janet, there are many other humanitarian aspects to consider.'

Janet quipped. 'It's going to be fun though, isn't it Oats?' She loved finding the softer side of Oats' weighty scientific considerations with thoughtful and sometimes frivolous, lighthearted digressions. Janet then asked. 'Michael, I remember Munkhan saying he would keep in touch with you on a periodic basis.'

'It's a little early, Janet. They're all still in transit.'

Then Janet said. 'Karina was just feeling a little separated from Mharn, but she's okay.' There was plenty of building enthusiasm, for the first group of explorers travelling towards Tamaryn's galaxy, however Janet could feel some empathy for Karina's position.

Oats added. 'Missions of this type have been a very rare experience, given the distances involved, even for this advanced global society.'

2
Some Limitations of Parochial Beliefs.

They all understood Karina's concerns were founded in the length of stay away for her companion Mharn. She was concerned that he may be gone longer than originally planned. The girls then left to go back inside. It was a hectic time, with many plans afoot.

A thought suddenly occurred to Oats. 'WIL must have planned this some time ago.'

Michael then recalled one of his recent conversations with WIL. The Great Spirit often spoke to Michael in elevated tones, leaving him a little perplexed about the full meaning of what was being said. Even Oats with his identic memory had cause to reminisce and ponder on these once spoken and revered words from WIL. They both settled as this gifted sequence replayed in front of them. Michael was in the Corillion Map Room at the time, not so long ago, when WIL appeared and spoke.

'A time has come for you to move on and leave temporarily your home galaxy and discover what lies beyond. Do not fear the unknown, Michael, embrace it. As you may be aware, there will soon be another Galactic Council Conference, and there are an infinite number of experiences for us all to share. One of these areas of enlightenment is to experience exchange programs, so that we can all understand each other, a little better.'

'These exchanges lead to more peaceful relationships while seeing further diversity, in challenging an intellectual and harmonious existence.' WIL paused. 'Michael, I want you to imagine a diversity of existence, beyond anything you have ever known before.'

Oats had several ideas running through his brilliant mind as we continued relaxing comfortably, on his back veranda. 'I wonder when Pim will get back to us.'

Oats's was thoughtful. 'I can tell Pim is already missing her son Mykron. Yes, Mykron and Velia will have a wonderful new future, together.'

Michael added. 'True, however they're going to be in the next galaxy. Pim's worried she might not see them for some time.'

'I can share her sense of anguish.' Oats alpine lodge had been a great escape for them both to unwind and go over the difficult adjustments, from their recent research findings on Earth's history of belief.

'I don't mind telling you Oats, I am feeling a little empty at the moment.'

'Why Michael?'

'Because we're left with a bunch of issues and so many unanswered questions.'

Oats smiled as he began. 'Not quite Michael. We have been able to de-clutter the history of many parochial beliefs. This gives us a better idea of what we are looking for.' Then Oats looked a little puzzled.

'What's up Oats, you seem perplexed? Oats was often able to think on several different platforms at once. Oats expression changed, back to a thoughtful posture.

'I believe we are going to find the compelling evidence, mankind has been searching for, about the beginning of Origin.'

Now Oats had Michael's undivided attention. 'Meaning?'

'Michael, for the remainder of this quest, let's ask with simplicity these questions. What are all the known and unknown Natural Forces in the universe, trying to tell us?'

Michael was puzzled. 'Both Mykron and Pim have mentioned this before.'

'Yes, I've just realized as humans, we talk a lot and often don't listen or pick up the subtleties, in the messaging from the living Natural Force.'

'What's on your mind, Oats?'

'These forces speak to us in silence. They gesture to us in hushed, quiet and calming tones, and they are often ignored, misunderstood or misinterpreted. This has been going on for thousands of our years, while we have focused on deities and evolutionary theories. Natural Forces speak to us with immense power and gentleness, as they control the very survival of all life, as we know it.'

Then remembering some of our ancient theological teachings Michael asked. 'You don't mean the continued teaching of ancient belief that Eve evolved from Adam's rib?'

Oats laughed. 'Nature predates our existence and all of our earliest beliefs. Nature was less well understood by our forefathers, in empires from our ancient times.'

'Has something changed for you now, Oats?'

'No, that's the point. Early belief continues to be passed on down from ancient planetary cultural experiences, while learning with an open mind, continues to be stifled. Natural Forces have remained an unchanging, universal enigma from the beginning of our times.' Then as if inspired Oats remembered. 'Also something else Tamaryn said about the way her galaxy followed natural law. Their jurisdiction predates early occupation in our galaxy. Michael, it's essential we talk to Mharn's father, Ki-sun Shi again.'

Michael sensed a hint of frustration. 'Oats?'

'It's something else Marmuron said.'

Michael laughed. 'You've covered quite a bit of ground with Marmuron so far.'

'Yes and she is the sweetest most instinctive spokesperson for the Natural Force, I have met here. Have you ever noticed how many people aspire to nothing in life and hit the target with amazing accuracy?' Oats began to reflect on his discussions with Marmuron about the evolving human race on Earth.

'In what way Oats?'

'Michael, just consider this. Since the publication of Darwin's flawed theory on the evolution of mankind, history has been full of examples, where humanity has unfairly poured scorn, on other less well educated cultural classes. While we waste our time, with this racial rubbish, we are learning nothing.'

Michael queried. 'So how did Marmuron help this conversation?'

Oats then remembered. 'It's in the silliness of our humanity. Alligators don't question, criticize or delegitimize crocodiles, for being foul, smelly, obnoxious or disagreeable. There's never any disputes between them over any color differences. Or what they believe in, or being just plain ugly or unfriendly. Do you ever see a baboon or a chimpanzee argue over their looks, color or class differences, their divisions or beliefs?'

Michael was reflective. 'Wow, yes, we really do look like the silly ones, don't we?'

Oats continued. 'Humanity on Earth will never discover its true roots, while we dwell on these nonsensical comparisons with biased correctness, as many have done, in our past. While we waste our time as a race, worrying about this kind of foolishness, we will never understand the unique, incomparable and remarkable design in the universe which is Nature's home. We are supposed to be the smart ones, Michael. We've lost time for centuries now, wasted on spurious quarrels over trivial irrelevancies.

Our history of trifling debates, over human origins and color differences, has been self-destructive.'

Michael sympathized. 'I agree Oats, but now it's time for us to move on.'

Oats had to get this last point out. 'Our humanity still struggles with itself and quarrels over tribal rituals and ancient beliefs on Earth, when we could be so much more effectively engaged.' Oats began to see with Marmuron's help, a more elevated view of the Natural Force when viewed against the weakening of our humanity's struggling global advancement. 'The folly, which our race has put its intellectual advancement through, has been acrimonious, unpleasant, disruptive and divisive.'

Michael agreed. 'Marmuron has really got you thinking.' Then 'Don't spend any more time worrying about all this, Oats. We have so many more positive encounters to look forward to.' It was a happy thought finish on.

3
Fond Memories for Absent Friends.

Amphitheater on the Planet of Kendagon, System of Kindred Spirits.

WIL's image suddenly reappeared and stood alone. He smiled with fond memories at his favorite place of solitude and he was in a happy, reflective mood. WIL was on a great quest of his own now. His cause was a truly grand one, for in the history of great causes, none ranked above the unrelenting search for the true meaning of life and its peaceful balance, within our natural co-existence.

It was due to this search for true character and quality in life that WIL met recently with some celebrated minds to question, if something had been overlooked. Was there a piece to this larger puzzle in Nature's Force, which had not been considered? It seemed to be an elementary contradiction that Nature was a powerful living force and yet at the same time animal classes are born with so many defenseless vulnerabilities. This was evident in the necessary caring nature, of nurturing, undertaken by so many species.

For as long as WIL could remember, this enormous amphitheater had become a place for unifying the spirit, of the human soul. Many advanced societies from diverse cultural backgrounds, had met here regularly and these truly great minds connected, to lift the hopes of civilization. WIL had watched, as his old friend Mykron, left on an indefinite mission to another nearby galaxy and this place retained nostalgic value.

Now, the foreground lay deserted and all the swirling masses, of engaging spirit activity had vanished. Tamaryn, the ancient and gifted oracle, would once again reconvene these welcoming reunions, from her own galaxy. Mykron, was now on Tamaryn's ship, with his new love Velia, returning to her homeland galaxy.

While this was the last gathering to be held, in this galaxy's cosmic region, WIL had many great plans, which were unfolding. The change of venue to Tamaryn's galaxy had been a brilliantly conceived and implemented choice.

Tamaryn, was instinctively brilliant and it was her guidance, which had inspired WIL. She advised, how we respond to the Natural Force defines who we are, our character, what we stand for and the future we leave behind. In this search for answers, civilizations must decide not only how they want to live, but also how we all survive.

Tamaryn was a treasured oracle and revealed a unique and positive way forward. Her ancient societies perspective on achieving natural balance, laid the groundwork for this insightful future change in direction. An advanced gathering of minds were now motivated, to build, on this broader understanding.

The desire to appreciate each other's cultures in growing friendship, was also strong among them. The most touching moments were found, when leaders chose to continue regular contact, by participating in future galaxy exchanges.

WIL smiled as he remembered his first meeting with Michael, who would now play an increasingly important part in WIL's future plans. In previous missions, Michael had been helped by Pim to gain an elevated cosmic view, exposing the inconsistencies in Earth's history of parochial records. Michael and Oats with Janet and Marmuron had loved these enlightening experiences. Now,

Michael and Oats in their quest for more answers, would soon gain an elevated perspective, on the vast history of universal origin.

As WIL's plans were still unfolding, his attention was being drawn to another image appearing in the amphitheater, some distance away. It was the beautiful, youthful and angelic spirit image of Pim. WIL knew, she would also be missing her son Mykron.

Pim cast a forlorn and lonely shadow of a figure, as her image continued to form. Her feminine heart was still a sensitive and tender place, as only mothers know. It seemed only a short time ago, since the myriad of visitors and envoys had left, however this giant amphitheater remained a treasured place, for Pim as well.

This was the third time Pim had returned here recently and she was now reliving her precious past experiences again. Pim had witnessed her son Mykron's mortality being miraculously renewed, on WIL's nearby primal planet of Giant Vines.

In a moment of reflection, this enchanting and virtuous creature, sat with a heartwarming smile on her face. Her building sense of fulfilling happiness, came from the well-known sacrifices she had made, in her own life so far.

This celebrated meeting place for unique minds from other nearby galaxies was now over and for Pim at least, her future felt a little uncertain. Mykron was one of a hundred delegates, departing on Tamaryn's ship, back to Tamaryn's nearby galaxy.

Now, Mykron would be able to recapture the innocence of his lost youth, once more. These treasured thoughts for Pim, came as she contemplated how her own life was about to change. She had felt cheered on and exhilarated at the time, in conversations between her mother Candolina and the revered oracle, Tamaryn.

Before leaving, Mykron and his new companion Velia had shared some warm and cherished moments at Benlay with Pim and it was this experience that was closest to her heart now. This moment of reflection was gripping her, as she wondered when and if she would ever see them both again.

Their primary duty would be to help Tamaryn's civilization adapt, to the future organizing, of these galaxy wide cultural exchanges and each of them left with so many cheerful hopes and dreams. Pim strolled around warmly with charged emotions on the site where she had last met the revered oracle Tamaryn. During the recent celebrations on Kendagon, the oracle had opened Pim's eyes to so many newer concepts of existence, within our greater universal expanse. These were the heartfelt memories, which would live on in Pim's mind, for some time to come.

Encouraged by Tamaryn, Pim had agreed to replace Mykron as the mediator on the Council of First Kings on the planet of Kendagon. Pim was still a little unsure of the overwhelming obligations and responsibilities, conferred on her, by this eminent position.

Soon, an ancient and sympathetic vision formed nearby. Pim called out. 'Mother!'

Candolina's image formed and immediately moved to comfort her loving daughter. 'Pim, you seem troubled and yet you have so much happiness, to look back on.'

It was true, Pim was now at the peak of a wonderful time in her history. 'When will I see Mykron again, Mother.'

Candolina said. 'We have an old friend nearby who wishes to speak with us both.' WIL, soon appeared and formed as an image. Pim and Candolina acknowledged the Great Spirit Leader, with enormous respect.

WIL smiled. 'Pim, your son Mykron is embarking on a most wonderful journey.'

Pim seemed a little uncertain as she appealed for some comforting insight. 'Can you please tell me WIL what it is like there?'

'Tamaryn's galaxy survives as a much earlier and ancient existence than our own. They abide by the most inspiring and unifying set of natural laws for shared environmental existence and self-governance.' WIL could empathize with Pim's heartfelt appeal, as he began to explain the situation a little more.

'Most of our planetary jurisdictions have civil laws, both at a provincial and regional level. By contrast Tamaryn's society realized long ago, the unspoken reality, of the universal laws of Nature.' WIL smiled as he continued. 'You will have many chances to see this for yourself, in your new position.'

Pim was momentarily heartened as though in need of reminding. She was cheerfully and pleasantly stunned. 'My new position?'

WIL began slowly. 'Yes, there are some things I would like to share with you now, that are not widely known. You need to understand what is being planned and what is currently happening. I would ask that you keep all of this, to yourself for the moment.'

'Yes WIL, yes of course.'

'Long before I first met Michael, Mharn's father Shi was sent to Tamaryn's galaxy for a very specific task. As you know, Mharn himself was a young child at the time.' As WIL spoke many images began to appear, showing WIL's first meeting with Michael on Earth. Also his offer, granted to Michael at the time, to follow his dreams of discovering the universes larger expanse.

More images appeared, showing the hardship Mharn faced, in growing up without his parents. Then the recovery of Shi from the disaster that overcame him and Shi's reunion with his son Mharn, on Michael's first mission. 'Shi was meant to return home much sooner than he did. Part of the reason for sending him there was so he could recover from this accident, you had already known about.'

'At the time Shi left, it was well known he had several adversaries and that was why Mharn was protected, in another provincial district, under adoptive care.'

Pim was visible in some of these images at Michael's first meeting, but not the earlier ones. WIL paused for Pim to consider this. 'WIL, you mentioned there was a task.'

'Yes. As you know our galaxy has been the host of these Galactic Council Conference's for several hundred generations. There had been some earlier planning for a new central location, for future conferences in another galaxy. Tamaryn's galaxy was being considered and she was very keen, to take back these responsibilities.'

'There are many developing and future obligations. This will be a vast and expansive program of recurring events, with appointments that can last for many generations to come. Understanding this, it was Shi's chosen duty to establish if and when Tamaryn's galaxy would be ready, to be the next host galaxy. Regrettably, Shi lost control of his measure of time, while he was away.'

Pim breathed. 'Now, it all becomes clearer.'

WIL continued. 'These exchanges have grown to be an enormous undertaking in an evolving process. There is scope for many more ongoing missions, between our two galaxies. Tamaryn's persuasive influence, will empower multiple civilizations to reconnect with their natural existence more peacefully. Her society is particularly adept at working with Nature's powerful forces.' WIL paused for Pim to catch up.

Pim felt a little overwhelmed with this evolving news. 'I don't quite understand my part in all of this, WIL?'

'Part of your new duties will be to help this ongoing changeover, become a reality in your influential role as mediator on our Council of First Kings. You will enjoy regular contact at many levels, to enable these continuous transfers of assignments.'

'Wow.' Breathed Pim as she suddenly realized how she would be able to see her son Mykron and Velia more regularly. Her heart lifted at the thought of being involved at an eminent level and the family reunion opportunities this would present for her. Tears began to grow in her eyes. 'Oh thank you WIL, thank you.'

Then WIL counseled her further. 'There's something else you need to know.' WIL seemed to hesitate and then. 'It's about Marmuron. As you know Tamaryn is a revered and ancient oracle. When you recently went to see Tamaryn at her mountain top residence at Benlay, Marmuron felt a strong and sudden connection with the Natural Force. The reason for this goes deep into Marmuron's ancient past. Marmuron's ancestry goes all the way back through countless generations, to Tamaryn herself.'

'Oh.' Breathed Pim.

WIL then continued. 'Tamaryn was born on her galaxy's primal planet and she has a powerful and fundamental connection, with Nature. It is not commonly known that when Tamaryn first went to the planet of Troth, as a young mortal, she was with child. As you know, all life contains essential foundations, from within elementary natural origins.

Tamaryn realized this hereditary connection with Marmuron when you were all at Benlay. Tamaryn also felt this early understanding of the history of living forces, growing within Marmuron.'

As WIL paused again, Pim thought to ask. 'Does Marmuron understand yet the depth of this connection with Tamaryn in her past?

'No, however Tamaryn has asked for our help. The transition for Marmuron will become quite rapid, once she reaches Tamaryn's primal planet. Empathy with the Natural Force has begun to impact on her perceptive consciousness and is becoming stronger.'

'These changes may cause some initial apprehension, as her mind becomes even closer to Nature. Marmuron will then discover a much deeper understanding of the messaging in the way Natural Forces evolve and progress, throughout the universe.'

Pim asked. 'Can we help her through this transition, in some way?'

'It is a beautiful evolution to behold, in becoming completely at one with Nature. The sense of disbelief, will be when she realizes the depth, of her privileged heritage with Tamaryn's primal planet.' As WIL enlightened Pim on the growing significance of this coming mission, Pim rapidly became more riveted, fascinated and engaged.

WIL then said. 'Remember, this is an evolving series of mission appointments and requires your upmost discretion and reasoned judgment. Can our council count on your discretion, to keep what you now know, in confidence?'

Pim's happy disposition softened. 'Yes WIL, yes of course. You can count on my complete discretion and support.'

WIL continued. 'Remember Pim, we are still establishing policy positions, for many other outgoing envoys and mission leaders. Your mind sharing has been elevated to level ten, to reflect the importance of your new position. No one yet to be appointed will be able to read your thoughts.'

'Thank you WIL. You can count on me.'

WIL shared a warming smile. 'I know we can Pim. You thoroughly deserve this elevation in position. We will speak again, as the need arises.' And then WIL's image just seemed to vanish into thin air.

Pim remained quiet, while digesting all of what she was just told. 'No one else knows Mother' then, as if completely shocked and stunned she repeated. 'No one else knows.' A tear formed in Candolina's eyes as well.

'I'm very proud of you Pim.' They both formed as mortals as tears of complete elation and happiness overcame them.

'I want you always to remain close to me, Mother.'

'I will Pim. I will always be nearby.'

4
Natural Forces, Influencing Marmuron.

Planet of Pimeron, System of Kindred Spirits.

Oats was still looking a little bewildered about something and so Michael took a further moment outside, to continue their chat on his back veranda. 'Oats, you seem a little preoccupied. Is everything okay?'

Oats was in two minds again. 'No, not exactly.'

'What is it then?'

'It's Marmuron. Ever since Tamaryn opened our eyes and helped us see the extent of Nature as a universal force, Marmuron's insightful outlook, has flourished and blossomed.'

Now Michael looked puzzled. 'But she is a picture of pure natural innocence.'

Oats grinned. 'Well yes, however she thinks you and I have some incredibly narrow-minded and parochial viewpoints.'

'Of course we would Oats, everyone has. It's our background and where we grew up. Everybody would be influenced by their own history. Did you talk to her?'

'Yes.' Then Oats paused. 'Tamaryn's compound in the mountain top hideaway at Benlay was like an awakening for Marmuron. Almost as though she discovered an entirely new and enlightening philosophical cultural heritage.'

'In what way, Oats?'

'Well, she's learning from it and at the same time having difficulty explaining it.'

Michael asked. 'She's not upset or anything like that.'

Oats seemed confused. 'It's more a fascination with her origins and the silent forces, which influence Nature's laws. Then out of the blue she asks me 'Do you still love me Oatsy?' Then I said 'Of course I love you.' Don't get me wrong, she's still very happy, it's just I find her views a little ahead of my own at the moment. When she recently came back from her walk in the forest, I asked her what she was looking at, and she said she just went out there to listen.'

Michael asked. 'Would it help, if we all talked about this?'

Oats replied. 'Maybe, I'm not sure where all this is coming from, just yet.'

Michael became puzzled. 'When did you first notice these changes?'

'Well, surprisingly when we were talking about Copernicus. After a while she just smiled sweetly and then went completely quiet, as though she could see through several million years of our history, hidden within the confines of Nature's Forces on Earth. Nature is a powerful living force Michael, with origins we don't fully understand yet.'

'Oats, Copernicus is not a very romantic topic, to be discussing with Marmuron.'

Oats grinned. He knew I was just jesting with him. 'It was Marmuron who helped me see those things differently, Michael. She just lights everything up for me now.'

Michael smiled. 'What brought this on, Oats?'

'Or, she's just gorgeous Michael. It's her enthusiasm and she loves my work.'

Something didn't add up. 'You mean, she loves research and the study of science?'

Oats was a happy old sausage. 'Yes, fantastic isn't it.'

Time for a little friendly sassiness. 'Does Marmuron understand our quest yet?'

'Not fully, but she's the refreshing catalyst for the energizing change we need.'

Michael with humor asked. 'Why?'

'You, Janet and me. We all come with an Earthly perspective. Marmuron will challenge us to look beyond our parochial borders.'

Then. 'We're going to need this refreshing sounding board, to find the credible answers, we are all seeking.'

Michael was curious. 'What still fascinates you about Copernicus, Oats?'

Oats became excited. 'Our planet has misinterpreted our historical analysis.' Oats paused. 'These are the enigma's I'm hoping to resolve. Some fresh input from Tamaryn will help us as well. She was brilliant in helping us interpret our early history before.'

'What is it you are hoping to learn, Oats?'

'We've spent the last five missions uncovering evidence in search of enlightenment, with considerable success. However, we could be looking at some of this the wrong way. Many on our planet still look on Nature as a local natural evolutionary phenomenon. A Darwinian evolutionary miracle. Our parochial view might be believable, but what if we have all been wrong? To appreciate the broader view, that Nature is a life force across the universe, makes our coming research mission, so much more thought-provoking.'

Michael could see Oats was still wondering how all of them working together, would play out. After all, science had been his first love. Now, he also loved his Marmuron. The thought of how his two loves in life would get along together, was causing him some confusion and some merriment, at the same time.

World Peace in Our Time: *The Logic behind Universal Creation*

Michael then said. 'Oats, beneath all the cheek and humor Janet throes up, she's exceptionally clever, when challenged. She may also give us a fresh perspective.'

Then Oats became side tracked. 'It's the way Marmuron talks about Nature, speaking to her in revered, calming and dulcet tones. It is a sensitive influence, without any condemnation, blame or criticism. There's inherent messaging of peace, calmness, tranquility and hopefulness. She is just consumed by all her life experiences. What makes her happy, is her reflection on the whole of Natural life.'

Dear old Oats, had at last found true love and companionship. Never in his past had he ever known such personal, romantic and kindhearted human warmth.

Oats continued. 'Marmuron has a greater cosmic understanding than I have. She's positively glowing with warmth and perception, about where we are going.'

This was one of the reasons why Oats, sometimes appeared to be in two minds at the same time. 'Our girl's spontaneous enthusiasm, with their heart felt affection, added fun for us all.' Oats still remembered the enchantment of her magnetic charms and the warming embrace she recently gave him. Her face just beamed with glowing emotion.

Then Oats blustered. 'Interpreting our history was easy compared to this.'

Michael laughed. 'This, meaning what?'

Oats remained puzzled. 'Marmuron's cosmic history is longer than our own. This is where Janet and Marmuron working with us, will help.'

Michael remained fascinated. 'What else did you and Marmuron discuss, Oats?'

As the girls came out, Oats said. 'Listen to her for a moment and see.'

Marmuron gazed at Oats and asked. 'What is it about Nature, you love Oatsy?'

Oats seemed stuck for a moment. 'When I look back, it's the mistakes I've made. Never once has Nature scolded me, called me out, or condemned me.'

'It reminds me of my pet dog, 'Bones', it was the first toy I gave him to play with. We were great friends as I grew up.' Marmuron looked lovingly on Oats as he dug deeper into his past childhood. 'Never a harsh word from Bones, when so many harsh words could have been said. All Bones wanted, was a kindly pat, a playful hug and some treats. A nudging cuddle now and then, with some food.'

'Nature is like that, complex, lovely and beautiful in its own right, while overlooking my faults and mistakes, almost as if I'm an adolescent, on a lifelong journey. I know Nature will outlast me.' Oats smiled. 'And I may even grow up one day. I'm a child struggling to understand the beauty, held in Nature's myriad of mixed messages. Then again I may never grow up, but I live for the wonder and fascination of these experiences.'

Janet was moved, with swelling tears. 'That is a lovely memory to have, Oats.'

Marmuron just grabbed Oats for a hug. 'We're going to grow up together, Oatsy.' Then she asked. 'When do we leave for Tamaryn's galaxy?'

Oats smiled. Marmuron was the essence of innocence and curiosity. 'Soon.' And then. 'I love you Marmy, more than you know.' Marmuron had an inspiring presence and a brilliant mind, as she looked lovingly back at her Oatsy. Marmuron blew another kiss to Oats as the girls quickly rushed back inside to finish their packing.

5
An Impossible Dream.

Oats smiled and his laugh broadened into an adoring grin. He was watching the building enthusiasm between their loving companions, as they shuffled around inside his cabin. Oats mind couldn't relax 'I wonder where Munkhan is now.'

From inside, Marmuron could hear Michael and Oats still chatting and asked, 'Why do Oatsy and Michael, both gaze out over this forest.'

Janet stopped and thought for a moment. 'It is part of their impossible dream. A dream of adventure, discovery and the loves, found in Nature's ageless character.'

Marmuron was puzzled. 'What dream?'

'It began long ago and what surprises them most, is that they are now living it. Also, they want to discover the true reasons behind universal existence, while remaining as open minded, as they can be.'

'What is it, they believe Tamaryn can help them with?'

'Their quest is to find, the intrinsic secrets, behind Nature's silent force. The laws, for compassionate moral decency and the courage, of this spirit to survive, over time and down through the ages.'

'There's an undiscovered intelligence in the universe and Michael and Oats feel inspired to learn about these origins.

Where human ignorance and weakness can be overcome with enlightenment. Also by understanding this silent force better. An open mind will bring out the best in human character, bringing our planet, peace once more.'

Marmuron questioned. 'And the forest?'

Now Janet understood. Marmuron had grown up on the dark side of Troth, with little or no life experience, in Nature's forests. 'Love, is found in Nature's culture of sharing. Nature fosters this love and the love lasts with hope forever and is built deep in our hearts. The sounds in the forest, come with compassion, in the birth of her creatures, in watching a newborn, being given life's care.'

Janet continued. 'This peace and the sounds of innocence, motivate loving parents from all species to come together, where warmhearted nurturing, is shared.'

'Nature's gifts come in silence, giving life with kindness, while sowing the seeds of love, from the start. Nature's freedom of spirit, gives us hope to stay strong. Where love, in each newborn, runs deep across the cosmos, for all creatures to share.'

Marmuron smiled. 'What hopes do Oatsy and Michael see for humanity?'

'Nature's love in the forest has passed on down through the ages. It shows the depth, to which creatures care. In defense of her young, a mother will risk everything, to protect them. In the forest, you can see this courage and spirit, everywhere.'

'Friendship and civility is built among her species in the forests and this is shown with early family respect. Nature cherishes our hopes, for peace to endure, where her forests are inspired, with many chirping musical sounds.'

Marmuron smiled. 'Have Oatsy and Michael, ever explained this dream?'

Janet then thought out aloud. 'Let's go out and ask them?'

Marmuron with her affectionate enthusiasm and innocence, quickly followed Janet back out. 'Marmuron and I were just discussing your visionary outlook, in these forests and wondered, what it meant for you both, regarding our quest.'

Oats began 'Our quest, is to find the ancient inspirational secrets, behind Nature's living force. You see there is only one enriching, natural, moral philosophy for creatures, in the universe. The laws, for compassionate moral decency and courage to survive, down through the ages and over time. This dream without question, describes the passion in our quest so far and the importance for us, in this mission to come.'

Janet smiled warmly. 'I can see why this mission, is so important for us all.'

Oats was feeling challenged. 'It's about the future of our home planet, Marmuron. Many of our people are still holding opposing beliefs, which are thousands of years old, about Origin in the universe. As you look out here, you can see acts of love and beauty everywhere, but some cultures don't seem to ever learn from it and we ask, why is it so?' We're trying to discover why Nature can get along with itself, but humanity can't?'

'Chronicled ancient history has created issues of relentless conflict, over many centuries, between various civilizations and now we, have a chance to resolve it.'

Michael felt some building empathy for the kindhearted warmth in his old friend. 'We're going to continue this journey of discovery together Oats, to follow this dream and find these answers, to regain the peace on our planet, we all seek.'

Marmuron then cheered Oats up, with her compassionate warmth. 'Don't forget us, it's our quest too, Oatsy.' Oats laughed as he recovered a little. This had become Marmuron's passion as well, to be involved and her desire to be included. Janet put her arms around Marmuron and gave her a warm hug of friendship.

'Yes Marmuron, it is our dream as well. We are all going to share it, together. We're looking for the deeper secrets in life and we haven't found them all yet.'

While Michael and Oats were preparing for their coming mission, Mharn's father, Ki-sun Shi and his companion San, were also deeply involved in these same plans. As the governing ruler of several diverse and advanced provincial domains on the planet of Kendagon, the Shi's lived in their provinces' Great Hall.

Shi had led an extraordinary life so far, filled with adventures, few in his system had ever achieved. As advanced as their society was, travel between galaxies was still seen as a rare experience. Shi had travelled this path before to Tamaryn's galaxy and he was now considering several emerging predicaments. While quietly delighted for his son Mharn's current mission to Tamaryn's galaxy, Shi was also very much aware of the issues of time loss, for all of the pioneering explorers, who left with the first group of adventurers.

6
The Eternal Compassion Found in Motherhood.

Great Hall, Planet of Kendagon, System of Kindred Spirits.

Mharn's mother San, walked purposefully into the elaborate private lounge of their extensive upper floor suite, in the Kendagon Great Hall. When she left a short time ago she was happy for her son Mharn. Now she was looking more troubled and a little distressed.

Her companion Shi, noticed this change in her mood and he asked. 'Has something happened San?'

'I've just received an imaged message from Karina who is worried she won't see Mharn again for some time. She wants to come over and talk to me about it.'

Kisun-Shi responded. 'San, they have only just arrived in the outer perimeter of Tamaryn's galaxy. There's so much for them, still to see.'

San could see a building dilemma. 'Shi, we know it is a brilliant opportunity to visit another galaxy, but remember we lost twenty one orbits of our son's life as he was growing up. I don't want to see this happen again between Mharn and Karina.'

Shi softened a little as he replied. 'All that you say is true and this is why each participant was warned about time management, before leaving.'

San was now becoming more emotional, as she could feel an impending doom, closing in on them, with this issue of lost time. 'Yes Shi, they were warned, but they all leave with such youthful exuberance, on an adventure almost no one else gets the opportunity to take. We just can't wait until it is too late, to try and rescue Mharn. He won't see this coming.'

Shi considered the emotional concerns of his beloved San. It was true they had both been thrilled for their own experiences and only realized the true life cost, when they returned twenty one orbits later. Would their son Mharn, get swept up in the same excitement, of the opportunities and the challenges there. Would he over stay his time and lose contact, as they did with their real world realities.

Was there a greater responsibility as parents, with some experience of these issues, to mediate in some way? Perhaps a timely intervention was possible, if for no other reason, than as a friendly mission, to remind them all, of time loss variations. Maybe there was a sense of balance Shi could bring, to help the others realize the cost of this opportunity in time management.

Shi relented a little. 'San, ask her to come over. At the very least we can calm her fears a little more.'

San smiled as she responded. 'I already have.'

Shi laughed as he moved to give his companion in life, a hug. 'How did you know I was going to say yes to that, San?'

San smiled. 'Because I know deep down in your heart, you're a big softy.'

Sometime later Karina was being escorted through the enormous open arched entrance and down a wide decorative corridor, to the Shi's elaborate private lounge.

'Karina has arrived Sir. Will I show her through?'

'Yes, yes of course, have her come in.' as the chamber doors opened the greetings, were very warm and friendly.

Karina smiled and said. 'Thank you both for agreeing to see me. I know this is silly, but I'm missing Mharn and was wondering if you had heard anything yet?'

San confided first. 'It's not silly at all Karina, come on over and join us.'

As the three of them settled comfortably, Shi continued. 'By our calculations, Mharn and the others, will have just arrived within the frontier boundaries of Tamaryn's galaxy.'

Karina added. 'Mharn told me he would be gone, for ten rotations of Kendagon.'

Shi quickly assessed the situation and offered this suggestion. 'Karina, would you like to stay with us overnight, until we hear from them. Then when we've heard, you may feel more reassured.'

Karina's spirits lifted a little. 'Thank you, yes I would love to.' Shi called the aide to carry Karina's small bag into the suite, where she had previously stayed with Mharn.

San quickly intervened. 'Come Karina, I will show you down to your suite.' There was a building warmth between San and Karina as they strolled together down the richly decorated internal corridors.

As they arrived San said. 'You were right to contact us Karina, but there's no reason to be concerned at this early stage.' Karina remained calm and a little relieved with several things running through her mind. San was quick to pick up on this. 'Everything will be alright my child, you will see. Have an early night's rest and we can talk in the morning, when more of these details are known.'

'Thank you San, you are very understanding.' San stood up from the side of the bed and went to walk out of the room. As she moved down the corridor something in her mind didn't seem, quite right. San knew Karina very well and anticipated she would have a happier outlook for Mharn, in this early stage of his adventure. Something was bothering San in the corridor outside and she turned to go back and then stopped and pivoted again and then waited. San then walked back to Karina's suite and could hear a muted weeping sound of distress, coming from inside. She tapped on the door to see Karina still sitting on the side of her bed, with a reddened face and evolving tears.

'Karina, what is it my child? There's something you haven't told me.'

Karina knew now, that this was her only real chance to share, her very important news. 'There is some other news.' Karina paused and then. 'And it's good news too. I only found out myself just recently.' Karina said, concealing a brave and lonely smile.

San was a loving mother herself and was quickly supportive. Many things ran through her mind as she remembered being away from her son Mharn and how Karina must be feeling, about being alone by herself at this time. Yes, Mharn was on a wonderful life changing voyage, but he must be told.

San smiled at her warmly. 'Oh Karina, really.' Then 'We must tell Mharn.'

Karina muffled. 'This is where I was hoping to get some guidance from you San. I don't have to tell him straight away and if he is only going to be away for ten rotations of Kendagon then it can wait, until he returns, can't it?' Having said that, there was a powerful and compelling question confronting them both. Mharn's parents had been to Tamaryn's galaxy before and overstayed their mission, missing out on much of Mharn's early childhood and early life experiences.

San suddenly thought out aloud. 'Oh dear, Karina'.

Then Karina said. 'I don't want him to come back early and break his wonderful mission experiences, just because he feels he has to.'

There was a growing protective maternal influence, building in San now. 'You want to carry this responsibility, all on your own, Karina?' and then 'He has a right to know.' Then 'He will want to know' then after a further thought. 'Do you believe you arrived in this condition, all on your own? Mharn loves you and.'

Karina then interrupted. 'Yes, I understand San, but do we need to tell him so soon?'

San moved to give Karina a heartwarming motherly hug. 'Oh my child, my poor child.' San was in tears now. 'Mharn is your companion in life. He would be heartbroken, if you kept this from him, while he was away.'

Karina continued. 'This is only for a little while. After all, I have only just found out myself.' Then. 'This is why I needed your guidance San. I'm not sure where to turn or what to do next.'

San considered the heartfelt concerns being raised by Karina and then on reflection said. 'Uri and Arkina are your close friends. Have you spoken to them yet?'

'Well, I have only spoken to Janet who suggested I might contact you both first, to find out, if there was any news yet.'

San smiled on Karina warmly. 'Thank you for coming to see us and for confiding in me Karina.' San paused. 'You can't keep this welcome news, locked up all by yourself. You need your friends around you now. This news needs to be celebrated. Have your night's rest now and we'll talk again in the morning.' San gave Karina a nurturing kiss on her forehead. As she left the room for the last time that night, San walked down the corridor with a great sense of purpose. She had lived through trauma, like this before and had to talk to Shi again.

As San reentered their elaborate private lounge, she was becoming distressed. 'Shi, Mharn will never get back here in ten rotations. It takes four rotations just to get there.' San had tears running down her cheeks as she added. 'We can't let the tyranny of distance destroy their lives Shi, we just can't allow it.' Shi moved with increased feelings over to give a comforting hug to his loving companion.

'Karina is with child, Shi.' Was as much as San could get out, as she blubbered with tears of emotional concern and delight.

Shi, was immediately overjoyed and delighted. However with a great measure of diplomatic experience, he was also shrewd and astute.

Shi had an ample number of highly placed friends and had already acted on San's previously felt concerns.

Shi was also very well aware of the distress caused to his son Mharn, when he grew up without them as parents. They had gone on a different mission, to the same galaxy, long ago. Shi had contacted a close friend of influence, while San was out of the room.

Shi smiled. 'An old friend will be here soon, to help placate and calm your fears.' And as Shi spoke, their galaxy's systems ambassador, Sun-Ky, appeared on a transfer medium in the corner of their ornately decorated, private lounge. Shi offered him a very warm welcome. 'Ah, you are just in time Sunny (Sun-Ky). Thank you for coming.'

San, wiping her eyes, turned quickly, as the image of Sun-Ky formed. 'Sunny, you are most welcome.'

They all quickly resettled as Sun-Ky began to speak up. 'I've only just come from a meeting with WIL. As our systems galaxy ambassador, I have been appointed to co-ordinate and control, all of our current mission objectives.'

Shi's face brightened. 'So you're going as well, Sunny?'

'Yes, no one else knows yet, however I will be joining WIL's ship with Pim, just before it leaves our galaxy.' Shi felt immediately reassured, that a friend with Sun-Ky's status and high standing, would be in a position to help direct and co-ordinate all events from Tamaryn's galaxy. If there was any need for help, then Sun-Ky would be there to help reinforce, time loss understanding and compliance. 'Let's keep this to ourselves for the moment, Shi. However I will be there to offer help, if needed.'

'Sunny, I don't want Karina to suffer. It would break her heart if Mharn was away for too long.' Sun-Ky smiled at these natural concerns coming from San. In his elevated position and being able to mind share these concerns, Sun-Ky already had an answer.

The two elder statesmen confided for a moment and then Sun-Ky asked. 'Do you believe Karina would like to go on Michael's mission to see Mharn, if this was possible?'

This was an answer to San's hopes and dreams. Her face, lit up with blissful excitement and cheer, at this suggestion. San held her hands beside her face. 'Why I believe Karina would love to go.' Somehow Sun-Ky was able to calm all the fears, expressed by San earlier on. The Shi's knew that Mharn was thrilled for this opportunity to go and remained youthfully unaware, of time management issues.

Sun-Ky thought to add. 'It would be so easy, to get caught up in the thrill of these experiences and put off coming back, till another time. For each delegate, their personal planetary visits to Tamaryn's galaxy, would be selectively different.'

Sun-Ky spoke to them both. 'We know the distances are enormous and we have become much better at managing opportunities. Voyages between galaxies is still a wonderfully new phenomenon, for our civilization. As advanced as we are, the discoveries and the marvels, of what we find, still remain unknown, to so many in our society.'

Sun-Ky paused. 'Many things have changed since your last mission to Tamaryn's galaxy. Distances are still of concern, however we are now much better prepared, for the consequences of time change variations. Both WIL and Tamaryn knew that some of these concerns would arise. That is why a compromise proposal was arranged for Michael, to take a second mission and follow, in three rotations of Kendagon.'

San was now more emotionally invested in these developing events and asked. 'Do Michael and Oats know, about all these other plans yet?'

Sun-Ky smiled back. 'The invitation from Tamaryn yes, but not all the details yet.'

San queried. 'Are there any other sensitivities and considerations?'

'Yes of course, there are several. As you know Pim's son Mykron also left with Velia to return to her home planet, in that galaxy. While some of the other one hundred delegates can afford an extended stay, several including Mharn will have to understand their choices, as these missions unfold.'

Shi asked. 'Do you know what the prearranged, schedule of events are?'

'Not all of them, but the primary obligations will be to complete the duties of council conference transfers. Many of the longer duration tasks include environmental and conservation sharing, creation of new animal shelters and scarce element recoveries. Michael's delegation could visit and bring home, some of those with shorter mission duration responsibilities.'

'As adventurer's they would see huge variations in rotation times, types of flora and fauna, the age and types of different animal species. Customs and language with differences in climate and temperature, due to distances from the solar mass. There would be variations in jurisdictional regulations, special gravity boots, for different planetary mass/density, elementary concentrations. That was before a language was known, or a word was spoken or a greeting was made, by welcoming authorities and dignitaries.'

San was elated. Soon, Mharn would have someone else to consider. Someone much younger and still in the earliest stages of development to look after and protect. Providing comfort and moral support, to his loving companion in life, would soon be his utmost consideration, among other immediate heartfelt thoughts.'

Thank you Sunny. 'Watching your companion in life, blossom into a state of motherhood, is perhaps one of the greatest of nature's given and simple pleasures. It grants a father the chance to teach guidance, in sound moral character strengths. Parenthood is one of life's most precious and powerful guiding motivations, in the evolving continuity, of moral decency.' San began to walk back down to check on Karina,

Shi then called Sun-Ky aside. 'Thank you Sunny, thank you for this. San will be so much more relieved.'

7
Uri's Tender Encounter with the Natural Force.

Ancient Forests Province, Candon Planet, System of Kindred Spirits.

Meanwhile, Urundayy (Uri), one of Karina's closest friends was facing her own life changing circumstances. Some time ago Uri and Herron arrived back from visiting Karina and Arkina. Now Uri had several things on her mind. She was comfortably seated, in the entry foyer of her clan's castle, as she began remembering some recent experiences with Herron.

Gallahant, Uri's elderly father, was wanting to pass on the responsibility, for running their provinces massive animal welfare sanctuary. This would pose an enormous responsibility on Uri, as the sheer size of this natural wonderland, covered almost the total land mass of their entire province.

Uniquely diverse animal creatures, filled the regions, as they roamed within the abundant fertile ancient forests. These drifting herds wandered, searching for food and shelter among a profusion, of colorful floral ground covers. The protective nurturing of these herds in these changing environmental conditions, would utilize most of her energy.

This generational passing of responsibility had not been entirely unexpected. There were many early accessible records dating back in their province. Each animal class had been reproducing descendants, long before her time. This subtle observation had been playing on her mind. The continuity of her family's guidance, in this province was paramount.

After all, a time would soon come when she too would have to pass on the reins of preservation and supervision, as her own time, came nearer. Uri now better understood this, as the elder of two sisters. This responsibility would fall onto her shoulders, one very painful and fateful day, when her father passed on.

Uri had recently celebrated her union of companionship with Herron and she saw him as the loving companion she needed, in this larger natural plan. Apart from being stunningly gorgeous, Uri found it easy to tempt, seduce and charm Herron. Uri knew that Herron was drawn to her physically, particularly when he held her close, while gently massaging and squeezing her buttocks.

Uri was now remembering an earlier experience with Herron, which included some playful and mischievous frolicking. She well understood how the male of the species saw the reproductive process, as more of a sensually stimulating and erotic pleasure, with their chosen female companion. However the larger natural responsibility of reproducing offspring, sometimes seemed to get lost, in the flurry and heat of the moment, for Herron.

After a moment of reflection, she smiled. The youthful exuberance and excitement of the chase, was a tantalizing and tempting moment, for her as well, to reflect back on.

Uri began to wonder if this mutual natural enthusiasm, was part of Nature's larger overall inherent plan, for the replication of the species. Perhaps it was, but tempting Herron to want to take her sexually, while staging a physical encounter, had played out in her mind.

Uri laughed out loud as she remembered how easy it had been to stimulate and arouse Herron's interest, given her seductive shapely firmness and natural feminine appeal. Herron adored her bodily magnetism and alluring charms. She knew where to take him and how their erotic love making, would play out. This recent memory continued to play out in her mind.

It had been several rotations of Kendagon since Herron and Uri had come back to her animal sanctuary on Pimeron. Once returning to her private island among the enormous aged trees and massive layers of floral undergrowth, they were completely alone. There were of course Uri's small animal friends on the island, who seemed to delight in her company and welcomed, the many visits she had previously made.

Herron had been here several times before, when Uri tempted him with her unique levels of feminine seduction. Now with building excitement, Herron was anticipating some early foreplay. However as they approached the small internal lake, near the waterfall, Uri hesitated with a mischievous grin.

At the water's edge Uri began to remove her outer clothing to finally reveal the beautiful rounds of her sensual and erotic naked form. Now covered in only the skimpiest, of under clothes, Uri turned with radiating sexual charm towards Herron, who had been passionately undressing her, faster than she could peel off her own clothes. Herron's face lit up with images of excitement, as to where this temptation may lead. He then started to remove his own clothes, however Uri didn't wait. As Herron paused to watch her, Uri was soon gone.

Within two body lengths from the sandy beach, Uri peeled off her top, while covering her full bare breasts. She then foisted the top back onto the beach with one hand, at Herron's feet. He was now having trouble undoing the rest of his clothing and became erect at the sight of this stimulating, suggestive and erotic display and the thought of what lay in front.

World Peace in Our Time: *The Logic behind Universal Creation*

Uri was absolutely gorgeous and knew exactly how to capture Herron's attention. As Uri swam further over to the gently flowing water fall, she stepped through and behind the cascading water, throwing back the bottom piece of her garment, leaving him with an image of her being completely naked.

'Wow' gulped Herron as he launched himself into the water in an effort to catch up. Uri was tantalizing and enticing in her tempting erotic display. Herron of course was now naked and rock hard as he reached through the waterfall to gently hold Uri's hand.

She laughed wildly as he pulled her tenderly through the pouring water towards him, in a rampant display of urgent desire. Herron turned her around and pulled her back as he rested his throbbing muscular expansion between her beautifully formed, rounded cheeks. Herron then pushed his hands between her arms from behind to gently cup her firm rounded breasts in the palms of his hands. Uri bent down further arching her back and fully exposing her beautifully rounded buttocks, for Herron's immediate pleasure.

Herron gently rubbed the palms of his hands all over her cheeks and then held her hand, lifting her back up. As the cascading water poured down on them both, Herron turned her around again to face him and kissed her beautiful, happy smiling face.

This was the moment Herron had been waiting for, as he lifted Uri up by her beautifully rounded cheeks to hug him. She quickly wrapped her legs around his waist and he placed his throbbing muscular expansion between them. Her soft warm tissue felt the exhilarating thrill of fervent excitement as Herron's massive, throbbing and thrusting expansion entered her.

He gently pushed himself deeper, as she began to breathe more heavily with each passing moment of groaning pleasure. Herron now thrust more purposefully, as he held Uri's cheeks to pull himself in, as deep as his throbbing expansion could reach.

Uri sighed heavily again with increasing pleasure, as this tantalizing desire, was now taking its natural course.

Herron continued to thrust himself deeper and deeper, with unrelenting pounding passion giving a throbbing climax, of lasting pleasure. Herron couldn't hold back any longer as he came, again and again and again. Uri felt this throbbing, pulsating, exploding mass inside her.

Herron's urgent desire was still gripping Uri, by her firmly rounded buttocks, as her beautifully shaped cheeks began to relax. She grinned with sensual pleasure, as she stood up in the loving arms of her adored Herron. He held Uri securely, pulling her close, while her warm rounded breasts, pressed firmly onto his chest. A loving smile was worth a thousand words, as he ran his adventurous hands, all over the magnificent rounds, of her beautiful form.

Herron whispered passionately in her ear. 'You're absolutely gorgeous.'

She responded lovingly. 'You're absolutely enormous.' This only served to give Herron the encouragement he needed to find his second burst of energy.

Uri took off and swam around to cool down, before leaving the water as she lay on the soft grass, under several large shaded trees.

Herron laughed as he caught up. 'You knew I'd follow here, didn't you? She rolled away giggling, as Herron lay down next to her, once more. There were moments of warm touching and sharing pleasures before she gestured, opening up to him once more. Herron moved in between her and Uri immediately wrapped her legs around Herron's waist again as his strengthening muscular expansion, grew firmer, with throbbing pleasure and desire.

He held her buttocks in the palms of his hands while massaging her body. He then thrust himself gently into her once more, pushing further and deeper inside her fleshly form. He held her close, as he began to satisfy, his urgent throbbing needs. The raw animal passions between them were intensifying again, as Herron thrust himself again and again, finally bringing a muffled whimper of pure pleasure from Uri's lips. She became tense and rigid, clinging onto him tightly, while sensing another, thrusting explosive gush coming.

Unable to hold back any longer, Herron exploded again and again once more, deep inside her, until he was completely spent. Uri felt her primal urges completely satisfied with this passionate seduction. There was an early experience of maternal desire, building slowly within her. **She began to wonder if this thrill of the moment, was part of the creative force, within Nature's Universe.**

How else would animal life continue, without this emotionally charged, sensitive and passionate bonding between consenting adults? The mutually erotic desire, giving an incentive to reproduce, between both the males and females of the species, must surely be part of Natures design? Uri saw herself as just one small part, among many life forms, in this miracle of life.

As they uncoupled and swam around playfully together in the pond, Uri paused just for a moment and held her abdominal region with warm maternal affection, as an inner glow swept across her face. It was only a fleeting sensation, but she felt certain this was the beginning, of a completely new experience for her.

The process of creating and building the next generation of her family, had now begun. As a gentle Natural Force, Uri could see evidence of Nature's presence everywhere, within her provinces' larger open sanctuary.

Uri and Herron had remained hidden for some time beneath the dense floral undergrowth on their private island. They decided to return to her father's grand fortress in the distant Highlands Game Reserve. This ancient castle, in the upper Cold Mountain Country offered greater protection, for the provinces many clan's people. The natives were trained from infancy to protect the larger animals, in this vast and friendly sanctuary. With her memories coming back to the present, Uri had arrived back at the castle, from these times with Herron.

As Uri's mind came back to the present, Varrek, her father's trusted head clansman, came over with some urgent information. 'Your father has asked me to let you know of an incoming imaged transfer, which has been stored for you.'

'Did he say who it was from, Varrek?'

'Yes Miss. It was from Miss Karina from the Kingdom of the Voices province.'

'Thank you, Varrek.' Varrek nodded with respect and then left. Uri then turned to Herron. 'This could be important. I'd better go and see father.'

Herron gave her a quick hug of support. 'I'll be here, when you get back.' And as Uri walked briskly away, Herron sat down, recalling the recent loving times they shared together.

As he had a moment to reflect on this, he was reminded of their previous erotic physical encounters on the nearby planet of Pimeron. He laughed as he remembered the two bulls, head butting each other for the right to inseminate the nearby female, of their species.

Herron had experienced these same primal urges, which had stimulated the bulls. He had a blossoming union with Uri and she knew how to thrill and stimulate, his natural sexual desires. Herron chuckled quietly to himself. He could tell by just holding her hand and sensing her alluring charms, that he was captivated by Uri.

Uri was stunningly gorgeous and adorable. He was mesmerized by her feminine appeal and now he began to wonder if there was a greater underlying and evolving purpose here as well. Deep down, Herron understood that one day, the strong bonds of their union would support the creation of children and when it happened, he would be ready.

However with his youthful mind and his innocent pent up urges, reproduction was the furthest thing from his mind at the moment. Then again, apart from his own acquired self-control, there didn't seem to be any personal control, over these deeply rooted and emotionally driven basic urges. As an animal class, it was as if he was part of an innate and instinctive, greater Natural Force, controlling the reproduction of life, within him.

Although Herron had been temporarily focused on his youthful vigor and energy, he had warm feelings for his union of companionship with Uri. There were many wonderful plans they shared together, in a loving friendship, for life's journey ahead.

It only seemed a moment, when Uri quickly came back to find Herron.

She smiled at him. 'Come, we need to talk to Karina and the others.'

Help from another Close Friend.

Province of Desolate Plains and Mountain Caves - Candon Planet

Arkina was the third, of these close friends with Karina and Uri. Each had grown up, as the eldest daughters, in the three largest provincial jurisdictions, on Candon. As the future heads of their respective clans, the girls became very close and met frequently. This friendly contact, gave them many chances to understand effective trading, in the other provincial areas. Meetings were often informal and welcome, as their parents were also good friends. So, the girls had grown up together and remained close with each other, over time.

As friends it was quite common to receive imaged messages, between themselves. Arkina arrived back home from her favorite plateau, where she had just spent some time with Kendy (Kendu). For Arkina, it was here, among the flowering blossoms and heavily shaded trees where she completely fell in love with Kendu. Both of them felt enormous empathy for this blissful setting and for the friendly creatures, which inhabited these pristine forests.

Hidden near this mountain peak, was a reclusive misty green haven which served as a shelter, for many innocent forest creatures. This warm and protected ecological sanctuary, had become their own. It was a natural environment, near the uniquely secluded plateau.

Arkina's family home was also an impressive castle like fortress, set on the distant valley floor below, run by her aging father, the Clan King, Oronsey. From the enormous colonnade leading to the ancient entrance, Arkina was greeted by her formal, tolerant and understanding aide, Dronka.

A slightly irregular-looking individual, Dronka was still trying to catch her breath. 'There has been an urgent image transmission for you Miss from Miss Karina. Your father said it had come from the Great Hall on Kendagon and may be important.'

'Thank you Dronka, I'll see to it now.' As Dronka left, Arkina recounted. 'That's where Mharn's parents live. Come on.' She moved quickly up to her private suite, followed closely by Kendu. Contact was soon established, and Arkina quickly asked. 'Everything okay Karina?'

'Yes, can you meet me on Kendagon, at the Great Hall? I'm staying with the Shi's.'

Arkina asked. 'Has Mharn arrived safely at Tamaryn's galaxy yet? Is everything okay?'

'Yes, everything is fine. I have something important to discuss with you and Uri. We have a unique opportunity coming up, to visit Tamaryn's galaxy with Michael on the Corillion.'

Uri was excited. 'Wow, when are you leaving?'

Karina laughed. 'No wait, this is one of the things I want to discuss with you both. Would you and Kendy like to come with Uri, Herron and me to see Mharn?'

There were moments of silence, followed by a quiet gasp. 'Wow, I mean yes.' Then after a hasty glance at Kendy and a quick pause, Arkina snapped back quickly. 'When?'

'We're leaving in about two rotations of Kendagon and we'll be away for about ten.'

Arkina jumped at this chance. 'I'll be over, as soon as I can.' Then the three dimensional image closed down. Arkina looked a little stunned and shocked. After all, she had never been outside the Kindred Spirits planetary system before. After a moment she turned to Kendu.

'Something's wrong and she needs our help, Kendy. I'm not sure what it is yet but something has happened and she needs us.'

Kendu was amazed and puzzled as well. 'Mharn could have arrived by now. We can't just leave for fourteen rotations of Kendagon? Then. 'We may never get this chance again.'

Arkina nodded in agreement. 'Let me talk to father first. Everything should be okay.'

Kendu then queried. 'I wonder what's happened, maybe Mharn needs our help?'

Arkina was decisive. 'Enough of this. Let's get over there and find out what's going on? Karina needs to talk to us, about something.'

Kendu looked a little confused and was still none the wiser. Then Arkina smiled at him and tried to clarify things. 'It's girl talk, but Herron will be going there as well.'

Kendu agreed. 'Yes, of course I'm coming. Visit another galaxy, try and stop me.'

9
Our Evolving Plans.

Oats' Alpine cabin - Pimeron Planet

From his cabin, Oats and Marmuron were still resting comfortably together on their back veranda, looking out at countless visions in the night sky. Oats was still trying to figure out Marmuron's charming and disarming ways, while she had a rapidly developing fascination for Oats' desire to unravel the great cosmic unknowns. Their loving companionship was delightful to watch.

As they looked over the beautiful mountainous terrain, observing the stunning ancient forest views, Marmuron thought out aloud. 'It is so easy to destroy something that cannot defend itself, with a voice.'

What are you saying? Queried Oats. 'All these trees take an eternity in our lifetime to grow. They contribute to so many animal classes, wellbeing and yet we can destroy them without any consideration, for the feelings, compassion or kindness to others.'

Oats was reflective. 'Yes that is correct, but so can a forest fire and that can do even more damage.' Oats was weighing several issues.

However, Marmuron understood the greater underlying sensitivities 'Yes Oats, however this is the connection of dependence.

We need to understand the impact on individual species, in the Natural Force. There is a balance, which holds the sustainability for all life together.'

Oats seemed distracted. 'I'm listening.'

'It's a nurturing process Oatsy. Many life forms need each other to survive and maintain the balance, of a cherished and cultivating existence.'

While Oats was giving this further thought the ancient spirit image of Pim appeared nearby and was greeted warmly. Pim was friendly, as she was charming and shared any mother's natural kindhearted warmth, for her son Mykron's future happiness. There was of course, a wonderful opportunity for Mykron to explore Tamaryn's distant systems and galaxy.

Oats, on seeing Pim arrive, bolted out of his seat. 'Hi Pim, any news on the others yet?'

It was the tyranny of great distances, which was on Pim's mind now. However, her son and his new companion Velia would be experiencing one of the most thrilling and unparalleled encounters, of their times together. With all these concerns still playing out in her mind, Pim was still able to focus on the concerns of the coming mission.

'By my calculations they're just entering the frontiers of Tamaryn's galaxy.'

Pim then seemed a little hesitant. 'There have been some other developments.' More questions began coming, thick and fast as Michael and Janet, came rushing out to see her.

Janet wanted to clarify something. 'Mharn is only going to be away for ten rotations of Kendagon isn't he?'

Pim seemed less certain about this now. 'These plans are evolving as we speak. I've just found out it is doubtful, that they will be back in another six rotations of Kendagon.'

Janet was feeling some concerns for Karina. 'Oh.'

The excitement was shared, then Pim advised. 'Michael, Kisun-Shi wants to see us as soon as possible. It's now over three rotations of the Kendagon planet, since they all left.'

Then Janet quizzed. 'We could still bring Mharn back with us, couldn't we?'

There was no immediate answer. Pim seemed in a thoughtful mood. 'We may well have some more passengers coming with us. I'll let Mharn's father Shi, explain it, as he has asked to see you all, as soon as we can.'

Oats just beamed with excitement. 'Now, Pim?'

Pim laughed. 'Whenever you're ready, Oats.' The four friends left with Pim immediately to find out the news, Shi wanted to share.

Pim confided as we boarded the shuttle. 'Remember Shi has been to Tamaryn's galaxy before and has some visionary insights, which may help us all.' It seemed as though there were many developing plans afoot.

Michael and Oats were now making plans for a quest, never before thought possible, by the ancient forefathers and philosophical scholars, in their earliest times of curiosity.

The heavens were indeed a more massive expanse, than many had previously visualized. A future full of gateways to discover, beyond any boundaries, previously thought possible.

Once aboard the Corillion, Pim quickly gave them a revised update. 'An image has just come from Tamaryn's ship only moments ago. Our friends on the first mission have just entered the outer limits of Tamaryn's galaxy. We hope to hear more, once they arrive within her inner planetary systems.'

Oats queried. 'Pim, what does Shi want to talk to us about?'

Pim smiled. 'We'll be there shortly. I believe he wants to ask, for your help.'

The Great Hall - Kendagon Planet

The Corillion descended into its normal orbiting path. They then shuttled down to the Kendagon planet below and headed straight towards the Great Hall.

Within moments, Pim, Michael, Oats, Janet and Marmuron were escorted by Shi's aide down the ornate corridor, to the elaborate private lounge, of the Shi's extensive upper floor suite. Janet, Marmuron and Pim were increasingly thrilled for the opportunities that this new quest presented.

10
Memories from Shi's Past.

As Shi greeted them, Janet was eager to find out how Karina was coping with her sensitive news. Pim and Marmuron also followed San, who had recently taken Arkina, Kendu, Uri and Herron down to Karina's suite. There were the sounds of joyful laughter and cheerful chatter coming from inside, as San brought Janet, Marmuron and Pim into the happy and heart-warming group. The natural response, of overwhelming love and support for Karina's exciting news, which lifted her spirits enormously.

After their initial greetings, Shi led both Oats and Michael, onto the large outside patio, set high above the grounds and overlooking the surrounding scenic countryside. Michael and Oats noticed Shi was a little hesitant when Oats erupted with enthusiasm. 'Shi, what challenges do you see for us, in our coming mission?'

'Let me come to that in a moment. You need to understand what it is like there.' Shi was casting his mind back, to a time long ago. A time when he also felt the vulnerabilities and the vastness of space and distance. 'You must expect to be over-whelmed, beyond your wildest dreams. Tamaryn's primal planet is a home to many thousands of small and larger villages. There is a natural splendor of ancient forests, with happy melodious sounds from many varieties of chirping birds and forest creatures. There is a sense of inspired cheerfulness, among the many clan's people. It's hard to describe, but you feel like you want to stay there forever and become part of this warm and natural, living experience.'

Oats began to wonder out aloud. 'Like a lost horizon, Michael?' Michael nodded while understanding Oats's meaning.

After a pause Shi continued. 'You won't understand it all completely until you arrive. It is a melody of competing musical sounds, appealing to the serene and peaceful. Singing birds, speak of innocence as creatures. It stimulates the heart and soul, for lovers of peace.' As Shi spoke he brought up some visions. 'There's a heartening and captivating warmth, with a composure of tranquility, found in each of these villages.'

Shi paused while recollecting other memories. 'Tamaryn's residence is a little more formal by contrast, with many elaborate and ornate settings, with a sweeping view over this natural wonderland.'

Michael was beginning to wonder why Shi wanted to speak to him and Oats in private. 'Shi, how hard will it be, to get Mharn, to come back with us?'

Shi was still looking a little troubled and unsettled. 'Michael, we went there ourselves for a very specific purpose and became lost in the natural wonder of it all.' Shi seemed a little saddened. 'It is possible to become overwhelmed, by all these inspirational visions, within the local surroundings. So much so, that you may not want to come back at all. It can really have that kind of influence on you.' Shi seemed a little more determined. 'Michael, this is where our family needs your help. To be able to guide the mission's purpose, as set out by WIL. A cool head will be needed, to see the higher purpose here and not give way, to emotional appeal and persuasive influences.'

Michael questioned. 'You don't want Mharn to overstay, do you?'

'It would break Karina's heart. She faces immense responsibilities, in her own province back here.'

Oats asked. 'Pim mentioned, that Tamaryn's galaxy, could be a hard place to leave'

'Yes it is true. They have created something really beautiful, which honors the Natural Forces of Nature. To be presented with an opportunity to go there, gives the chance to look into the soul, of an exquisite natural beauty, in all of its forms.'

Oats was still puzzled about something. 'Shi, Pim also mentioned, their system of natural justice laws.'

Shi paused. 'You are referring to their jurisdictions, of natural compliance laws?'

Oats agreed. 'Well yes, I guess so.'

'There's little for your expedition as guests, to be concerned about. It's wisest to actually see it for yourselves. Tamaryn may arrange an expedition, giving you a thorough understanding of the levels of conformity, their systems abide by. These ancient systems of guidance and coaching are taught from an early age and are based on an individual's understanding, of their own choices and boundaries.'

Michael was reflective. 'Pim once told me about choices and boundaries, on my first mission. At the time it seemed a little daunting and unnerving.'

Shi was thoughtful. 'It can be, if you are not use to observing Nature's universal laws.' There was something else on Shi's mind as he led our two researchers further out onto a sheltered marble terrace, surrounded by an elaborate and decorative balustrade.

Michael couldn't contain his enthusiasm any longer. 'Shi, have there been some other developments?'

'Yes, but not quite what we were expecting.' Oats and Michael looked perplexed as Shi paused and then. 'Can I speak to you both, in complete confidence?'

They agreed as one. 'Why yes, yes of course.'

Shi then opened up. 'Michael, my family needs your assistance and experienced discretion, with an issue of the upmost delicacy and sensitivity.'

Michael was supportive. 'Why yes, yes of course.'

Shi began to explain the most recent events, concerning Karina's more recent news.

After a moment Oats asked. 'Shi I don't quite understand, all the issues here yet?'

Shi was understanding. 'On your planet Earth, the last frontier begins with discovering what lies beyond your solar system and if there are any other life forms out here. Also considering the elementary composition of other bodies and the dynamics of our galaxy in general. For us, it is more about visiting other nearby galaxies and discovering more, about their origins.'

Shi thought back to an earlier time, long ago. 'For San and me in our time, we didn't realize how lucky we were, just going there. It was truly overwhelming and we lost track of time. Not because we didn't care, but because, so many things were different.'

Oats became more enthusiastic. 'What was different, Shi?'

Shi sighed. 'Oh many things really, rotation times, life expectancies, orbital path times, animal class types, the changing sense of gravity, from one planet to the next. Our children have no idea, of the wonders they will all face.'

Shi then refocused. 'The thing for Mharn is this. It is one chance in a lifetime to be selected to go, to be promoted and to be honored. Mharn has achieved all of this on his own.' Shi was becoming emotional with a father's pride, in his sons achievements. 'Without any help from anyone else he has achieved this and as his parents we love him dearly, as does Karina. We don't want him to lose this chance and neither does Karina. However sometimes things just happen, beyond our control and this is what we are trying to prepare you for now.'

As Shi explained further, Oats said. 'Thank you for confiding in us, Shi.'

'There's something else.' He paused and then said. 'We believe it will help our cause if Karina and Mharn's four closest friends come with you as well. Mharn may well need friends close by, to talk to. They will need to be briefed and made aware of the importance of Mharn, wanting to come back home, on your return voyage.'

'Do you mean, Uri, Herron, Arkina and Kendu?'

'Yes, they are all inside now, offering Karina support.'

Oats and Michael were beginning to wonder how problematic and challenging, this mission could become. 'Has there been any contact from the first mission yet?

'Let's go back inside and find out.' Shi then said. 'WIL has also asked to see you before you go.'

'Thank you Shi.' And as they left to go back inside with Shi to find the others, Michael whispered to Oats. 'We'd better keep this conversation with Shi to ourselves for now. We might need a little help, to dig ourselves out of some fairly tight spots.'

Oats quickly nodded. 'Yes, let's see how everyone is getting along, before we're all missed.'

Back inside, there were celebrations for Karina's happy news.

Janet, Marmuron and Pim were still down in Karina's suite learning as much as they could from San, about all her experiences, so long ago in Tamaryn's galaxy. As we arrived we overheard.

'Karina, why not just tell him?'

'I will, but I don't want him feeling as though he has to come back. I want him to come back, because he wants too.' And as her tears grew. 'Because he loves me.' Tears continued to run down Karina's cheeks, as she began to wonder how this would all end. Karina knew that Mharn was very excited about going and she was thrilled for the opportunities this chance gave. What she needed now, was the counsel of close friends?

It was soon time for them all to move on and they thanked San and Shi for their firsthand experience and cherished insights, of what to expect during their travels.

Planet of Pimeron, System of Kindred Spirits.

As they headed back to Oats cabin, everyone knew of Karina's news and how to keep it confidential. Then Oat's explained his primary concern. 'Back on Earth, you can live your whole life and some people will not even see their own country, let alone their own planet, in one life time. How can anyone, go to a new galaxy, for such a short period of time and not get swept up, in the experience?'

Michael was puzzled. 'I just don't know Oats. This is one of the great unknowns isn't it? One chance in a lifetime and only a limited time to see it. Some of these answers may come to us when we understand the boundaries of this mission a little better.' The wonder and fascination, kept growing between them all.

Like so many others, Oats and Michael were packing up now and getting ready to leave.

11
A Meeting with WIL.

Oats' Alpine cabin - Pimeron Planet, System of Kindred Spirits.

Apart from the hopes and dreams of others, Oats and Michael were planning an inspiring mission of their own. To find answers they could trust. Yes, there would be moments of compassion and adventure, however the next step was in gaining some insightful guidance from WIL. They had received a vision from Pim, to expect him soon.

WIL's vision appeared on Oats back veranda and after initial greetings they waited in silence. WIL watched, as their elementary innocence and limited knowledge of universal origin, was on full display. A thought came to him. 'You are about to enter another galaxy Michael. **It is important that you become more enlightened, about the origins of our universe, from a galaxy perspective. Sun-Ky will be able to help you all, during your coming voyage.** I would urge you to take this opportunity, to build on your parochial perceptions, about the history of our universal existence. **Sun-Ky has a unique understanding of your planetary history and it is important that we all arrive, with the same informed vision, from a galaxy perspective.'**

WIL became more thoughtful for a moment while remembering generations from his own past existence. WIL began to explain the history of Tamaryn's galaxy. 'Their inner societies have survived for many thousands of generations, within eight inner star systems, containing twenty three inhabited planets. These planets include all their known life forms and their cultures vary, in their embracing, of Nature's laws.'

'The wonders of Nature are a fascination to behold. You can understand more about Nature, in a moment of peaceful tranquility, than in a lifetime of activity.'

Then WIL went deeper still, with his explanation. **'The experiences, that many citizens cherish the most, are the wonders in life, they understand the least.'**

Oats then asked. 'What is it like there, WIL?'

'I want you to imagine a place further away, than many of us have ever been before. A time which existed, before settlement in our own galaxy began. Imagine a people who have learnt the secrets, of survival, without conflict. Consider, a jurisdiction which is at one, with the Natural Force. Their endurance is a celebration of life, in all its forms.'

WIL continued. 'Don't be surprised, be amazed at the wonder of the unknown. With an open mind and a compassionate and understanding heart, you will find the soul of existence, in your coming travels.'

Then Michael asked. 'Can you give us a better understanding of what to expect?'

Even WIL was overwhelmed with admiration. 'Tamaryn's galaxy, has planetary systems, similar to our own. There are some differences in elementary formation, size and mass compositions. The influencing Natural Forces, with star systems which support early planetary life forms, closely resemble our own. You know that I was born on our primary planet of Giant Vines, in our Lodan system. This is what enables me to continually renew, as a life force.' Oats was fascinated.

'Yes, yes of course and is Tamaryn's history much different?'

'Tamaryn still lives on her primary planet and it is very similar to Giant Vines.'

Michael asked. 'What are the people like, there?'

WIL continued to be amazed. 'They are part of the many different forms, to look out for. Everyone who visits, will come away with a slightly different perspective.'

Oats asked. 'Is it hard to leave their society?'

WIL then said. 'It can be. Just understanding the diverse life forms and elementary differences, in climate. Their environmental ambiences, priorities of cohabitation and scarcities of resources. Their attitudes to life, can be like beginning all over again.'

Now Janet was more curious. 'Humanities attitudes to life?'

WIL replied. 'Not so much. It is more their natural choices in life.'

Janet asked. 'What do they have there, that you found most thought-provoking?'

WIL paused and then. 'Having a social order with a longer settlement history than our own, gives a very well developed understanding of what makes communal living, exist productively. This has been achieved through a closer understanding of living, within our Natural Forces.'

Marmuron was now even more motivated. 'How, WIL?'

'Consider the number of jurisdictions on your planet and consider their early cultural history. Much of it is consistent with human development only. What you will find on this mission, is a clearer understanding of essential natural laws for all living classes.'

Oats then asked. 'What is it, about animal behavior?'

'Examining the history of multiple animal class behaviors, is important in their galaxy, because their culture represents the origin of choices and boundaries.'

Michael reflected. 'That's what Mykron introduced, as the first clan leader on the Candon planet, in this system.'

WIL then confirmed. 'Yes, these are the personal choices we all make and our subsequent self-control, decides how we adapt, in a social order. At an early stage, their youth are grounded, on these choices.'

WIL then elaborated. 'It is not only about behavioral issues. It is the choices we make, that decide where and how we live. Those, who choose a different path, will leave an unspoiled land, of blissful enlightenment and utopia.'

Oats murmured quietly. 'Paradise.'

Michael chuckled. 'Well maybe, or a version of it anyway.' Then Michael asked. 'WIL, what immediate differences would we as new inhabitants see?'

'Well there are traps for the unwary. You will need to be on your guard. This is one of the reasons why we are sending you on this mission. To bring home those with shorter mission durations, or those that can't adapt, conform or assimilate quickly. Tamaryn's highly ordered societies have another outer system planet, which better suites dissenting or opposing approaches, to existence within the universal Natural Force.'

'Individual life choices, become your own duty of care, with the obligation of self-responsibility. In higher orders of simple existence, survival between animal classes is considered, a shared communal responsibility.'

Oats then observed. 'Destiny and fate, are an existence, within our own control.'

Then Michael asked 'How does this society, see itself?'

WIL paused momentarily. 'Their greatest achievement, has been to perfect a culture of social cohesion. One of the most important unspoken laws in this community is to achieve a closer understanding of how to survive with each other, under natural law.' WIL hesitated as he felt some warming sensitivity, with this fundamental existence. 'What comes within a moment of passion, in the evolution of human life, is the discovery of a moral decency and self-discipline. This is created in the nurturing protection, of the next generation.'

'This develops from a progeny's innate feelings. An instinctive right to exist with an early fight to survive. Instances of this self-preservation can be seen in many animal classes, where a mother will defend her offspring, sometimes at the risk of her own life.'

'This willingness to protect the next generation against early harm, is found in the highest instincts of character and its fundamental moral principles. **For without renewal, the evolution of Nature, as a living universal force, would cease to exist.**'

Oats became a little confused. 'I'm sorry WIL, I don't quite understand. Is there an overriding concern, here?'

'There are two. The primary objective is for a smooth transition and we are sending our highest diplomatic representative Sun-Ky, to take charge of this mission. At a personal level, my private concern would be for the Shi's son Mharn. A long time ago I sent Kisun-Shi on a similar mission and Mharn suffered, because they overstayed their time there.'

WIL paused. 'I have lived through this before with his parents. Mharn will be caught up and highly motivated to stay for longer and Karina will not want to hold him back or to stand in his way. Of course their child would be the one, who suffers the most.'

Michael, mumbled quietly to himself. 'Oh dear.'

WIL smiled. 'We believe that Karina needs the chance to explain her circumstances to Mharn. Having some of Mharn's closest friends as support, will give them all a chance, to broaden their outlooks.'

Oats agreed. 'Yes, I'm sure they would be a great support, for Karina.'

WIL smiled. 'One final thought before your mission leaves in one rotation of Kendagon. Pim has yet to be fully briefed on the duties of her new position as mediator on the Council of First

Kings. Both Pim and Sun-Ky will join your mission through the Map Room portal, just before the Corillion leaves, the outer boundaries of our galaxy.'

WIL's image smiled and evaporated, as he left us in deep thought. While still not completely familiar with our new challenges, WIL had certainly given us all plenty to think about.

12
A Nervous Start to a Dream.

Time had passed quickly for them all and their plans were gathering pace. All of Karina's closer friends had now come aboard the Corillion and were busy settling in for the long voyage ahead. Oats and Michael were keen to catch up with the first mission, however, Michael was a little unsettled, with Pim being away.

The two friends met in the Map Room and sealed the entrance behind them. They had been under way for some time now and Michael was looking puzzled.

Oats asked. 'Michael, you seem concerned, about something?'

'We've never started off on a mission before, without Pim.'

'Yes, that's true however WIL said Pim would meet with us, before we leave the boundaries of our galaxy. She will come through the Map Room portal.'

'Oats, from the beginning of my missions, I have enjoyed the close counsel and leadership guidance from Pim. She has been my friendly and mystical guide to our galaxy.' Michael paused. 'Every question has been answered and every obstacle has been overcome. She has been like an encyclopedic reference to our cosmic challenges. I have come to know her history, her hopes and her dreams for the lost people, in her ancient civilization.'

Oats pondered for a moment. 'Yes, there's a lot for us all, to look back on.'

'We have been through immense challenges together and now I'm losing her.'

'Yes Michael, we've become like family together, however we are not losing her.'

Michael was feeling frustrated. 'Oats, this is crazy unless we have some help and guidance. As much as I'd love to go on more missions, it doesn't make any sense, without some level of celestial guidance and support. Now we are having to think and act for ourselves. While in most circumstances we could easily manage, neither of us have any idea of where we are going, how to get there or how and when we'd ever get back.'

Michael continued with his concerns. 'Yet now we are charged with having to be self-assured, calm and confident on a mission of discovery, while we are alone, until Pim joins us later.'

Oats sounded curious. 'What is it, Michael? What's up?'

'Oats, we're leaving our galaxy, mate.'

Oats was brimming with enthusiasm. 'Yes, exciting isn't it?' Oats must have thought Michael was nuts.

Then Michael added. 'Remember when WIL told me that Pim would be taking on newer responsibilities, after our present mission is completed?'

Oats seemed puzzled. 'Yes of course.'

Then Michael reflected. 'Oh, it doesn't matter Oats. I'm just being silly.'

Oats was very reassuring. 'We'll be okay, mate.'

'Oats, both you and I have barely left Earth as explorers, to discover our own galaxy. Yes, we've been to some other planetary systems, but now we are planning to leave our own galaxy, to discover another one. Isn't there some part of you that thinks we're moving, a little too fast here?'

'Michael, this is just a case of nervous excitement. Don't forget we were invited by Tamaryn, to visit her galaxy.'

'Oats, remember what it was like for us many years ago, visiting South America. For a moment, imagine you are alone touring around their regions. All I'm saying is that it would be easier, if we had a local guide with us. Someone who knew the languages, the local customs, where to go and what to expect.'

Then after a pause. 'Up here, we don't know where we're going. We don't know how to get there. We don't know who to meet, or even what language they speak. If we get back we don't even know where we've been.'

There was a short pause. Oats was trying to be supportive. 'Or, Michael.'

However Michael was digging in deeper here now. 'We don't know how long it takes to get there. We don't even know the climate, how to react to their customs and traditions. We may not even be able to find our way back.'

While Michael was trying to adjust to the absurdity of their present predicament, Oats just laughed at this. 'Helps you understand what it was like for Christopher Columbus, doesn't it and he didn't even, have a map.'

'Oh Oats, be serious for a moment. Remember when we were students, we couldn't find our way, around the local shopping mall.'

'Or Michael, we can always get co-ordinates and ask questions in the Map Room. Then there's Captain Champion to refer back to, for help as well.'

'Oats, none of us have been outside our galaxy before. There's a hundred thousand questions we haven't even thought of yet. When it comes down to it, our universe of knowledge is still so primitive. People on our home planet, haven't even left our system yet. Just consider the vast dimensions up here, in any direction, with no end in sight.'

Michael paused and then. 'Distance and direction are our challenges and time is our enemy. We are a microscopic speck in an enormous multi-dimensional expanse. This is what's frightening the crap out of me.'

'Michael, you're becoming unnecessarily alarmed and upset.'

'Rubbish Oats. Sure I want our future missions to work out. I'm just considering what this voyage would have been like, without having Pim's guidance.'

'This is unlike you Michael. Pim hasn't been there before either. We are all on an adventure, exploring the universe.'

'That part I can handle Oats, but we are also going on a mission with enormous responsibilities, where many people will be depending on us to succeed. Remember how important this immense transfer of conference responsibilities is to WIL and Tamaryn's galaxy. We can't afford to muck this up, or disappoint anyone now.'

'Don't get me wrong, I'm a confident person, I'm just a little fearful that these mission objectives will be beyond our ability and experience to achieve, given all the things everyone is hoping for.' Oats just smiled and seemed completely relaxed.

'Michael, ever since I joined you on these missions, I've had the feeling of an unassuming and inconspicuous supporting guidance in the background. It is a gentle supervision with a discreet, absorbing and driven focus. I know what we are doing up here is important to many others and I can promise you, we are not alone in our efforts here. There is far too much at stake for them, to just leave a couple of monkeys like us on our own, without any higher levels of support.'

'I sure hope you're right Oats.'

'Confidence grows with experience, Michael. It'll work out, you'll see and remember, we are on WIL's ship.'

Michael's outlook, suddenly changed. 'Yes, yes I had forgotten that for a moment.'

World Peace in Our Time: *The Logic behind Universal Creation*

Oats became more reassuring. 'Pim will be here soon with Sun-Ky and we still have many things left to plan.'

While Oats and Michael had been completely self-absorbed in a certain amount of naval gazing, Pim miraculously appeared through the Map Room portal.

Pim was lovely. 'We must have reached the outer limits of our galaxy. This truly was like leaving home.'

Pim was quickly followed by Sun-Ky, then she gasped. 'Wow, we just made it in time.' Having Pim on board now was very reassuring for Michael. None of them had ventured this far out before. There was more comfort, building in his hidden anxieties.

Sun-Ky then said. 'I'll be in my suite for a while, waiting for any news from the first galaxy mission group. We'll have a briefing after that, when we have further news.'

Pim immediately sensed my building nervous energy. 'Your fears are completely unfounded Michael. It is quite normal, on a first voyage, to have lingering concerns.' Then she added. **'Is it because, no one has ever explained the universe, to you before.'**

Michael was momentarily startled. 'Well no, plenty of ancient beliefs, theories and philosophical concepts.' Then. 'It comes from the innocence of ignorance I guess.'

Then Oats added. 'Michael and I were brought up to believe in a heavenly presence and we found out the truth of that, on our recent visit to Benlay, with Tamaryn.'

Pim smiled. 'You both really have no idea what's up here, do you?'

Oats could tell Michael was now in a lonely place 'I guess that's right. With all the things we've been taught since our childhood, it would be fair to say, we have no real idea.'

Pim was extremely self-confident and Michael adored her for it. It reinforced Michael's earlier thoughts about, where they would be without her.

Pim smiled. 'Michael, we need to correct all these misunderstandings now on this mission, while we can. A clear mind will help you understand all of this.'

Oats jumped at this. 'You can explain all of this.' Oats seemed stunned.

'Why yes of course. Your ancient history has misled you both, from the beginning.'

Their sense of adventure was just reignited. 'Wow.'

They both spoke together in one voice and asked. 'When.'

'Let us settle first. While we are between galaxies, we will go over and correct your history of belief and any other theories. Sun-Ky and I will answer all of your questions.'

Pim watched the excitement building on their faces. Oats and Michael were thrilled. Then she counseled. 'Everything you have been taught to believe, is from an ancient, narrow and parochial perspective.'

Getting to the next galaxy was a completely different experience for our researchers and they would be ship bound, for some time. There was a growing wave of nervous energy and boisterous excitement, building among Mharn's friends, as well.

13
Understanding the Clean Beam.

Leaving their home galaxy, was a first time experience for Karina's support group of youthful adventurers. Herron and Kendu were amusing themselves by preparing to rediscover the Clean Beam. They waited for Karina to walk through first to clean, renew and restore herself.

However when Karina approached, there was a gentle and ominous, warning sound of caution. The visible beams stopped, the process shut down and a low echoing, reverberating, warning signal, sounded out. The system had stopped and perplexed by this, Karina went to find Pim. Alerted by the sound, Pim rapidly developed a broad smile when she heard and then quietly coaxed Karina aside, for a chat.

Karina was confused. 'Did I do something wrong Pim? I haven't broken it, have I? Pim quickly gave Karina, a warm hug to console her.

Pim appeared a little teary as she held Karina carefully. 'No, not at all Karina.' Then becoming a little more emotional, Pim began to explain. 'It is important to understand that the first function of the Clean Beam is to just clean you, without you having to change, or the need for any liquid.'

'Remember though, that this is WIL'S ship. As you may know WIL comes from our galaxy's primal planet of Giant Vines, which is part of the Lodan system. The ability to renew back to a version of your former self, is available to all their inhabitants. This is what ensures their ability to prolong life and extend the age of maturity, to many times what would be considered normal, on all other planets.'

'Wow, so that's how they live for so long.'

'It is just culturally accepted, as a function of their life's existence there. When the Corillion was constructed, WIL installed the Clean Beam to both clean and renew back to an earlier version of his former self.' After a short pause Pim said 'Karina, all the regular officers and crew on this ship have used the Clean Beam previously.'

'The primal nature of the planet of Giant Vines, is that it originates from Nature's living force. This force is also present in the structure and formation of the Clean Beam. So the beam can restore life, to a version of its former self.'

'However as a Natural Force it is contrary to its fundamental essence, to destroy embryonic life.' There was a short pause as Karina was trying to absorb what was being said when Pim probed back to a previous conversation. 'You're pregnant aren't you?'

Suddenly Karina realized what had happened. The beam shut down because it could not destroy, her unborn child. 'Oh dear.' Karina muffled as tears began to grow.

Pim smiled more broadly now. For as much as WIL was widely considered in their system as the Great Spirit, there was a greater silent Natural Force in existence. A dominant force with its own established guidelines, which supported all life in the universe, including WIL's.

Pim smiled. 'I don't believe that WIL ever envisaged that his ship would carry a crew member who was expecting a child. Most of us are older by comparison to you and your friends.' And then. 'You can clean and change in my quarters if you like, Karina.'

Karina was a little overcome as she said. 'Thankyou Pim, thank you.'

As they shared a warming smile together, Herron appeared at the door. 'Pim, it looks like there's something wrong with the Clean Beam. Uri has just tried to use it and it still doesn't work.'

Karina became emotionally thrilled as Pim asked Herron to bring Uri to her suite.

Herron continued muttering to himself. 'I hope we can get this fixed, otherwise it's going to get very uncomfortable, for some of us.'

As Herron left, Pim and Karina continued with a happy and adoring embrace. 'Herron doesn't know yet.' Karina revealed, in some surprise.

Then it occurred to Pim. 'Maybe Uri doesn't either. Let me explain this to her and we'll see how she responds, to the news.' It was only a few moments later and Uri came down to Pim's private suite, where she was immediately met by two, lovely smiling and happy faces, staring back at her.

'What's happened to the Clean Beam?' was all Uri could get out. Pim quickly explained again, the historic ancient function of the Clean Beam, so that Uri understood what had just happened to her. A broad smile erupted on Uri's face as this thrilling and welcome news reached her conscious thoughts. Uri already knew of Karina's pregnancy and went over to give her a warm supporting hug. The two girls enjoyed an enduring friendship and took immediate pleasure, in the future sharing of the next stage of their lives. Karina was absolutely thrilled, to think their children would grow up, being a similar age and sharing, life's experiences together.

Karina gasped. 'Uri, this is absolutely wonderful news. It's just marvelous.'

Coming down the passageway were the rising muffled voices of Herron, Kendu and Arkina as they continued to Pim's suite.

Pim quickly asked Uri. 'Does Herron know, anything about this yet?'

'Oh dear, Herron.' Uri exclaimed with surprise.

Uri was momentarily caught off guard, as Pim then took control. 'It's alright, I've been through this before, with my son Mykron.' Then 'Uri, I want you to calmly explain why the Clean Beam stopped for Karina so that everyone understands what has just happened and then let Herron work the rest out for himself.'

Uri and Karina were looking a little hesitant and tentative. However Pim was quickly supportive and developed a broad happy smile. 'Remember, this is magnificent news. Everyone will be tremendously happy for you both.'

As the others came back in, Herron, Kendu and Arkina were amazed to see a couple of happy faces greeting them in Pim's suite. Herron began with. 'Pim, can we fix the?' then completely puzzled he queried. 'What's going on? What are you all so happy about?'

As Uri explained once again, the extent of preservation coming from the Clean Beam, some looked more puzzled than others. Men aren't very quick sometimes. Herron then interrupted with. 'But it didn't work for you either, Uri?'

Everyone burst into laughter as Herron seemed to be the last one to figure it all out. Herron's earlier concerns about the Clean Beam not working, quickly evaporated when he discovered the reasons why. His face glimmered and glowed as he watched the natural loving innocence and pure joyful happiness, developing on the face of his adored Uri. The look of loving happiness grew rapidly, as he hurried over to give Uri a comforting hug of warm support.

'Oh Uri, really.' The others quickly gathered around offering congratulations and cheerful wishes. This thought of emerging adulthood, brought a sense of change to the faces of their youthful innocence.

Then Pim said. 'Nature's purpose is to create life, not destroy it. The natural formation within the Clean Beam, will not run contrary to the Natural Forces purpose.'

As Herron and Kendu left to go back to use the Clean Beam, the girls stayed with Karina in Pim's suite. Janet asked. 'How are you feeling, Karina?'

Karina seemed so much happier now, with all her friends around and she was going to see Mharn soon, as well. 'Okay, I guess, it's all good.'

Janet was reassuring. 'Telling Mharn, is weighing on your thoughts, I can see that.'

Karina paused 'It's not just that. I have known Mharn since we were children together. Much of his early life has been a lonely struggle to succeed, to become educated, despite his parents demise. Everything he has achieved, including being an Ice Ball champion, has been a struggle, all of his own. This chance he has now, is an immense opportunity for him. No one in our province, has ever had a chance like this before and I don't want to spoil it for him now. I want him, to choose, when he comes home.'

'I know you love Mharn, but he can't make this choice unless you tell him.'

Karina started to softly cry with tears running down her cheeks, as she noticed the privacy they shared. She had seemed happily engaged with Janet. 'I will find a way.' Then she stumbled with a growing reddishness on her cheeks and a look of uncertainty. 'I don't want to be the cause of him breaking his mission experience, to come home early because he feels he has to.' Karina seemed to stumble now as she hung on to every emotional feeling of love, affection and tenderness she possessed. 'I want him to come home, because, well because he loves me.'

Janet was more sensitively moved now, than she had been for a long time. This selfless act of love, loyalty and devotion caused tears to come to her eyes, as she reached out to put her arms around Karina, in a hugging embrace. 'Maybe you will let me help you find a way, Karina?'

Karina was feeling a little emotionally alone and lost, as she agreed. 'Yes, however I want him to hear the news, from me first.'

'This is a very personal choice Karina, as it would be for any expectant mother. It is your news to share with Mharn and it will be your choice to share.'

A broadening smile erupted on Karina's face, as she now found an even closer friendship, in an understanding confidante. 'Thank you, Janet.'

A Galvanizing Change in Plans.

Michael and Oats had come back from the Map Room to a vision of happy smiling faces. Once the experiences of the Clean Beam were explained, everyone settled and Pim then said. 'Now that we all have heard this wonderful news, Karina has asked that she be allowed to tell Mharn herself.' Everyone understood it was her news to share and these were, her choices to make.

Oats and Michael were both fascinated with intergalactic travel. 'Pim, we have just left our galaxy. Can you advise the best way, to manage our voyage?

'We all need to prepare for a dormant state of deep sleep. It is the most efficient way to rest and stabilize ourselves. The course has been set and the crew, will maintain a rotating security watch. We will exist in this dormant state with breaks, for about three rotations of Kendagon. Once we are within the outer systems, you will all be reawakened.'

Momentarily Sun-Ky re-entered with a fleeting note of urgency. 'There's been a change of plans with the first mission.' We all went quiet and then. 'Their ship will orbit Velia's home planet of Prisium first. The planet is named after one of the most beautiful and colorful floral species there, It's a prominent feature and flourishes everywhere.'

Oats queried. 'I don't understand, why did they have to go there first?'

Pim then quickly followed. 'Yes Sun-Ky, what's happened to them?'

Questions came from everywhere as Sun-Ky continued.

'The captain of Tamaryn's ship has reported an incident, with their Clean Beam.'

Then. 'It is just a precautionary measure before going to Tamaryn's primal planet.'

Pim's face glowed with excitement. 'Is everyone in good health?'

'Yes, all will be explained when we arrive.' Then. 'Our captain has also requested an early landing clearance on Prisium. We will have a visual image coming through here shortly, of the first mission on Tamaryn's ship.'

Then as Sun-Ky spoke, a vision suddenly appeared. 'There's Mykron and Velia.'

Karina's spirits lifted, as excitement built. 'I can see Mharn.'

Oats became cheerful and exuberant as Herron asked. 'What is it like there? Are we going to stop there also?'

Sun-Ky felt it was time for our first briefing. 'Prisium is very close to Tamaryn's primal planet in natural beauty. There are many aged rocky outcrops, amongst the high mountainous regions. There are enormous forests of tall aged floral trees, with copious amounts of changing seasonal coloring. Buried within the natural scenic blooms are many old, well established villages. The population lives simply and Velia's parents are the provincial leaders, of the largest province.'

Pim asked. 'Sun-Ky, what was the reason for the diversion?'

'Velia set off an alarm in the Clean Beam and so she could not be taken directly to Tamaryn's primal planet. The ship's captain decided that in the best interests of all, it would be better for us to regroup on Prisium. We will make our own choices, when we get there. Tamaryn's ship will leave shortly afterwards, with the other envoys, for her primal planet.'

Pim, was absolutely thrilled for Velia and Mykron. 'Oh dear, how lovely.'

There was a low murmuring among everyone else. 'Wow.' Now Pim began to wonder about the unforeseen dangers for Uri and Karina in being exposed to the primal planet. Pim quickly explained to Sun-Ky what had happened with our own Clean Beam.

Janet queried. 'But surely, pregnancies occur everywhere, even on primal planets?'

'Yes Janet, however there are slight differences. If you become pregnant on the primal planet and stay there, then your condition remains safe as it does anywhere else. However to go there without forewarning in a pregnant state, it may place an unborn in harm's way. We don't understand all the reasons yet. This is about preventing risk.'

Then Pim agreed. 'Some of you may have to remain on Prisium as well.'

Sun-Ky advised. 'Yes that would be prudent for the rest of us, to meet the first expedition, before we go onto Tamaryn's planet.'

Karina and her friends left the Map Room and returned to their quarters to finish changing. A building fascination occupied Janet's mind with a change of topic. 'Pim, can you please tell us more about how Tamaryn's society, follows natural law.'

This was going to be a difficult conceptual vision to understand. 'Well let's suppose you have ten thousand trees in a tropical rainforest. These trees never get emotional or angry, they never have silly disagreements or argue like bats over who owns the tree they share.' Pim stared at our puzzled expressions and then continued. 'I know this sounds obvious and trite but consider. A tree has never had a fight with anybody. A tree has never won or lost an argument with anyone and a tree has never had a difference of opinion with anyone else.'

Janet went first. 'Pim, what is the point of all of this?'

'I want you to consider the diversity of living things and why some prefer to live in a natural environment. Look at the variety of living species in the complete entirety of the Natural Force. **Humanity with all of its competing issues, could have evolved in a much more understanding, intelligent, motivated and cheerful manner. We could be so much more constructive, in how we engage with each other and with other living species.**'

There was another pause and then. 'I want you to consider the enchantment of the galaxy, you are about to enter. You will see types of existences, never before encountered. I want you to regain an open mind and be inspired by the depth of natural beauty. Consider other species life cycles, the tests they face and the forces they have to endure.'

'Ask how they survive in an environment, which can be just as rewarding as it can be unforgiving. You will also meet some celestial visionaries and may not comprehend their purpose, until we leave sometime later.'

'Remember, a tree can live longer than humans without mobility, without vision without the ability to question or to listen and resolve. A tree doesn't reason, doesn't construe, vilify or cause harm to their kind. A tree contributes to life's purpose, without thought of compensation or gain. A tree can't speak, has no opinions and can't hear, yet where we are going, humanity can't exist naturally without them.

Karina had arrived back at her suite now with her friends and was moved to open up, about her long history of friendship with Mharn. These earlier years with Mharn had brought many tearful and happy memories for her.

15
Early History between Karina and Mharn.

Karina and Mharn became friends from their early times in childhood. While Karina enjoyed a strong family upbringing, Mharn had battled through life, on his own. For reasons unknown to him at the time, Mharn's parents had been on an important preliminary mission to Tamaryn's galaxy.

While Mharn's parents had lost track of time, experiencing the sheer beauty and splendor of Tamaryn's planetary systems, Mharn had struggled as a child, growing up without them. Life in his early years, was an emotional ride for Mharn as he strived to succeed, without the normal parental encouragement and close family supervision.

Understanding these difficulties, Mharn had enjoyed many personal successes, particularly with his skills in the local inter planetary Ice Ball team. Karina had watched his self-motivated progress with increasing fondness, because at heart, Mharn exuded all the warmth, of an honorable and decent friend.

Now with his successful inclusion in being selected to go on this first mission, Karina thought more warmly about his aspirations, than the early stages of her own maternal condition. Within the deepest walls, of her own inner being, she loved Mharn as the soul mate of her companionship. She felt this sense of empathy and compassion with emotional depth, for a close friend, which she had never felt for anyone else before.

It's hard to describe your innermost feelings sometimes, as words don't seem to do justice to illustrate, the compassion held in experiencing life's hardships.

So here she was now, on this mission, only because of Mharn's achievements. Now that she was pregnant with their first child, Karina was torn between telling him now, or after he had completed his early duties.

Yes it was happy news, yet she still felt she had time. Her hidden concern was that Mharn too, like his parents before him, would also lose track of time. Having made up her mind to come, Karina wanted to tell Mharn in her own way and in her own time because; well because it was her news and her choices to share.'

Within the privacy of her suite, Arkina asked Karina. 'What is going through your mind at the moment?'

Tears of tender love came to Karina's eyes, as she grappled with her choices. 'I have grown to love Mharn, ever since he was very young and all through his times as an Ice Ball champion. He has struggled courageously and gallantly on his own, to get somewhere in his life. Now he has been appointed as a junior ambassador, to represent many of us on a mission to another galaxy and he is the only reason why, we have all been invited to come along now.' She began to weep openly.

Arkina tried to comfort her. 'Oh Karina, you will have to tell him at some time. This will be his child too.'

Karina didn't want Mharn to feel forced to cut his mission short and return home early, besides she believed time, was on her side at the moment. None of this seemed to make any sense to her friends, however she understood Mharn's struggles now, better than anyone else. She knew Mharn loved her and they had shared many intimate, caring moments together.

As Karina's two closest friends, Uri and Arkina came closer to comfort her. They both understood this was a difficult situation for Karina and offered her every support. Herron then remembered another point of view, which might be helpful. 'Karina, just before your union of companionship, I listened to Mharn pouring his heart out, over his friendship with you.'

Karina smiled at Herron. 'What did he say to you?'

'Mharn described you as loving, trusting, warm hearted and compassionate. A source of his greatest friendship and his true companion in life. A friend everyone looks for and rarely ever finds. Mharn said he counted himself extremely lucky to have found you and I know for certain, you are always in his thoughts.'

Karina sighed. 'How lovely, thankyou Herron.'

Karina's girlfriends came together, to give her moral support in her time of need.

Then Kendu asked casually. 'What's happening back in the Map Room with Michael and Oats?'

Karina continued wiping away her tears. 'Oh they're just being enlightened on the fundamental and essential differences between our two galaxies.'

Herron quickly followed with. 'Shouldn't we be there as well?'

Arkina added. 'Yes, wouldn't that be worth listening to?'

Karina smiled. 'Well it is more about planetary differences, Natural Forces and the unravelling of their own planets, ancient historical beliefs. I believe Sun-Ky is preparing them for the reality, we are all going to have to face, in our challenges to come.'

The friends continued chatting about the fortunes of destiny and what a brilliant opportunity this was, to be able to come on this mission. It was indeed early times for them all and only high ranking officials, had ever made this trek before.

Meanwhile back in the Map Room, Sun-Ky and Pim were having a quick revision on the historical significance of Michael and Oats present mission when Oats asked straight out of the blue.

'Pim, what is going to happen in the next five hundred generations for us?'

Pim had a remarkable mind and ever since they met her five missions ago she has displayed exceptional insight into Earth's past, present and future.

'Just consider how far you have all come in the last hundred generations.'

Janet was becoming more intrigued with Pim's further explanations about Nature as a silent force, in the universe. 'I don't quite understand all this yet, Pim?'

Pim smiled as she continued her explanations of the cosmological natural environment. 'Have you ever noticed that trees can live in peace, serenity and harmony for their entire lifetime? The forest communicates with self-control. Individually trees teach us to consider the benefits of solitude, privacy and seclusion. They can be tall, masterful and strong. This ability to grow and contribute to life's purpose helps us all to understand and continue with biodiversity. Trees on your planet Earth, have been in existence, far longer than humanity. Ever wondered why? Nature was not a parochial accident as some may believe and still suspect.'

Marmuron was excited and asked. 'Sun-Ky, what is it like on Tamaryn's planet?'

Sun-Ky was reflective as he began. 'To begin with, the natural splendor is breathtakingly beautiful. It's the closest existence we have, to our own Foundation Forest on WIL's home planet of Giant Vines.'

Marmuron was fascinated. 'Can you describe these Natural Forces for us?'

Sun-Ky smiled. 'Don't look at the universe from the viewpoint of just one of its species. Try to see the visual reality of natural existence from all the others and keep asking, why is it so? Nature as a force, is the essence of humanities existence and survival. However it is so much greater than this.'

Sun-Ky then asked. 'Do you have some more specific mission objectives of your own, in Tamaryn's galaxy?'

16
So, what's our Quest, Oatsy?

Marmuron moved to the front of her lounge chair as she was drawn to Oats broader interests. 'So, what's our quest Oatsy?'

Janet grinned. 'Oats is only just getting warmed up.' We all laughed. Even Oats chuckled. Oats was loving this exchange, between us all.

Oats's emotion showed, as he collected his thoughts. 'It's something really big. A quest, no one has found the answers to yet. Michael and I are so close. We began in our early years, by questioning the logic of our human origins and our recorded history. It didn't make sense. Finding dependable and reliable answers became our dream. Now we can forecast and visualize a path forward, to finding these answers and it's exciting. Our plan is to make our dreams possible and our future depends on which enlightened steps we take now.'

Then Oats felt motivated by one of our great former leaders from the past. 'Mahatma Gandhi once said. **The future depends on what we do in the present. We must become the change we want to see.'**

Oats continued. 'Consider the evolution of thought, among our own planetary cultures. Ask why we still have native tribes on our planet, who've celebrated primitive rituals for more than eight thousand years, with almost no change in their evolutionary understanding or progression? Yet in other more developed cultures, architecture, telecommunications, medicine and transportation alone have progressed rapidly, in only the last five thousand years, beyond any comparison.'

Sun-Ky's thoughts seemed cautious and almost reserved. 'The answers to your dilemma Oats, has its roots in the likely intervention, from a different intelligence, at another time, to lift the conceptual visions of some cultures over others.'

Oats was reflective. 'Yes, some of us believe, that this is possible.'

Janet queried. 'What is behind this?'

Sun-Ky smiled at Janet's eagerness. 'There is good reason to believe, that there was higher intelligence, at the time of the formation of matter Janet, because it is logical. The elementary formation of matter, suggests it.'

Janet was first. 'Where is the logic?'

'There are multiple levels of intelligence in the universe, as early as its beginning. Some questions require a depth of understanding, we are all still searching for.'

'Natural origin suggests a higher level of intelligence in the universe, beyond anything we have ever known, even if you just consider, motion and gravity alone.'

'Any analysis of matter in the universe, will show a geometric symmetry of motion. Whether it is found in particle matter, in orbits of moons, or planets orbiting around a star system, or even larger orbits of star systems around galactic masses.'

Sun-Ky laughed. 'Our society is also looking for answers as to how, when, where and why elementary matter and molecular structure, was created in the first place.'

'Consider the evidence which comes from the original creation and dispersion of matter. The architecture and design of star systems across the universe, the gift of life in all its forms, as we know it.'

'Then there are all the sources of energy. The forces in place, to support and sustain our survival and existence, in this enormously complex design. It's extremely important to keep asking questions of the how, the when, the where and the why in all of this.'

Then. 'Sorry if I'm running on a bit.'

Oats was fascinated with the unknown. 'This is why I love research. It's an acceptance of the reality of the yet to be discovered and a desire to search for answers we can trust. You have been of great help to us, Sun-Ky.'

Sun-Ky then said. 'Oats' your questions about evolution, in traditional communities concerning intervention on your planet, are worthy of further consideration.'

'Evidence of cultural differences can be found in our own societies. Some cultures are more motivated than others, to search for an enlightened interpretation.'

Janet asked. 'Motivated in what way, Sun-Ky?'

'In many ways Janet. Language, communication, architecture. There are several clues. Remember, Nature does not motivate or impede us from doing anything. In life we have a most brilliant opportunity, to probe, search and explore, a greater understanding, of the environment, we all share.'

'There is an abundance of natural resources to observe and experience. We are part of an imaginative Natural design, which asks the gifted minds how they would like to live, to learn, to adjust, to progress and to explore, without any limitations.'

Oats then realized something else. 'These forces in the universe, exist in an almost timeless and weightless vacuum? There's reasonable certainty of planetary movement and predictability of motion with gravity. However, when considering how these forces in Origin began in the universe, something is still missing.'

Janet asked. 'So what's still missing, Oats?'

Sun-Ky was amused as he offered this thought. 'The reasoned logic behind it all.'

Janet immediately came back with. 'The logic?'

'Yes Janet, it's a very large and important part of the cosmological conundrum, but first we need to listen to the rest of Oats descriptions of your quest.'

Something Sun-Ky just said triggered a thought in Oats mind, however he could not work that out just yet, as he continued to try and understand the complexity of evolution. There were many puzzles, mysteries and enigmas which required further research.

Marmuron then asked again. 'What's on your mind, Oats?'

17
Understanding the Natural Force.

'Many things really, however let's start with this. We are trying to interpret and learn from the calming silence and unexplained harmony. Also the infinite tranquility which exists, within many regions of our Natural Force.'

Janet quizzed warmly. 'Is this the short version, Oats?'

Oats smiled. 'It's truly fascinating Janet. There are many laws in the cosmos which govern existence. Guidelines that have been held in a timeless and observable silence. Laws that go back before any recorded history which we have ever known. The laws are methodical, systematic and precise for the existence of elementary atomic matter and the orderly replication of the species.'

Janet was lovely as she tried to help Oats reach the point of his deliberations. 'Can you please give us some worldly examples, Oats?'

'There's a perceptive and even visionary serenity, contained within Nature's layered and silent existence. Living species of multiple floral plant life varieties, in old growth forests, exist with extraordinary diversity. Tall aging trees, speak in calming tones with solitude, strength and seclusion, while forever maintaining a tranquil, composed and unflustered peacefulness. There are of course, numerous contrasts.'

'There's the extreme violence of predatory and carnivorous behavior, in many of Nature's animals, on the open plains, in search of existence with survival. All these living examples can be different again in other geographic regions on our planet. There remains a biological smorgasbord of undiscovered life forms within our tropical rainforests and on our deep ocean floors. There's an almost visionary existence, of exotic and vulnerable living species everywhere.'

Sun-Ky asked. 'Do either of you believe, existence has a purpose?'

Oats then asked. 'Michael?'

Michael laughed. 'You're on fire, Oats.'

Oats continued. 'Our planet has a long history, of cultural diversity. Both Michael and I have always been fascinated, as to how it all began.'

Oats paused, but only for a moment. 'Once again, Charles Darwin believed we began from a single celled organism about three and a half billion years ago. That the ancestry of mankind, had its origins in Africa. The brilliant contribution from his work, was in the formation of the initial discussion, on Origin itself.'

'Darwin's research was invaluable, however his speculative hypothesis remains completely unconvincing and inconclusive on several grounds and helped create decades of unnecessary racial tension, conflict and division between different ethnic cultures.'

Marmuron questioned. 'Why, Oatsy?'

Janet then offered this. 'It's the many remaining unanswered questions. As a human race, if we were all from the same source of primate as theorized, then why do we have different facial structures and appearances? There is a diversity of cultures, a history of languages and varying times of existence, all by geographic region alone?'

Janet was more involved now and began to explain the differences. 'Yes we evolved, but not in the way theorized by Darwin.

So we discovered that all these theories have flaws. The question is, where do we go from here?'

Oats suddenly blurted out. 'Tamaryn was right. Our planet, has misunderstood our origin, in the universe, ever since our earliest philosophical beginnings.'

Janet saw the confronting challenges and it seemed almost overwhelming. 'Changing our planets mindset and on this scale, is virtually impossible on our mission.'

Then Oats asked. 'What are we missing here, Sun-Ky?'

Sun-Ky paused. 'It is the life force you see every day. The unexplained Natural Force, which has a universal presence. Life motivates us to reason, to question, and to reproduce. Life enlightens us to think and to rationalize, while encouraging us to find harmony and accept each other with understanding, in peaceful co-existence.'

'Nature is a force, with an instant captivating charm and an all-embracing presence. The force is your first breath and last gasp of fresh air. It is a lifelong education, for those who choose to explore, the origins of Nature's living messages.'

Pim seemed hesitant. 'There's something else Michael'

Oats turned. 'About Nature?'

'Yes, it can be an unstable force.'

Oats queried. 'In what way, Pim?'

'Both small and large, I'm afraid.' Then. 'It is so easy to destroy, what can be so inherently hard to create. You may well ask why our culture interferes, why we encourage, why we nurture and motivate Nature to exist, thrive and multiply.'

Pim continued. 'It is because Nature needs friends to survive. There is a common vulnerability and fragility in this force, as existence is not always guaranteed. Characteristics of survival in Nature can often be destroyed. Life may not be sustainable, without this cultivating, fostering and nurturing program of support.'

Pim paused. 'Just as it is so easy to destroy tree life, it is also easy on a much grander scale, to destroy the orbital path of planets, only to see them slip out of course and be consumed by their central solar mass.'

Janet became a little concerned. 'But how could that happen, Pim?'

Pim was moved. 'An opposite force moving against the orbiting planets direction.'

Then. 'Something small, like an erupting volcano is unlikely to cause this change. However a massive collision could. These forces can work, both for us and against us.'

'Our relationship with Nature is one of nurturing and self-help, for our own survival. You will find these differences, in the social complexity of Tamaryn's varied societies. This is not a judgment, either for or against, one social order or another. Each of the planetary visions you will see, have different approaches to life and Nature. It comes down to the individual choices they all make and the boundaries they are, or are not prepared to cross.'

Janet asked. 'Is that the main focus, to look for Sun-Ky?'

Sun-Ky said. 'Perhaps there is one other larger influence to mention now. It is the capacity to care, which lies within each one of us. Caring offers a diversity of emotional choices. Just as there are harmful influences, which bring disillusionment and disappointment, there are also enormous and overriding benefits, found in nurturing.'

Janet seemed puzzled. 'How does it begin?'

'It is in our capacity to love, which will define who we are and what we become. Watch carefully, at all levels in these societies, which you see. Animosity and ill feeling will destroy some hopes and dreams, while poor leadership will accelerate this demise.'

'This is about each individual's interpretation of choices. Peace, freedom, love, honor, moral character and decency are all personal life choices. Some species will deviate from higher moral choices, however they will lose something, when they do.'

'It is only when you come back to a natural environment, you realize how close you are, to the endurable and ecologically sustainable, Natural Force. In a moment of self- evaluation, there comes a level of candor and sincerity, in your isolation with Nature.'

'The most perfect example of this can be found on Tamaryn's home planet, where harmony lives with tranquility. Patience, tolerance and restraint, live with forgiveness and compassion. Always remember that Nature never passes judgment on its species. Our own conscience will eventually pass judgment, on the life we have led, as you will see.'

Sun-Ky then revealed. 'You will observe this, when you see the planet of Isolation. It is a home for those who are prepared to live without Nature's basic character.'

Oats queried. 'Is this like a prison planet?'

'No Oats, it is important to remember, Nature does not criticize, condemn, deride or pass judgment. Many of the people on Isolation, live in a happy sense of denial and self-acceptance, while overlooking Nature's silent messages and overtures.'

Then Sun-Ky gave some further insight. 'Nature as a force, survives in each one of us, through the continuous reproduction of the species. All living things including plants, flowers, trees, vines and every animal class would perish without replication, reproduction and breeding. In higher order animal classes, choices are made and some boundaries are crossed, however future existence would be lifeless, without the emotional incentive, sensual stimulation and capacity to reproduce, among many species.'

'Throughout Tamaryn's many planetary communities, civilization engages with Nature, on different levels. Those closest to Nature, on her primal planet, possess and appreciate the most wonderful sense of simplicity, in existence. Others who challenge the Natural Force in their character or behavior, find their own level of peace, within the boundaries they choose to set and the paths they choose, to cross in life.'

'What does that mean?'

Sun-Ky smiled. 'All will become clearer, soon.'

Sun-Ky realized we still had many unresolved questions and reservations. It was over the multiple and inexplicable differences, in the way our planet's cultures viewed their own history, verses our global history, particularly, our views on Origin.

18
Key to Unraveling, Earth's Recorded History.

After a pause, Sun-Ky began. 'Many societies on your planet Earth have conflicting views of world history and naturally enough, many believe their own version of history, is correct.' Janet looked puzzled as Sun-Ky's thoughts became more reflective. 'We do need to clear up a few things, before we arrive, in the boundaries of Tamaryn's galaxy.'

Then Sun-Ky said. 'Throughout your ancient history, it has been believed that a God in mankind's image, created Heaven and Earth. Following a quick review we will show you overwhelming evidence, that these beliefs are logically unsound. We will also reveal some visionary insights, which show that no God, could have created this.'

Janet gulped. 'What?'

Oats became fascinated. 'Hold on Janet.'

Sun-Ky continued. 'Michael, we need to look forward as visionaries and not just back, as historians. To find real answers to the origin of the species on Earth, we must first review your past creative existence, to correctly identify how programed belief began. We need to reveal the reality of existence, as it was and enlighten your perceptions, about the universe as it is, before we reach Tamaryn's galaxy.'

Michael was immediately inspired, to have an intelligent debate and resolve some of our, age old dilemmas about origin.

Janet became more inquisitive. 'So, our recorded history is incorrect?'

'Often recorded history is written, for how some in the past want their own times to be remembered. We must use this opportunity now, to correctly interpret these past narratives and false impressions. It is essential for everyone to recapture an open mind.'

Oats cheered up. 'This is one of the reasons why we are so excited about seeing Tamaryn again. She had a very powerful and eloquent explanation, for the history of deities, from our ancient times and helped us understand why Copernicus struggled, with his own discoveries.'

Oats often wondered why, this period of Earth's enlightenment, seemed to languish and stagnate, when so much more of an explanation, could have been found.

Pim asked. 'We have noticed you are all still struggling, for reliable answers?'

Oats revealed his frustrations. 'The current narratives just don't make any sense. Our different cultures, can't all be right, about origin'

Pim smiled. 'Sun-Ky has a deeper understanding of galaxy history than most and I've asked him to help explain all the outstanding doubts and queries you may have. Sun-Ky comes with a strong reputation for making difficult concepts, easier to understand.'

Oats and Michael smiled broadly as Sun-Ky explained. 'From the earliest of times in your ancient history, many saw heavenly existence, as a creation by a loving God, with the Earth at the center of the heavens. Without help from telescopic enlargements, magnification from satellites or advanced, sensing technology; changes in the movement of regional bodies provided the limit of their cosmic interpretations. Many advances since those earlier times, have uncovered the magnitude of what we now understand, as the universe of galaxies.'

'Michael, so much of your history is still remembered, inside the records of early mythology and belief in traditional folklore. It's now critically important, to correctly interpret this historical narrative and to see things, as they really are.'

Janet was mystified. 'We covered all this before, with Tamaryn.'

'Not quite Janet, Tamaryn helped you see back through almost seventeen hundred years of your history, to show that Jesus of Nazareth, was created to be the Son of a Roman god.' Then. 'Remember an old saying of yours, about wealth, power and control.'

Sun-Ky paused. 'Your civilization has a collection of ancient records which began over three and a half thousand Earth years ago and were summarized in the 'Holy Bible'. This reference book, claims to understand what happened from the beginning, at the point of Origin.'

Oats was absolutely glued to his seat at the thought of further illumination on these issues. Sun-Ky noticed this growing level of enthusiasm as he continued. 'It is imperative we clarify your understanding of Origin, against how we see the universe, as it really exists. We have a more logical interpretation, if we can review it for you now?'

Michael watched Oats gripping his fingers with excitement. 'Yes please.'

Sun-Ky laughed. 'Janet, your ancient astronomers have been trying to understand the origin of the cosmos, for thousands of years. We are going to another galaxy and it is important we review this elevated celestial vision of Origin, with you all now.'

Oats was becoming effusive in his enthusiasm. 'Janet, this is what we are searching for, a more enlightened interpretation, of the universe and our place in it.'

Janet was happy to share an open discussion, as long as the errors in our early recorded history could be clearly and logically explained.

Then Sun-Ky asked. 'Oats, what are the pressing concerns propelling you both forward, so we can see where some of these past visions differ?'

'It is the unknown axioms, from several well-constructed past truths. For thousands of years on Earth, life has existed, with an unresolved vision, of enlightenment.

Oats face beamed, as Sun-Ky asked. 'So what are the relevant axioms?

Oats then began. 'I'm hoping to understand the hidden visionary concepts, behind these often quoted references, from our past.'

I. 'As long as there's been 'One True God', there's been killing in his name.'
II. 'A lie gets halfway around the world, before the truth has a chance to get its pants on.'
III. 'Power corrupts and absolute power, corrupts absolutely'
IV. 'History is written, by the victors of wars.'
V. 'To the victor, goes the spoils of war.'
VI. 'If we open a quarrel between the past and the present, we shall find we have lost the future.'
VII. 'Out of intense complexities, intense simplicities emerge.'

Oats paused. 'I want to understand, how these references relate to our past creative beliefs and why so many conflicts, still remain, over how it all began.'

Sun-Ky smiled. 'Oats, there is a fundamental answer, for all of these proverbs.'

Michael became intrigued. 'Just one answer?'

Sun-Ky watched our perplexing looks. 'I can see that none of you have ever lived through, a brutally aggressive regime change before.'

Then Michael added two more. 'There are other documented sayings, recorded down through the ages, consider the unembellished significance of these also.'

VIII. 'The first casualty of war is Truth.'
IX. 'All roads lead to Rome.'

Sun-Ky then said. 'To find the answers to all these proverbs, we need to re-examine key aspects of Roman History. After centuries of warring brutality, **truth** for the Roman Empire became interwoven with the acceptance of their earlier beliefs and mythology.'

Oats was fascinated. 'What aspects in particular?'

Sun-Ky was profoundly diplomatic and gracious in his response. 'From the early stages in life for humanity, the meek and mild in existence, never sought brutal change. Power was never handed over, it was seized. Victory over others was imposed. Wealth was not earnt, it was stolen and control was not sought, it was decreed, where many brutal proclamations were enforced.'

'Before Rome's often ruthless intervention, civilization was made up from many varied ethnic cultures. After centuries of conflict, Rome believed they could continue their empire's vision of greatness, by enforcing peaceful change.'

'Until the present time, Rome's creative wisdom in reshaping their past, has been written into history and been very well concealed.'

This struck a chord with Janet who became more absorbed. 'I don't understand?'

'Janet, if an empire under an administration of ruthless tyranny, wanted peaceful change, what would they do?'

Janet struggled. 'Most of this was revealed by Tamaryn recently as well.'

'No Janet, what Tamaryn helped you with last time, was to give you a more accurate understanding of Rome's influence around AD325. To find the answers you seek on planetary origin, we need to reconsider how institutionalized belief, in ancient cultures began and why these faiths vary so much, between one faith and another.'

While Oats and Michael were still on the edge of their seats, Janet remained puzzled. 'Many people on Earth believe we already have the answers to all this.'

Sun-Ky smiled at the innocence in Janet's response.

Oats began. 'Janet, these unanswered questions, have lingered in the minds of prophet's, philosophers and researchers on our planet for well over three thousand years. One great historic site, remains divided, over these differences in belief. Jerusalem is the only city which holds great status for all believers of the three monotheistic religions, Judaism, Christianity and Islam. The gathering believers, flock to the sacred sites there, holding different views, on our natural origins.'

Oats continued. 'Origin, in the Holy scriptures, claims there was divine intervention. Some in science, are still looking for the 'God particle' and parallel universes. We still don't understand this expanse, which we are all living in. Globally we are yet to agree on all these findings. The most reasonable position to take now, is to look for more clarity in our history, against recent discoveries.'

Michael asked. 'Sun-Ky, can you give us clarity, on this most profound of debates?'

Sun-Ky was very quick to respond. 'Yes, I can.'

Oats was jubilant. 'Brilliant, Janet, there are many thoughtful minds looking for greater clarity and resolve on Universal Origin. What we need is enlightenment on this quest. The endless wars and confrontational crusades, need to come to an end.'

Janet was considering many levels of this complex debate. 'Sun-Ky, can you really answer all these questions and resolve, all these doubts?'

'Yes Janet, the logic behind enlightenment has never been fully revealed before. The Roman Empire had a strategically brilliant and disciplined fighting force. Centuries of conflict had come, at high cost. They faced many choices between the preservation of myths, held in your ancient history of beliefs and the yet to evolve enlightenment.'

Janet asked. 'What is it that we don't know?'

'Janet, what we would like to do is give you a true reflection of Origin, in the universe. This may be hard, however until all minds break free, from the collection of historical beliefs, none of them, will see future enlightenment.'

Oats became more absorbed, as everyone instantly settled.

Sun-Ky continued. 'You need to understand how and why Rome took this path, to continue building their empire, through peaceful means and why Copernicus's discoveries, were never allowed to be completely examined, explored or scrutinized.'

Oats went first. 'You are right, we have never lived through times of barbaric behavior and cruelty and there are so many contradictions, in ancient belief.'

Sun-Ky smiled. 'We can help your search, with a more inspired and uplifting perspective of Origin?

Then. 'We look at the universe a little differently than you do and we need to explain this view, for you now.'

Michael grinned. 'If you can help us understand these axioms from our past and help us find out where peace was lost on our planet, then we will be eternally grateful.'

Sun-Ky smiled. 'Let's begin now.' There was a building enthusiasm in the mood among us. Many things didn't add up, from past analysis of our planetary history. Could Origin have been misinterpreted by mankind in our past? Both Oats and Michael were thrilled for these chances, in this moment of discovery ahead.

Sun-Ky began. 'What motivates you personally to rediscover your history, Oats?'

Oats face reddened as his eyes became more tearful. 'Exactly for the reasons you mention. An informed open discussion, has long been overdue. There's been a concerted effort by biblical scholars in our past, to shut down or restrict any questioning over the history of belief. We won't unify as a race on our planet, until these answers are found.'

'If we could find the answers and help our planet stop fighting with each other and resolve their differences peacefully and unite, that would be worth something?'

'How will humanity ever learn anything new, if we are just taught to believe and remember, without any questioning, of our ancient past? If we spent more time as a race on our future, rather than on the imaginative mythology of past cultural beliefs, then more young lives could be saved.'

Oats then reflected on another historical reference. 'One of Earth's great early philosophers, Omah Khayyam (1048-1131) also questioned our written history. As a renowned Persian mathematician and astronomer, he wrote.

> **"I sent my Soul through the Invisible.**
> **Some letter, of that After-life to spell: And**
> **by and by my Soul return'd to me. And**
> **answer'd: I Myself, am Heav'n and Hell"**

Oats regathered his thoughts. 'Until we struggle as a race to resume this search for historical truth, our planet will never discover real peace. With global unity, humanity could look forward to an inspiring future, once more.'

Janet developed tears as she gave Oats a hug. 'They are lovely reasons, for us all to move forward, Oats.'

It was then that Sun-Ky answered. 'Together on this voyage we will find these answers for you all, Oats.'

19
How did Mythology, become Established on Earth?

One of Oats' recent discoveries was now weighing him down. 'How do you change, such globally entrenched ancient beliefs, with a more modern conceptual vision?'

'How do you help a world, believing in multiple, sacred and religious differences, that they are just observing the past, from a different ancient perspective, in time?'

Oats was now puzzled. 'Michael, do you remember when we both went to see Ayres Rock in Central Australia, named after Sir Henry Ayres.?'

Sun-Ky watched with growing interest. 'Tell us about this example Oats.'

Uluru (Ayres Rock) is one of Australia's most recognizable natural landmarks. The largely sandstone formation, stands 348 meters above ground, rising 863 meters above sea level with most of its bulk lying underground, to a depth estimated to be about six kilometers. The rock has a total circumference at the base of about 9.4 kilometers.'

'This rock has great cultural significance, for the traditional indigenous tribes and forms part of their ancient Aboriginal dreamtime, in the area.'

Janet declared. 'I've always wanted to go there, Oats.'

'Yes Michael and I loved the experience, however entrenched belief is not new. I raise this because the rock is believed to date back over five hundred million years.'

'It has been deemed hallowed ground and sacred to the indigenous tribes for many thousands of years, before the pyramids in Egypt were built, before Christ was born, or many other religious orders, ever began.'

Janet's thoughts softened. 'I'm still trying to understand the point here Oats.'

'Well, how are we ever going to find enlightenment on our planet, when the major debating points revolve around, who discovered it first, who owns it and what we call it?

'It is just one of many examples of how some societies, living with past ancient beliefs, can hold their own progress back. If we are ever going to learn more as a race, we should be far more interested in, its origin, the rock's geology and how it got there.'

'If some of us can't move beyond sacred historical beliefs, then insight for our future generations, will never be found and universal enlightenment, will be lost.'

Janet sounded a note of caution. 'People still have a right to believe, don't they?'

Michael answered. 'Yes of course Janet. However, some of our civilizations have been fighting with each other, over different religious beliefs, for thousands of years.'

Oats paused. 'Our search is an ancient one, more ancient than humanities time on Earth. A time before men and women made proclamations about anything and a time before natural existence for us, all began.' Oats paused as he smiled warmly. 'We're looking for a more reliable and dependable explanation for universal Origin, than some of the versions and theories, we have now.'

'Unraveling this search for conclusive evidence, has been forced underground, even before the times of Copernicus.'

'This is an adventure of discovery Janet. We don't know all the answers yet, but the future is not about changing past beliefs. It's about finding breakthrough answers with reliable research. Michael and I both see a better future for humanity, if we're all united. Historical references are extremely helpful, in interpreting the future.'

Janet smiled. 'There's more to this driving you Oats, isn't there?'

'Yes, the history of belief is considered sacrosanct, and can't be touched. It is the only field of learning on our planet which conditions a person's mind to believe blindly in the past, without any questioning of reality, or a re- examination of the evidence.'

It was time to move on and Sun-Ky asked. 'Oat's let's go back and look at some more recent beliefs. You both just learnt about some aspects of ancient Roman history. Can you quickly summarize these findings, for the rest of us?

Oats began. 'Early in the fourth century, Rome wanted non-violent change, across their empire, to enable a peaceful withdrawal, of their Roman legions. Much of the early teachings about Origin and creation for many cultures has not changed since those times. Our only interest here, is in finding a more logical and enlightened perspective.'

Something else suddenly jolted with Oats. 'Remember our recent discussions on the history of other fields of study. Ask why we have had major advances in medicine, architecture, construction, travel, communications and electronics, just to name some examples. In the last two thousand years, humanity has conducted research for fresh and innovative answers, to improve our knowledge, in these fields of interest.'

Michael had been reflecting on this past history as well. 'Oats, just consider modes of transport alone. Look how far we've all come in the last few hundred years, since horses and carts.'

Oats agreed. 'Yes, as a race we have challenged ourselves to find answers in all these other fields of endeavor, with research. Why not look for logic in Origin as well?'

Michael explained the quandary he was still having. 'If the stated records are accurate and the Bible is a true representation of faith and belief, then why as a global race, do we still remain so divided? We have endured a history of Holy crusades and religious wars, going back over a thousand years with differences in this belief.'

Janet queried. 'What's missing, is the why in all of this?'

Michael paused as he realized the enormity of this quest. 'Janet, many researchers before us, have tried to discover the answers, we are still searching for now.'

Then Marmuron asked. 'Why do these ancient views, live on through generations?'

Oats replied. 'It is because we are coached and programed from an early age, to learn, to remember and to believe as children, in what we are told.'

'Can you give us an example of this, Oats?'

'It begins from the very first line, on the first page, of the book of Genesis in the Holy Bible which describes in detail, a belief of what happened in the beginning. Children will never learn anything new, if adults keep programming them to trust and accept these ancient beliefs on Origin. Surely concepts must be open to revision of thought? This repetitive mind programming, to future generations, is restricting children to a concept taught, since our ancient times.'

Marmuron queried. 'Why were these ancient beliefs, completely accepted across so many, ancient Roman lands?'

Sun-Ky asked. 'Let's quickly review this history briefly and limit it to the narrow perspective of belief about Origin. I'd like you to consider some questions. How did this memory of creation evolve and why have so many generations believed, in images of superior human beings, as creators?'

'We know ancient belief misunderstood orbital positioning in the cosmos, so why in the modern era instruct children, to continue believing this ancient version of events?'

Oats agreed. 'Humanity has been looking for these answers for thousands of years and in ancient times, some great minds believed in their own version and interpretation.'

Janet then asked. 'How was the evolution of thought, compromised?'

Michael said. 'Ancient philosophical belief, had the Earth positioned at the center of the Heavens, until it was challenged by Copernicus. The important point is that inquisitive minds were shut down, by biblical inquisitions, claiming blasphemous disrespect. A free thinking mind was blocked from questioning any new evidence, for centuries. This is the reason why Oats and I are searching for cosmic reality. We want to find common ground, with which everyone can work.'

Sun-Ky said. 'Your planet's transition, from an age of belief, to an age of reasoned enlightenment has been stalled.' Then 'Michael, always begin by asking who had the most to gain, from creating your historical records, in the first place and why?

Janet agreed. 'With so many different cultural backgrounds, it has become almost impossible to find common ground, on what to believe. However, social order has advanced enormously, over these past centuries.'

Sun-Ky said. 'Oats, enlightenment begins now, on this mission. The answers will be found with common understanding. It begins by questioning the how, the when, the where and most importantly the why, these records, were created in the first place.'

Oats and Michael were amazed. 'You can explain all of this, Sun-Ky?'

'Yes, let's look a little deeper at who advanced and encouraged these records and why. Ask how these changes would impact on their powerful interests and importantly, what were their motives? There's an important part of your history, which has never been explained. During the times of Copernicus, the church was protecting the very foundations, of these ancient beliefs.'

Sun-Ky then said. 'In Copernicus's time, he was not prosecuting a case against religious beliefs, he was searching for enlightenment. His efforts were being stifled by the church. So the question remains, what was the church concealing and why?'

Sun-Ky smiled warmly as he invited Oats to begin, by disclosing his most baffling of concerns. 'Oats, why don't you start first.'

20
Why was Copernicus, a Wasted Opportunity?

Oats paused, but not for long. This was one of his most favorite subjects and finally with Sun-Ky's help, he might be able to resolve this timeless conundrum.

Oats began slowly. 'Okay, so Copernicus was able to establish with almost complete clarity, that all our ancient society's views on Origin were creatively conceived. Prior to A.D.1543, all claims made in our past about the astronomical positioning, of heavenly bodies and how the universe was formed, were imaginatively conceived.'

'We've since learnt that our solar system is a true reflection of geometric symmetry and design in the universe. What we want to know more about now, is how and why.'

'Our system?' breathed Janet.

Oats continued. 'No, it's slightly more complex than that Janet. We would love to know more about design; what is the conceptual purpose and what are the other forces in place? Copernicus witnessed, a revolutionary breakthrough from existing beliefs, with his research, into the movement of nearby heavenly bodies.'

Marmuron queried. 'What do you mean nearby, Oats?'

'Planets in our solar system, named after their gods, were being influenced by invisible Natural Forces, which explained, continuous planetary motion.'

Michael added. 'These observations led to a revision, moving away from ancient belief in creationism, where Earth, was thought to be, at the center of the Heavens.'

Sun-Ky smiled. 'We can help you with a logical interpretation of this later.'

Pim then moved to clarify something else for Oats. 'Oats, your world has had the answers to this, since the times of Copernicus. The visionary evidence, just wasn't logically considered, at the time.'

Oats became more engaged, if it was possible 'In what way Pim?'

'It is in the way your planet has prosecuted the limitations of your discoveries. Living Natural Forces aren't global, they are universal.'

Janet seemed puzzled. 'Can someone please explain this simply?'

Sun-Ky responded. 'Maybe I can help?'

Janet smiled with increasing curiosity. 'Please.'

Sun-Ky said 'Oats, the discoveries which Copernicus's research revealed, also have to be considered against the background of the times in which he lived. It is important to remember, that he survived at a time, of persecution and oppression, where trust in God, was held without question, by the highest authorities.'

Immediately Janet agreed. 'Yes of course.'

Sun-Ky smiled. 'This belief had existed unchanged for more than a thousand years and was held in place by the institutionalized teaching of the Apostle's creed, celebrating acceptance, of their ancient beliefs.'

'In Copernicus's time, anyone who questioned belief, was charged with heresy. Inquisitions were held by the church. The whole concept of a living existence at that time was based on a doctrine of faith, in the worshiping of God, as the creator of the heavens.'

'It was inconceivable in those times to challenge authority. Freedom of thought, of speech and of expression, were not permitted in these times, of cruelty and persecution.'

Janet nodded. 'Yes, I hadn't quite considered it like that before. So something has been left out, or not yet explained?'

Oats agreed. 'Yes we're still searching for a reliable vision of how the universe was formed. Some well-established beliefs, yes. Many theories, but no definitive answers.'

Janet began. 'Many still live with this belief and ancient religious acceptance.'

Sun-Ky asked. 'Janet, if we could continue this illumination with you supporting these earlier beliefs, then I can help you all find the visionary enlightenment you seek. Are you prepared to help, in this process?'

Janet willingly agreed. 'Why yes, yes of course.'

Sun-Ky then patiently began. 'Remember what happens at birth. Our thinking minds exist as a blank canvas, where observation, training and teaching begins.'

'What we need to do now, is to un-muddle our minds and reconsider the reality of existence, as it truly occurs, in the universe.'

Janet became even more focused. 'Reconsider what in particular?'

'Well we weren't born to believe. We have been given minds to reason with, to question, to observe and resolve doubts. We are here to enlighten the next generation, not to confine their minds to be prisoners of the past. We must start with an open mind.'

This caught Oats by surprise. 'So it's a missing logical deduction then?'

Sun-Ky countered. 'It's a little more complicated than that, Oats.'

Oats expression brightened. 'Okay, so what are we missing?

'True enlightenment, will rarely come to a made up mind. The vision Copernicus saw, never had the chance to be fully explored, in his time.'

Janet responded. 'Yes it was.'

Sun-Ky could quickly read Michael's thoughts about being gentle with explanations to Janet, because of her higher levels of existing belief. 'No, no it wasn't Janet.' Then after a pause. 'His research has been suppressed, with little wide spread debate since. He was censored. About three hundred years later, Charles Darwin presented more parochial findings, on the 'Origin of the Species' and on Origin itself.'

Then. This further planetary self-examination, was largely restricted to the evolution of life, on your planet. A better insight on Origin comes, with a more far reaching and insightful vision.'

Then Sun-Ky noted. 'Consider a cosmic view which was not allowed to be considered during Copernicus's time, due to religious dominance and repressive rule.'

Even Janet wanted to get to the bottom of this now. 'You have this insight?'

'Yes Janet. Copernicus's discovery, came at an unprecedented turning point.'

Pim then shared some of her deepest thoughts. 'Michael, when we first met you, we were able to capture, much of your planet's amazing, recorded history. We would like to reexamine this evolution of thought, with you now. Some of your secret societies in earlier times, tried to become more enlightened.'

Oats felt inspired. 'How, I mean what happened, Pim?'

'The narrative of mythology, needs to be reconsidered and revisited. This became the secret societies, new challenge. To find logical answers, which they could trust. With increased determination, more began to meet in secret as new findings, helped inspire the many inventions and discoveries which followed, like medicine.'

'Oats interrupted with building excitement. 'Yes but what was discovered?'

'I'm afraid that biblical records, while filled with empathy, good Christian values and kindness, don't accurately reflect, the reality of Nature.'

Oats agreed. 'Yes, for minds willing to search and think for themselves, there still remains, so much more to learn.'

Sun-Ky countered. '**Our battle to survive a living existence, is only matched by humanities struggle to understand it. By any account, Natural Forces are our closest link yet, to understanding Origin better.**'

'It is important for the future of humanity to correct, the rewriting of your history. Consider, if your history of belief is an accurate reflection of Origin, then why do so many culturally divisive and contentious issues still remain, over these differences in belief? To understand, it is essential to go back and reevaluate ancient times, in the Roman Empire.'

'In the following analysis consider this. To remain great, Rome did everything for strategic reasons and tactical advantage. Throughout the following re-examination of historical images, remember, Rome transferred wealth and power to the bishops to maintain control, for future authority and governance. Finally, if mankind never questions, past mythology on Earth, humanity will never find an illuminating future.'

There was a warm enthusiasm building between Marmuron and Oats as Janet queried. 'There's an illuminating future, Sun-Ky?'

'Yes, however let's firstly clarify the omissions made in the past, Janet.'

Oats was in several minds again as Michael asked. 'What's on your mind Oats?'

Oats was reflective. 'In my early years on our planet, if you read comic books there were both super heroes and evil villains. All designed to appeal to your imagination. Some chose to believe in these characters while others didn't. For thousands of years we have been subjected, to folklore and mythology. Some of it gave our people hope and inspiration to believe in a better life ahead.'

Janet didn't want to lose this thread. 'Yes Oats, but where's the illumination?'

Oats continued. 'About five hundred years ago some brilliant minds uncovered a different world. A natural planetary concept, that more closely resembled reality. Belief is a very personal thing for some and what they are prepared to accept, in their own hearts and minds, is their choice. Some will want to live in the past, but I'm on the edge of my seat waiting for an explanation I can trust.'

Sun-Ky looked kindly on Oats. 'That will come shortly. Firstly let's consider some famous examples of how biblical mythology began and why your history, was rewritten from AD325.

21
The Continuation of Greatness, in Rome's Empire.

From freedom, to slavery then, freedom once more.

Sun-Ky created some more images. 'Rome began with a conceptual vision of greatness and over the centuries, achieved this greatness.'

'The influence of accumulated wealth, absolute power and complete control had filtered, from the emperor down, where greatness was widely seen as the preservation of privilege for the elites. Survival began, for those whose cultures and societies were oppressed, victimized and overthrown.'

'Over centuries of conquest, the consequences from invasive hostility, had also been great. There was an enormous suppression of feelings, built up from a surviving sense of loss and suffering. In this new repressive order, free men went from having liberty to surviving with suppression and slavery, under an autocratic and exploitive rule.'

'There were other greats, including the courage of the vanquished. **After centuries of rule, the patricians in AD325 appreciated, if true peace was to be restored, then the conditions of acceptance for change, must also be great.** Early in the fourth century, past records of belief began to be accumulated. Rome knew the oppressed cultures, living in their empire; caught up in this tyranny, were desperately pleading for change.'

'It became clear to the patricians that there was a missing sense of loss and compassion, mutual respect and a host of guiding ethical values, including hope, kindness, love, warmth, peace and belonging.'

'Now faced with this need for change, Rome sought an even greater vision. One that would attempt to explain Origin, with a memory of their empires, place in it. This new vision for transformation, after centuries of brutality, required a revolution of ideas.'

'This was the beginning of a different era, with a new idea. Just for a moment, let's reexamine this greatness, which took the Roman Empire from its beginnings, to be one of the greatest empires of all time, on your planet.'

Influences of the Roman Empire.

I. 'The Roman Empire stands today and throughout history, as one of your most enduring jurisdictions, of all time.'

II. 'Their influence over western civilization and culture has been profound, by any measure. It was the most powerful economic, cultural, political and military influence in the world and arguably the most influential, in world history.'

III. 'At its height, it covered almost five million square kilometers, and ruled an estimated seventy million people. Or at that time, almost 21% of the world's entire population.'

IV. 'From AD325, Rome was moving from a range of ancient pagan beliefs, to a more acceptable, newly defined and inclusive version, of legendary mythology.'

V. 'While there are many great things to admire about the Roman Empire, there's a cruelty, built into the concept of wanting to control someone's desire to be free. Historically from an elite's perspective, control leads to power and this power over others, lead to wealth accumulation, which was then used, to preserve privilege.'

VI. 'Think deeply on this, as to how power was used to create change. An ordinary individual's mind becomes captive, to a greater legendary belief in mythology.'

VII. 'Humanity, was born into an existence which extended anywhere between poverty and privilege. Existence for many, was often a struggle to survive and the power held by the patricians, or aristocratic elite classes, had always understood this.'

VIII. 'For hundreds of years this empire instilled a lasting influence on culture, reverence towards gods of mythology, architecture, philosophy, law and customs.'

IX. 'From the period around AD325, an evolving Christian civilian culture, spread further on a global scale, playing a crucial role in the progressive evolution of Christianity, in the modern era.'

Pim now brought up many more images, showing an age where there had been literally centuries of conflict. 'Many captured cultures, were truly sick of it all. The promise of this revolutionary change for peace took hold, where the legions could be withdrawn, belief could be instilled and the defeated won their freedom. Some records from these times were preserved and enshrined, for eternity.'

'The patrician's could visualize what the conquered and the slaves among them had lost, in their struggle for freedom. It was the persecution and cruelty that the empire's brutality, had created. But what was, this new vision?'

'Freedom, wanted deliverance from evil and an inspirational concept of Origin that the conquered and enslaved could believe in. Also, that peace can exist with hope, that a vision for social harmony could be reborn.'

Pim continued. 'The Holy Bible's collection of printed records, took on a global perspective of Origin, as it described the 'OTG' and how life began with creation.'

Janet was looking bewildered. 'Pim, I feel there's a big but, coming.'

'Yes, this is really important to remember, these views came from an empire representing about 21% of the world's population.'

Oats had been thinking about a recent statement and developed a stunned look on his face. 'I've just realized something. So the views of about seventy nine percent of the World's population, were not represented in the Holy Bibles founding records, either as a record of closely held spiritual beliefs, or other cultures beliefs, on planetary origins.'

Then another, thought blasting moment from Oats. 'So these records began just under the authority of the Roman Empire. These are their authorized biblical records?'

Sun-Ky was measured. 'You could look at it like that Oats.'

Oats began mumbling to himself again. 'This history of creation, dating from before AD325 has never been critically examined. Children are just educated to accept and believe, this version of Origin.'

'We have never been taught to question, the accuracy of these ancient beliefs, or how the universe was actually formed.'

Then a further thought. 'Could this be why this history of belief in the 'OTG' has caused such provocation, with contentious debates, over time?

Sun-Ky smiled and nodded. 'Quite possibly, Oats.'

Pim continued. 'Let's consider the first of many perspectives of this narrative?

A global perspective from Earth.

'Janet, you asked us how the Roman Empire could be accused of rewriting history. Your planet is still living in the times, of the Roman Empire's rewritten history.'

'Consider this. If an empire were to compile a book from their manuscripts and ancient records, which declares and proclaims it to represent a view of creation from the very beginning of time, this would certainly be a celebrated work of its age.'

'However, what if this book does not represent all cultures, other faiths from other historical records. There's too many to name, however the other seventy nine percent of the world's population, would have a cultural history of their own views, to consider.'

Janet's puzzled expression asked. 'Some examples would help.'

'Well the Egyptians, the Chinese, Aztecs and Middle Eastern cultures for example. Then there's the America's and other Asian cultures. What if this book did not represent the beliefs of all cultures? The historic views of the other seventy nine percent of people on the planet at the time, can be different, from those expressed in the biblical records.'

'Especially from the times of these earlier meetings, in Nicaea.' Janet was still coming to terms with this observation. 'If a book on belief and faith, ignores the other cultural views, of a global society, could this not create an eternal conflict, over these differences?'

'What if this book seeks to include, but fails to be inclusive, or seeks to be illustrative but is not completely representative. Then it could be rightly argued that the testimonies and assertions made in this book about Origin, are from ancient records yes; but only speculative of the best assessments of Origin, at that time, in their opinion.'

'This book has become the most widely read and accepted book, ever printed and preaches, moralizes and instructs humanity about belief, in the 'OTG'.'

'Isn't it time, seventeen hundred years later, to reconsider this history, to find a perspective and a reality, which is more globally inclusive and universally accepted?'

Michael had been listening quietly to this and responded. 'Yes, maybe it is.'

'Oats, just consider how hard it was for Copernicus, or how hard it is, even now to ask a planetary population to step back for a moment and then move forward, in a united way. **We are not rejecting an empires history, we are seeking a more inclusive society.**'

Sun-Ky and Pim watched quietly while Oats, Janet and Michael rationalized and reasoned, between themselves. This in itself had been an instructive, helpful and enlightening moment.

Sun-Ky then questioned another aspect of recorded history. 'You asked me to draw a distinction between rumor and fact. Let's begin by questioning a story, which became a legend, many hundreds of years ago. As we progress, I want you all to question all these issues with logic, as they are raised. Whether it is true or not, depends on what each of us is prepared to believe. These stories, myths and legends have been retold and confirmed in biblical records, since ancient times. Children are programed from an early age to remember this version of events, from Christian records only, which vary from those records, held in the Quran. An Arabic central religious text of Islam, which Muslims believe is a revelation from Allah (God). So let's review the following.'

A perspective of the narrative, from the Middle East.

'This powerfully created memory, of an unnatural birth, to a virgin woman, on the borders of Rome's Empire, is worthy of further consideration.'

I. 'Why would Rome's gathering in Nicaea in AD325 immortalize and glorify a death with the sanctity it implies, in the heartland of differing cultural faiths?

II.   'Then ask, why would, the 'Creator of Heaven and Earth' allow this act of the death of his son, to occur in a place and at a time, which could provoke endless hostility, with continued violence in this region, rather than bringing peace for all people?

III. 'That his child is recognized in Biblical records, almost three hundred years after his death and immortalized as the 'SOG' becomes a very defining and powerful memory.

IV.   'Whose interests does it serve, to endorse the origin of Christian beliefs in this area from AD325? As an act by the 'SOG' to forgive centuries of hostility committed by Rome's Empire, while creating havoc on the border, among other empires and cultures.'

V.   'For over fifteen hundred years since, humanity has fought continued outbreaks of violence, over contrasting beliefs, in this region.'

VI.   'The created immortality of the 'SOG' remains disputed, by some cultures and is not recognized by some other faiths, with their own differences in their history of beliefs.

VII. Could this series of events, in that part of their empire, have been a strategically important account, for the patricians and elites among the Roman aristocracy, to preserve at the time?

22
The Preservation of Rome's Greatness.

Janet was puzzled. 'I'm still feeling a little lost?'
'Okay let's stop for a moment to summarize and review. I'd like you to consider Janet, that your history on Earth, has been selectively rewritten, since AD325.'

Janet seemed bewildered. 'You can't rewrite history.'

Sun-Ky smiled at her innocence. 'Yes you can, Janet. Remember, in the last moments of Jesus's life the Roman Empire did not know who he was.' Sun-Ky then paused as if he wanted to emphasize something. Michael and Oats both felt an important breakthrough, coming, as if they may have missed a critical turning point, in history.

Sun-Ky continued. 'Oats, what does common science on your planet believe took place, in the beginning of the creation, of the universe?'

Oats was initially puzzled. 'Well many believe that there was a Big Bang, a massive explosion that resonated, throughout the universe, which helped explain the expansive motion of matter.'

Sun-Ky smiled. 'No Oats, what happened before this?'

Oats developed a completely blank expression, as Sun-Ky continued. 'Atomic matter had to be originally created.' Then 'So let's collect some evidence. It is very important to consider the fundamentals of design in the universe. There is a geometric symmetry of motion, with matter as discussed.'

Janet remained puzzled as Oats explained. 'Yes, there are rotating forces in motion with atoms, solar systems and galaxies. All matter is influenced by motion.'

Sun-Ky then queried. 'There is also a stability in movement, which sustains perpetual planetary motion. What I'd like you to consider is that the Big Bang theory may well be wrong. It is quite possible, that Origin's conceptual design is not yet, well understood.'

Now Oats was intrigued. 'Sun-Ky, are you able to enlighten us on this?'

'To improve understanding, we need to further examine current beliefs on your planet. The greatest collection of ancient beliefs comes from Biblical records, where your planets history, was rewritten to explain Origin. What happened in the beginning? The evolution of humanity. The exclusion of pagan gods and the fact that these records largely served the interests, of the Roman Empire at the time. Are you ready for this analysis?

We all glanced, as Janet nodded hesitantly. 'Yes.'

'What was not commonly understood at the time, were the strategic interests, of the Roman Empire.

    I. 'Centuries of conflict, was having an impact, on their treasury reserves.'
    II. 'The creation of a far reaching vision, giving hope through peace was needed.'
    III. 'This new vision, was to bring about a cessation, of ruthless hostilities.'
    IV. 'The gradual ceding of freedom, giving a sense of hope, to the enslaved masses.'
    V. 'Belief in change was essential, to limit the potential of popular uprisings.'

VI. 'This could be achieved with a peaceful end, to hostility across their empire.'

VII. 'Past pagan gods, would have no moral authority, for this uniting vision.'

VIII. 'An inclusive forgiveness, for Rome's centuries of conquering brutality, while safe guarding their accumulated wealth, would for all time, record their classical greatness.'

IX. 'Preservation of power, with a peaceful transition of authority, to the Bishops.'

X. 'Maintenance of control over human behavior and the suppression of rebellion.'

XI. 'An acceptance of a 'One True God', greater than all previous pagan gods.'

XII. 'Accepting of a superior being, who had created, Heaven and Earth.'

XIII. 'A loving, forgiving Father who provided a path to deliverance, to all from evil.'

XIV. 'Everyone, except the Roman aristocracy, needed to pray, for forgiveness.'

XV. 'In the creation of institutionalized belief, there was a path to an afterlife, in God's Heaven.'

XVI. 'This elevation of values, became the vision, for the unresolved mysteries of the heavens in their time and this was the first step in their era, to universal enlightenment.'

XVII. 'The First Council, included Christian bishops and was convened in the Bithynian city of Nicaea, by the Roman Emperor Constantine I, in AD 325. **As was the history of the Roman Empire; any transition towards a peaceful change, must also be great.**'

XVIII. 'The plans were comprehensively devised, built on and executed. From the beginning of time, Rome's history on Earth, would be protected, memorized and accepted, by becoming recorded, forgiven and forever remembered.'

XIX. 'With the rapid evolution of scientific discovery since those times, the moment has now come, for this written history, to be reconsidered.'

XX. 'An elevated discussion, to continue universal enlightenment, must be examined.'

In almost stunned silence, Oats queried. 'So this revolution of thought began around three hundred years after 'JC's' time?'

Sun-Ky smiled. 'For the Roman Empire, yes Oats.'

Janet was almost completely taken by surprise and had never before imagined that the Roman Empire had thought this whole change through, in strategic terms. It just never seemed to occur to her. This time in their history had always seemed to be measured, by its achievements and not so much by its strategic planning for change. Janet was still curious. 'How can you say, our planetary history was rewritten?'

Pim said. 'It was rewritten with the collection of biblical records. Consider the history of global conflict and wars, continued since those times. Also the dissenting beliefs and views of others, their sentiments and their history, outside of Roman influence.'

'Consider other civilization's with their own beliefs about Origin, who weren't part of Rome's empire. In AD325 a vision of the 'OTG' was not a globally conceived vision. Ancient Egyptian history, had their own beliefs, along with many others. Ask what the other seventy nine percent of the world's population, chose to believe at that time?'

'The accumulation of archives into Biblical records, when first printed, was a lasting written endorsement of the Empires history of beliefs, for this vision of the 'OTG'.'

'At the time of first printing, few other jurisdictions on your planet, held the sphere of influence, or spoke with the power and authority of the Roman Catholic Church.'

'It is a reflection of this power, accumulated wealth and control over process that inspired these beliefs, to remain in existence, even now.'

'There is a fundamental desire on your planet, to protect these given freedoms from persecution, which were held with the advancement of inspiring human moral values. These Biblical records, which confirmed the elevation of principled and moral decency, would bond with the core of humanity, for centuries to come.'

'Life for future generations, would be changed forever, as a result of these profoundly inspiring mythical images, of how Origin began. An all-powerful and loving 'O.T.G.' was indeed, a meaningful and creative vision, to motivate a sustaining recovery.'

'These visions of peace with harmony, of hope with an everlasting life and of forgiveness from sins, were encouraged by Rome's church. The memories over centuries of Roman ruthlessness and brutality, were gradually swept away, from your planets memory, in their ancient history.'

23
Mythology of Biblical Proportions.

The Impact of the Holy Bible:

Janet was still trying to work through these revelations and asked. 'Are you saying that the Holy Bible, rewrote part of Earth's history?'

Pim was kindhearted. 'It became a protection for humanity against a return to Roman brutality, while giving hope through belief. Bible stories were a civilizing and protective influence for the masses. It is important to remember under which jurisdiction these records began and were widely accumulated and then circulated.'

Janet seemed a little perplexed. 'Well there would have been many contributions from ancient scrolls and manuscripts over time, I expect.'

Pim smiled. 'It is often the case that history is written, by the victors of conquests. Let's consider other aspects of these changes and their consequences, to the present day.'

Janet queried. 'We're going to keep this simple, aren't we?'

'Do you remember who first authorized these Biblical records to be collected?

As many more images were created to help explain, Pim began 'Much has been written, but let's go back to the times of the creation of the Nicene Creed, by the first council of Nicaea in A.D.325.

This had everyone's attention, as Janet asked. 'So, how did these records begin?'

Pim responded. 'As discussed, it was Rome's chance, to reshape their history.'

Janet mumbled. 'I'm still trying to understand how they rewrote this history?'

Sun-Ky added. 'Remember Christ's dying words were entered from A.D.325.'

'Rome's existing pagan gods, had little influence over the broad cultural tribe's throughout their empire. The cost of maintaining control with their powerful legions over their empire, was impacting on their treasury reserves. There had to be change.'

'There was increasing support for this change. Rome needed a powerful, peaceful and progressive transformation. They sought help from the bishops to maintain social order, discipline and control. Remember, these decisions were about the preservation of wealth, power over others and control over process.'

Sun-Ky continued. 'At the time of 'J.C's' existence, the Roman Empire believed in pagan gods. Many oppressed cultures could not believe, they were brought onto this world, just to suffer at the hands of cruelty and oppression. Many believed in a different vision and a different future. A different version of creation. One that offered them hope, that one day, peace may be restored, in their own lifetimes.'

'After centuries of enforcing an often brutal and authoritarian rule, Rome sought change which began as a reform of conceptual visions, to withdraw their legions. To put a halt to fighting over old ideas and unite the empire, with a new idea. 'A One True God'.'

'A God, who in the beginning, created Heaven and Earth and a God that would belong to the masses. A created vision, which would give inspirational peace, love, hope and goodwill for all of humanity. The foundation of this belief was a loving heavenly father of human form. A single powerful God who created the Heavens, for all creatures.'

'Embracing this belief, would require an evolving change in human behavior which fostered civility. Importantly, a new belief, which forgave centuries of Roman brutality.'

'Receiving forgiveness, for centuries of invasions and conquests, including the mistreatment of humanity, from a much loved and highly respected spiritual figure, would have been an important conceptual vision, for the Roman Empire.'

With many blank looks, Sun-Ky continued. 'To be forgiven for all their past sins, with a historical revision from a newly endorsed spiritual figure, was a strategically brilliant and tactically clever, change in direction.'

'Local power and authority, would be held by the bishops, with the backing of Rome and would change for all time, the way civilization would be peacefully regulated.'

Janet was astonished at these revelations. 'But how do you change history?'

Pim had an understanding smile. 'What if you were able to reconstruct records, which were now taken from the beginning of time, to not only describe Origin, but with an explanation that seemed plausible? And at the same time, begin the institutionalized teaching of belief for the masses, to control outbreaks of behavioral violence or revenge.'

Sun-Ky continued this explanation. 'After centuries of conflict, the Romans knew how to break, a person's spirit. The question for them became this. How do you influence a person's defiant manner and their disrespect for authority? To change their opinions, attitudes and behavior by appealing to their hopes and dreams?'

Then. 'This revision of history would bring about change, while softening the memories of centuries of past conflicts. Rome not only revised the narrative of the past, but found a way to reinvent itself, from ancient paganism, to Christianity.'

'Adopting a Christian history of belief, which was supported by the bishops with the acceptance of the 'One True God', became their vision. Many believed Heaven and Earth were originally created and this conceptual belief could be widely embraced throughout the Empire, by other provincial leaders.'

'The championing of hope through peace, as a pathway to Heaven would be seen as an uplifting change from repressive and authoritarian rule. However Rome needed to maintain control through the church, while implementing these changes.'

'It became the most profound example of change, in the history of their times.'

Oats began mumbling to himself. 'So the compilation of these manuscripts, was an accumulation of existence, as seen in ancient spiritual beliefs.'

'Yes, it was during this time that Emperor Constantine1, ordered these scriptural records to be compiled and kept, including references to the testaments of belief.'

'Over hundreds of years these testaments were accumulated and cataloged. What remains of the original foundational documents, are held within the archive vaults in Vatican City. Many parchments and ancient manuscript records, are kept in these vaults.'

Pim continued to explain. 'From these and other records, the first mass produced copies of the Gutenberg Bible appeared around A.D.1455. It began a revolution in teaching and acceptance, of these ancient collected works.'

The visions continued as Sun-Ky said. 'The republishing of historical records into one Holy Bible, was seen as an immense and lasting achievement. To bring together thousands of years of ancient records. This concept, to try and understand the history of origin, from the beginning of time, was and still is remarkable.'

'The publication laid out a powerful summary of stories, recounted back to before Roman times, including their understanding of life's origins, from the beginning.'

'For centuries the Holy Bible has been circulated, republished and distributed in many languages with the support of church leaders and biblical historians. The Bible gave credible support, to early cultural, societal and planetary beliefs. It was seen by many, as an inspiring and civilizing, reference work.'

'The contents tried to bring mankind together, under the authority of the church, where repentance and the forgiveness of sins, led to promises of an afterlife for the future of humanity in a civilized society. These records created some divisions between other cultures. Some of the Bibles claims and spiritual theology, led to disagreements between other faiths. However, with goodwill, the authority of these accounts, brought many cultures together.'

'This was until the formation of the heavens and the path of orbiting celestial spheres was questioned by Copernicus in A.D.1543. Even so, for hundreds of years till the present, the Holy Bible is treasured by many followers, who take these messages of peace, hope and everlasting life, as their chosen reality.'

Pim paused. 'We will explain in a moment, why creation of the universe, by any God, is unsupported by new evidence.'

Janet was mildly stunned. 'How could anyone prove that God doesn't exist?'

Pim watched this baffling expression building on Janet's face and smiled warmly at her parochial innocence. The two had become close friends over recent times. However despite this Janet, was amazed and queried again. 'Beyond any reasonable doubt, Pim?'

Pim's reassurance was just as firm. 'Yes Janet, beyond any reasonable doubt. However, for the time being, let's continue this historical reexamination.'

Michael, Oats and Janet were all stunned now, by this last comment from Pim.

But for now, they were happy to quickly revisit biblical history.

Pim continued. 'The Bible also contains many examples of high moral character values. Teaching courage, compassion and standards of good behavior. These values have existed, as a timeless legacy throughout mankind's cultural history.'

'True companions, friends and family, have searched for these principles and ideals in each other, from the beginning of existence.'

'Some of the more contentious issues, have come from the instructive way mythology has been recorded as fact. The Bible's records are stated with legitimacy and conviction, reinforcing a view that certain events and experiences, actually occurred.'

'These accounts were compiled by the scribes, as a summary of what had been believed and told at the time, from around AD325.'

Janet questioned. 'Why are we talking about belief? I thought we were reviewing a new vision for Origin?'

Sun-Ky leaned forward to sympathize with Janet's heart felt concerns. 'Janet, there is nothing wrong with your planet's history. We are not judging either the rights or wrongs of belief. However, unless we can examine the logic behind institutionalized belief, then you will find the minds, at many levels of society, will remained trapped. **There is no path to future enlightenment, by training your mind to live in the past.**'

Then Pim said. 'Your planet will never break free from historical belief, unless we face this now. Some continue to believe, because 'It is written', the Bible for them remains an article of faith.'

Oats found his voice. 'And for others?'

Sun-Ky paused and then. 'I'm going to ask you to consider several other perspectives of the same narrative. This may take a moment, however I would ask you to question your own observations and perceptions, with a more careful self-examination.'

Janet was almost speechless, but not quite. 'Are we going to find out why ancient belief about Origin, is incorrect?'

Sun-Ky smiled. 'Yes Janet, this became the most concerted effort in history to rewrite it. To revise the memories from the past and to transform change, for the future.'

Janet was flabbergasted. 'How could Rome, do this?'

'Simply because the Empire wanted change. The creation of 'The One True God' became a vision, to civilize their empire, across their domain. In many respects it has been a remarkable success. Educating the great unwashed for more than a thousand years to become a morally bound, highly educated, character driven society.'

Pim asked. 'Are you ready to uncover this mystery now?'

As a dedicated researcher, Oats became animated. 'Unbelievable.'

'Let us reconsider the more obvious points first.'

Janet still remained cautious and was still puzzled by something. 'I still don't understand yet, how you can say actual history, was rewritten?'

24
The Narrative of 'The One True God'.

'Janet, the origins of the Holy Bible, go back to a time over twelve hundred years before 'JC; was born. The records in the Holy Bible's Old Testament, come from the original Hebrew Bible, the sacred scriptures of the Jewish faith, written at different times between about 1200 BC., and 165 BC. These records, portray Earth's history from its earliest creation, to the spread of Christianity in the first century A.D. So the references go back to the god Yahweh and cover the creation of the Earth, through Noah and the flood, Moses and much more, finishing with Jews being expelled to Babylon.

From around A.D.325, a conceptual vision of the 'OTG' as a loving heavenly father was willingly embraced by the persecuted, the victimized and the oppressed. Never before in the history of their lifetimes had the poor and the downtrodden, found a heavenly being in authority, so caring for their welfare, their happiness and the future of their survival.'

'This vision became the new idea, which the Empire's humanity had been searching for and the Empires civilization stood ready, to embrace this change. That values of honor, decency, character and civility, could not only be taught, but could be seen to be held at the highest levels, were a blessing for the future, of their empires humanity.'

'Civilization throughout the Roman Empire's invaded lands, were motivated and inspired to accept, love over hate and unity over division. To accept an inspiring belief over tyranny with compassionate warmth, over invasive brutality. Rome's revision of humanities origins, would escalate this transformational change, in coming centuries.'

'If you believe in the Roman God's existence, then it can reinforce the conviction held, in your own views. However if you believe in one of Earth's other cultural deities, then you may find this belief provocative.'

'What has most certainly happened over the last fifteen hundred years, is that Rome has continued her greatness on your planet, across many other borders through both war and peace.'

'It's important to dissect the meaning of the expression, 'The One True God'.'

'If Rome had only said, 'The One True Roman God.' This would limit the scope of the grievances, felt by other global faiths. However, this was a strategically brilliant shift by Rome, to expand their Roman Empire's influence and greatness, with a transformational narrative, to a more peaceful existence in their empire.'

Janet quizzed. 'There's no historical reference, about Roman strategies?'

Sun-Ky smiled. 'Well there wouldn't be. This was about reformation of thought.'

'Just for a moment, consider the offensiveness, created by the terminology. For any Empire, to claim that their God is true and righteous, above the gods of all other planetary cultural societies. This may well be seen as confrontational and provocative.'

'Many other societies at the time, including the Egyptians, the Greeks, the Norse and the Germanic tribes, to name but a few, could well have taken offense at this claim by the Council of Nicaea, decreeing 'J.C.' as, the only Son of this 'One True God'.

'It is as if Rome placed their version of history and creative vison of Origin, above all others. Also by this claim of the 'O.T.G.', Rome was suggesting there wasn't any truth in the beliefs, of all the other cultural pagan gods. This had the potential to create conflict and so, this is how they tried to change the course of history, in their time. They tried to rewrite the narrative, of original existence and belief.'

'As long as there's been 'One True God', there's been killing in his name.'

'To understand what happened, we need to understand Roman strategy. There was little long term economic prosperity and security for Rome, to be bound up by endless conflict. The cost of relentless wars, had a mounting impact on their treasury reserves.'

'It was increasingly felt by the ruling elites in Rome, that a shrewd and pragmatic transformational change in policy and direction, was essential.'

'The question became this. How do you adopt a compromise, which motivates change in social order and how could this be achieved?'

'If change was to take place, then it was important for the continuation of both peace and security, that one controlling force, would be replaced with another. A different kind of force. The withdrawal of their legions, for a more peaceful force. One which would help avoid uprisings and attacks, over issues of revenge and reprisals against Rome.

Janet asked. 'An example of rewritten history, would help?'

'This is the most important example of rewritten history. At the time of 'The Last Supper', the Roman Empire did not know who Jesus was and yet now he is remembered as the 'Son of God'. Remember Jesus wasn't created to be the 'Son of God', until about 300 years after his death, around 325A.D. How is it possible that close to his death, the Roman Empire had no idea who Jesus was and yet 300 years later, this elevation of his memory, is used to forgive the Roman Empire's, history of cruelty and oppression?'

Sun-Ky paused and then. 'The Empires revision of this history, was embraced for its vision but soon began to impact on other cultures, outside Rome's direct influence. Egypt had a unique ancient history, of their own beliefs and faiths in gods of Origin.'

'While Christianity created an all-embracing path forward for many, power over belief became the battle ground, for control over civilizations, in their future conflicts.'

Oats began. 'So how does logic, see this history? I'd love a clearer understanding?'

'Consider the logical inconsistencies in your recorded biblical history.'

Janet leapt at this. 'Inconsistencies?'

'Yes Janet, some of your historical records don't make sense, when compared to a range of different perspectives, which we will consider now.'

Sun-Ky continued. 'There are several very strong biblical narratives, however to find the reality in all of this, we need to consider the following different perspectives.'

'In these scenarios, I'm going to ask you to question, what it is you have been taught to believe and to consider, **fact from fiction**, remembering, **'All roads lead to Rome.'**

25
The Creation of Institutionalized Belief.

The Roman Empire's Perspective

'Consider the decisions made in their times, from a tactical advantage, Rome's strategic influence and their power over others. The Roman Empire did not fall, they made a choice. Do not look at these times, through the eyes of the Roman elites as being ill-considered or lacking judgment. The elites and patricians, at the time were astute.'

> *'Always remember this logic; this is the reasoning key, which unlocks all doors. If you have the power to create, then it also follows, you would have the power to create change, whether it be the Roman Empire, or 'The One True God' Himself.'*

I. 'Belief in the many existing pagan gods, would not secure the peaceful change that was needed by Rome. A more fundamental and inclusive, far-reaching vision was required. At the conference in Nicaea, it was held that an all-powerful and loving deity, must have created natural existence, from the very beginning of time.'

II. 'For all the oppressed peoples in the empire, faith would accelerate with belief in this elementary change. Coexistence and harmony would come, with an equality of social inclusion, as well as freedom from Roman persecution and the end of tyranny.'

III. 'The change in belief, from all pagan gods, to the 'O.T.G.' was not brought about by God. The 'O.T.G.' was a Roman creation, at Nicaea from around 325A.D.'

IV. 'Ask why, after almost 300 years would Constantine, have decreed that 'JC' died in the Middle East, as the 'S.O.G.'. The Roman Empire killed people everywhere, so why in Judea. The celebrated 'S.O.G.' died in this location of cultural diversity, for strategic and defensive reasons and to forgive the Roman Empire, for all their centuries of hostility.

V. 'It was essential in the rewriting of history, that Rome be eternally forgiven and that the ascension of 'JC' as the 'S.O.G.', elevated this forgiveness, to the highest levels.'

VI. 'Remember also that throughout history, millions of other people have died tragically during these times of conflict, yet this one incident is remembered, recorded and taught above all others. It was the revision of this history and the elevation of this forgiveness, which was the foundation of the Empires teaching, of institutionalized belief.'

VII. 'The history of belief from the beginning of creation, was recorded for a calculated reason. These teachings have continued, from one generation to the next, Humanity may well ask, how much longer, do these entrenched teachings of ancient created belief, hold back humanities future, of enlightenment on Earth?'

VIII. 'The 'O.T.G.' was Rome's most open-minded explanation at the time, to rationalize the creation and evolution, of natural existence, on your planet.'
IX. 'An enlightened account, founded to create hope, where there had been none. To give believable spiritual salvation to the poor and needy, which had not existed and a promise of forgiveness and an afterlife, to motivate a change in their behavior.'
X. 'Authority for implementing these peaceful changes, would be passed on down from the Roman legions, to the church leaders. A move sanctioned by Rome.'

As the visions paused, Sun-Ky said. 'Rather than existing by decree, let's accept for a moment that 'God the Father Almighty' actually exists. Then I would ask you to consider this perspective, from this point of view.

A Perspective of the narrative, from before A.D.325.

'By advancing a narrative of creative history, since the times of Adam and Eve; biblical records, have left verifiable logic, open to critical analysis. Most famously by Copernicus. Let's now question this history, from these earlier times.'

I. 'Prior to the acceptance of the 'OTG' from A.D.325, many regional orders lived in a time of self-belief, with a broad range of culturally different pagan gods. The 'O.T.G.' as a Roman God, reflected, the Empire's transformational motivations.'
II. 'Ask yourself this. If 'JC' was known to be the 'Son, of God', at the time of his crucifixion, would the Romans, still have killed him anyway?'

III. 'If 'God the Father Almighty, Maker of Heaven and Earth', saw his Son being crucified, for advocating high moral values, why would he watch, in these circumstances without defending his own son, as any parent would? No loving father, would stand by and do absolutely nothing, in these circumstances.'

IV. 'A decision by a paternal God, not to help his son, would be inconsistent with all the natural Christian values for good character, supported by spiritual guidance.'

V. 'So this revision of history is contradictory and only makes sense if you consider the narrative, from the Roman Empires perspective, as discussed earlier.'

VI. 'The past was rewritten, for the benefit of Rome, principally and humanity generally, to create a morally bound change, in character behavior which forgave Rome.'

Sun-Ky then asked. 'This part of the narrative doesn't make logical sense either.

A Perspective from the Son

I. 'If 'JC' truly was the 'Son of God', why would he seek change by going to a village in the Middle East, which has been left in religious turmoil, ever since.'

II. 'The only reason for Rome's strategy to control or induce change there, would be because at the time, the Middle East was a diverse cultural problematic issue for Rome.'

III. 'If the 'S.O.G.' was all powerful, why would he not go directly to the Roman Emperor and demand widespread change and reform from Rome?'

IV. 'What tactical purpose does it serve for the 'S.O.G.' to endure an unnatural birth, in a remote village and then allow himself, to be crucified there, by the Romans?'
V. 'This narrative was created to immortalize a figure, perpetuate a myth and celebrate a legend, to help stimulate, motivate and inspire, peaceful change for Rome.'

Janet was gob smacked. 'I just never considered, interpreting history like this.'

Pim then asked us to reflect on a different aspect. 'There is another more logical view of the universe, other than that held by your ancient mythology, which we will share with you in a moment. However, I want you all now, to put yourselves in the mind of a creator, because the logic here doesn't make sense either. If you are in any doubt about the existence of 'God the Father Almighty', then this may help.'

'The first of Ten Commandments. 'Thou shalt have no other Gods before me.' If 'God' ever existed, then consider the logical inconsistencies, from his perspective.'

A Perspective from 'The One True God'.

I. 'If you were God the Father Almighty, why would it be, that Jesus Christ is your only son in the universe, because the Roman Empire decreed it to be so, around AD325?'
II. 'If 'The One True God' existed, he would have the power to create change. How would watching your son being killed, at the hands of tyranny and brutality, help your vision, as being a loving and compassionate, Heavenly Father in creation?'

III. 'According to Biblical records, the Roman Empire, had no idea who Jesus was, at the time, of his 'Last Supper'. How then, could Rome possibly know, in A.D.325 that Mary was a virgin, at the time of Jesus's birth? These are the legends of folklore and mythology to glorify an unnatural act. While less known at the time, fertilization in the reproduction of the species, is one of Nature's central and fundamental laws.'

IV. 'It was not until A.D.325 when Rome decreed, that Jesus Christ be immortally remembered, as the only 'Son' of 'The One True God'. The resurrection of Jesus's memory, to forgive the Roman Empire, was created for these words of forgiveness.'

V. 'Father, forgive them, for they know not, what they do.'

VI. Logic shows that the greatest single beneficiary of these everlasting words, were the Roman Empire. Almost nothing in reparations were ever paid by Rome, while being forgiven, for their centuries of conquering brutality, against humanity at large.'

VII. 'On the question of compassion. What purpose could possibly be served, in the creation of the universe, for the 'One True God' to allow his only son, to be killed on planet Earth, in a remote Roman garrison outpost, in Judea? This forgiveness of sins only makes logical sense, from the Roman Empire's, beneficial perspective.'

We were all completely numbed, by these visions and revelations as Janet queried. 'What was at the heart, of Rome's determination to preserve their greatness?'

Sun-Ky answered slowly. 'To preserve their **Wealth**, to maintain their **Power** and to ensure there was no challenge to their **Control**.

The Roman Empire had to be forgiven, by the highest authority known, in Earth's creation, as imagined by them at the time.'

'Wow', Oats' expression changed, as he began pulling these perspectives together. 'To forgive the Roman Empire for centuries of cruelty, oppression and abuse. To control this transition to peace, without any judgment against Rome, from the highest authority, the 'O.T.G.'. Rome would be instantly forgiven from A.D.325 for any fault, or a sense of guilt, while taking no responsibility, for centuries of cruelty and oppression.'

'This creation of biblical folklore, began as a narrative, to ensure the eternity of this powerfully recreated, act of forgiveness. By encapsulating belief and faith from the beginning of time, in their Biblical records of Origin, Rome sought to avoid any uprising, erupting from their history of conquering brutality, or any recompense for stolen wealth.'

'This narrative, is still causing divisions, between other faiths on Earth today.'

Pim asked. 'Consider these axioms, repeated throughout your history.'

    I. 'Power corrupts and absolute power, corrupts absolutely. Any study of the history of wealth, power and control will reflect this.'
    II. 'History is written, by the victors of wars.'

We remained in stunned silence, as Pim observed. 'We also need to consider this.'

A Perspective, for the future of Humanity

    I. 'The important part of this whole narrative for civilization, was the adoption of civilian Christian values, which have lived on, throughout your history.'

II. 'Jesus is remembered as a spiritual survivor, with lasting warmth and reverence, throughout the history of mankind, since those times.'
III. 'People from all walks of life will meet at different times of the year, to celebrate shared values, in memory of his kindness which changed the outlook, to an evolving peaceful living existence, for humanity.'
IV. 'Many of these fundamental values, share the same laws, held in Nature and are found by observing many other natural species. Social cohesion, is an essential ingredient for the advancement of any communal order.'
V. 'Proclamations supporting creeds, for moral behavior and character values including the institution of marriage, still survive in many places on your planet.'
VI. 'With this narrative locked in place, Rome could bring home her legions and the Empire would not be blamed for their history of conquests, violence and abuse.'
VII. 'Although not agreed to by all faiths, biblical history remains treasured and remembered by many, as are Rome's architectural achievements, art, culture, language and the civilizing of humanity, in their empire.'

Oats just discovered something else. 'This is why we have had wars for centuries, over belief. It is because a change in cultural belief was imposed on the Middle Eastern region, by Roman intervention, trying to change that regions own past.'

The images continued. 'A narrative that is remembered differently between cultures and passed on down to their young. While these myths continue, from one generation to the next, a hostile environment throughout the Middle East, may never be settled.'

Janet was looking distressed, by these continuing revelations. 'But miracles from the Holy Bible have had such high levels of acceptance and belief in their authenticity.'

Pim asked. 'Do you want us to pause for a moment, Janet?'

It took a smile from Pim. 'No please continue. I'd rather find out, than not know.'

Sun-Ky began again. 'You have to go back to the times, when these records were first accumulated. Remember, many believed in supernatural feats during the times of pagan gods. The publication of biblical records began at a time, of momentous change. These miracles became more widely accepted, because they were confirmed and printed in the Holy Bible. We realize this is a lot for you to accept, all at once Janet.'

Janet sat in a state of almost complete shock. She was having her long held beliefs, systematically pulled apart, dissected and reduced to the mythology of the times. She was feeling confronted, while Oats and Michael enjoyed this challenging debate.

Janet remained composed. 'Jesus's fondest memories, are as a man of peace?'

Pim acknowledged this. 'The Roman Empire came up with a healing for oppression, in an ancient time when the persecuted were yearning for and willing to accept believable change. This change by those in power, altered, your planet's historical records. Have you ever wondered whether power, does corrupt?'

'Were the people just being told, what many of them wanted to hear at the time? Ask if there is another answer, which may more correctly resolve the mysteries of our universal expanse, with its conceptual and visionary design?'

Sun-Ky looked on Janet kindly. 'When you have grown up being indoctrinated from childhood to believe something all your life, it can be hard to see a different reality.'

'We touched on this earlier, regarding the connection between Wealth, Power and Control. If you can convince the masses to believe, then this creates power over their thoughts and deeds, in both their mind and responses. If you can levy taxes on them, this creates wealth and if you can create jurisdictional authority, to legislate over their freedoms, behaviors and prosperity, then you have a level of control over social order.'

'Well you need a certain amount of order to create social harmony, in society.'

'Yes Janet, that is true of many societies. However the benefit is almost always for the elites in the creation of their privileges. The creation of tax free income, wealth, power and control is fashioned, to protect the influential, among the privileged.'

Janet was a little more open minded now. 'But if you had no human regulations or control, other than the laws of Nature, what else would you have?'

'Why you would have an advanced global society, Janet. A community which prided itself, on self-worth of the individual and mutual respect. These friendly and warm-hearted societies we are going to visit, can co-exist with complete freedom and a sense of self-responsibility.'

'Under your regional and global systems you have man made laws. Where we are going, they place the emphasis much more on self-control, self-worth, self-interest, self-respect and self-reliance. If humanity can learn, that life originates with self-development, then the only laws that matter are the Natural laws and Natural justice.'

'You will come to understand this more, when you see it for yourselves. All that is needed is an open mind, willing to ask, why is it so?'

Janet asked. 'Can you explain these natural law's a little more for us please?'

'Natural law is there to protect the common sense, in us all. Natural Forces are easy to learn. You are taught to protect yourself from drowning, falling from a cliff, being poisoned or being eaten in the wild. There are so many things to be careful to look out for, however if you can learn this knowledge and find your place in life. This is their dream. When we get there, you will see how different people, see their dreams unfold.'

'Some of them make good choices, while others make more difficult ones.'

Pim then created some more visions. 'For the moment, let's complete this review by summarizing this research.'

The amassing of early Biblical records

'This explanation of origin, began for humanity, with the narrative of the creation, of Adam and Eve. Rome had the changes she needed and so a culture of religious instruction, belief and faith was born, which still exists and lives on today.'

'While many references contained in the testaments go back several thousand years, it was around 325A.D. that the largest accumulation of biblical records began.'

'It was about this time, that an outline of beliefs including miraculous events were summarized into referenced records, which formed the basis of their official archives.'

'Many ancient scrolls, manuscripts and parchments were secured. It was a coming together of both faith and belief, in a championing of ideas, to find a new way forward, from centuries of hostility, created under a life of a cruel reality.'

'The surviving archives from ancient times, formed the foundational documents that became included in biblical records. It was during these times that Constantine1 ordered several manuscripts to be translated and held. The first printed bible, had its foundations from these originally created references.'

Oats lamented. 'We don't seem to have advanced our perspective of Origin, in seventeen hundred years. Even today our science is still looking for the 'God' particle.'

As the visions continued Pim said. 'It was Rome's way of recrafting the history of cruelty and oppression in their past, while bringing to an end, all hostilities. This would begin a program of reform in faith, prayers, hymns, psalms, gospels, books and creeds of belief, which were created to celebrate this new vision. A rectification with a narrative, where even the Roman's would be forgiven by the 'S.O.G.', for their sins of the cross and against humanity in general.'

Janet asked. 'Why were these changes so widely accepted?'

Pim moved to explain simplicity. 'It was Rome's chance, to recraft her greatness.'

'Moving from multiple regional and cultural deities to the 'O.T.G.' of the people, had enormous influence in Rome's Empire. Equally for the legions to gradually withdraw, leaving the bishops in charge of this peaceful change, had a greater calming effect.'

Janet sat there looking almost completely bewildered. Never before had she felt so challenged. It wasn't the logic so much, it was an empires attempt to revise and amend history, in such a calculated way to change the course of history. It wasn't a question of right or wrong. It was to continue a vision of greatness, to reach the minds of the many, who wanted transformational change and this change, was largely accepted by them.

Janet finally asked. 'Why doesn't any of this, make logical sense now?'

Pim was moved to offer Janet the comfort of friendship with further clarification. 'It does make sense when you consider the order of events. Jesus was made the son of a Roman god almost three hundred years, after his death in AD325. Rome tried to unite the whole of Christendom, with the authority Rome had at the time.'

'It was so long ago, these details are not commonly understood. The Roman Empire at the time were trying to unite their different cultural regions, under the concept of 'The One True God'. Remember your axiom. **'All roads, lead to Rome."**

Finally Sun-Ky added this. 'By utilizing the best explanations at the time, the patricians inspired the plebeians in their empire, to seize hope over fear with this concept of creative origin. A plausible and unifying view of origin in their times, which their many conquered cultural backgrounds could believe in.

26
Because, 'It Is Written'.

Pim said. 'The concept of creationism to unite Christendom away from a history of violence, conflict and brutality, was Rome's answer to establishing a new sense of social harmony, a new order, with a unity of belief, among all their cultures.'

Then Sun-Ky looked on Janet and asked. 'Since those early times and considering the many discoveries made since, I want you to reconsider the following. In a universe governed by Natural Forces and Natural Laws, we need to question whether any of the following myths and legends, were real and still make logical sense to you now.'

Sun-Ky then began. 'Janet, you asked about the course of history being changed. Miracles were part of an evolving folklore, in ancient times. Entrenched belief in the Holy Bible's version of creation, has grown to become an institutionalized obsession.'

Pim then said. 'Let's consider some examples of these beliefs. For hundreds of years, inquisitions were formed to crush acts of sacrilege and disrespect, to protect biblical records. Janet, you questioned why there still exists such high levels of belief?'

Janet mumbled. 'Well, yes?'

Pim smiled. 'There is no evidentiary support, for any feats of miraculous events, outside Nature's own laws. Look for a living experience, as it naturally occurs.'

'For the reality of existence in the universe, we must look beyond ancient mythology, legends and folklore, to discover what actually happens in Nature.'

Then Sun-Ky said. 'When you review the history of society's pagan gods, across many cultures and the importance for Rome to get the change they sought, it is easier to see how some verses were written, with inventive imagination.'

Janet was intrigued. 'Some examples of this folklore and invention, would help?

As Pim began with more images, she watched our searching responses. 'Let me quickly summarize examples of the more famous, unnatural biblical narratives.'

'Ask yourself if these examples, are fiction or non-fiction. Each of you must decide this, for yourselves.'

'Noah's floods?'

'As a massive flood, or protection of the species two by two, did this happen?'

'The parting of the Red Sea.'

'Once again to miraculously divide the Red sea, as part of the biblical narrative of Exodus, with the wave of a hand. The escape of the Israelites, led by Moses, from the pursuing Egyptians in the Book of Exodus, across the floor of the Red sea.'

It was now that Janet decided to question. 'Why in historical times, could this not have happened?'

Oats began first. 'You mean why can't a man wave his hand and divide the waters?'

Janet was now struggling. 'Well this is one of religions, foundational beliefs.'

Now Michael found the answers he'd been searching for. 'Because the world in which we all live, is a natural one and if you believe in Nature then it is not logical. Like many of these other miracles, it is founded in mythology. There is little difference here than in the super heroes, we allow our children, to believe in and read about today.'

'The virgin birth?'

Pim then asked. 'Always question, how mythology compares with Natural Law?'

'This is one of the most famous examples, found in early mythology. In ancient times, two thousand years ago, minimal public records were kept for the plebeian classes, on their births and deaths in Judea.

According to Biblical records in Jesus's final days, the Roman Empire couldn't even identify who Jesus was, at the time of 'The Last Supper', without the help of Judas Iscariot. So how could anyone have possibly known, that at the time of Jesus's birth, his mother Mary was a virgin? Yet some hundreds of years after Jesus's death, at the Council of Nicaea in A.D.325, Emperor Constantine decreed that at the time of Jesus's birth, his mother Mary had been a virgin. This helped confirm Jesus Christ as the only son, of 'God the Father Almighty' the 'One True God'.

The birth of offspring, without impregnation and fertilization, is against all the laws for Nature's natural, principles for biological reproduction?'

'Feeding the five thousand'

'To feed five thousand people with two fish and five loaves of bread, is not possible in a Natural setting. Is this just another example of ancient mythology?'

'Walking on water?'

Sun-Ky speculated. 'This fable of Jesus walking on water in the gospels, is in contravention of all the Natural laws of gravity, in the universe. Each of you must question the reality of this. In Copernicus's time, he would not have been able to discuss any of this, openly and freely.

'Turning water into wine?'

'Ask yourselves if this would have happened, in a Natural universe?

Janet asked. 'What is the simple answer, to these miraculous events?'

'Over a thousand years since these were first written, has anything changed? If any of these miracles took place during the times of 'JC', then the Romans would have found out about it at the time and not have had to decree them, three hundred years later.'

Janet asked. 'You don't believe any of these myths, legends and fairytales, do you?'

Pim responded after a moment. 'Janet, you weren't born in Heaven, so why would you return there? You were born naturally in Nature's environment and that in itself is a miracle. Nature has its own laws and its own miracles to discover. Enlightenment began with the interpretation, of some of these laws.'

'No-one before 'JC' has been able to defy gravity and walk on water.'

'It is folklore in the Natural world to believe that you can stand in front of a large body of water, like the Red sea, wave your hand and miraculously divide it to escape the approaching, Egyptian forces.'

'In the history of Natural reproduction, it is pure folklore to believe that Nature plays no part in the procreation or breeding of children, where impregnation for fertilization is essential.'

'No-one before or since has been able to alter Nature, to miraculously create wine out of water. To live with a closed mind that locks in these ancient legends of past belief, traps the minds of humanity, into that past. We are on a mission to learn more about the reality of the past, the present and indeed the future. Biblical miracles are real, in the minds of those souls, still captured in the past by these created beliefs.'

Sun-Ky closed with this. 'Each of us must decide whether we want this doctrine of theology to continue to have power and control over the minds of our children, into the future. Copernicus was never able to explore this in his time. Now we have this chance and this choice. How much longer is humanity going to give up asking questions and just believe these ancient myths, legends and stories?'

Oats was measured. 'These stories were told and the legends created, much as it is today for children with their own super heroes. These imaginary beliefs, were a recreated spiritual vision, of past unnatural events from ancient times, to enable change and to influence and control, social behavior.'

'Michael, you once asked what the church was trying to protect in Galileo's time.'

'It was the Holy Bible and access to 'The 'One True God' through the Roman Catholic Church. This is what the church elders found themselves defending, over time.'

'Ask yourself this. In the institutionalized creeds of belief, from these ancient times, how is it possible that the Romans could know, that 'JC' was God's only son in the universe, unless this story was written and conceived out of mythology, for a strategically considered purpose?'

'An envisioned creation, to control the minds of the empires civilians, who were so desperate for hope and change, at the time. By giving humanity this supreme vision, that peace was at hand, cruelty was at an end and that forgiveness, compassion and mercy, had come, from the very origins of existence.'

'And so it was written. This divine intervention, offering an afterlife for those who sought forgiveness, became the groundswell for this change, which so many had sought. For the soul of a persecuted empire, a vision that decreed peace, love, hope and forgiveness was accepted. This vision was believed, by a population ready for change.'

'It was a brilliant transition over time, from slavery to freedom for so many. Now finally, I want you all to ask yourselves, if the following occurrences seem natural.'

A Perspective, since the times of Copernicus (A.D.1473-A.D.1543)

I. 'Is it natural for the 'O.T.G.' as a male deity, to have had, no women in his own origins? Consider the logic, as stated in early biblical records, with the creation of Eve as the first human female, from Adam's rib.' Is this natural or even logical?'

II. 'In Nature, the female of the species is central to the evolution of humanity. So it would be unnatural to have Adam as a male form first, before Eve.'

III. 'Is the creation of the universe, by a God in human form, a logical interpretation when God himself, did not come from a mother, of Natural origins?'

IV. 'Consider that biblical history from the beginning of time, almost ignores cultural beliefs, in pagan gods. Pagan god's were themselves also imaginatively created and were considered responsible, for many unknown occurrences in ancient times. With the advent of enlightenment, does this not seem like, just another extension of paganism?'

V. 'Can the creation of 'JC' as a Natural biological reality, be considered as a logical evolutionary experience, without any insemination or fertilization ever having taken place? These legends from ancient biblical times are celebrated and lauded, because in the Bible. 'It is written'.'

VI. 'The reality that your history around the times of 'JC' has been rewritten and embellished, altered and amended in the Holy Bible, should beg the intelligent mind to question why. Yes, why was history recrafted to include acts of mythology to support belief?'

VII. 'Enlightenment, challenged biblical history with a scientific discovery from Copernicus. His astronomical model, placing the Sun at the center of your solar system, captured the reality of existence. However, only a small part of this research has been examined so far, to reveal a greater enlightenment on origin.'

After a pause, Sun-Ky continued. 'From the times of Copernicus, the church felt this rising tide of building doubts, from the discoveries of Nature and felt compelled to act. Growing research and the study of local astronomy, suggested an alternate reality, which would have challenged the memory of biblical mythology forever.'

'If people were allowed to think differently for themselves, it could be the undoing of the foundations, of what the church had represented for over a thousand years. This conceptual belief in their 'One True God' had to be preserved and defended.'

Janet was flabbergasted. 'For over a thousand years, ordinary people have been taught to trust and accept these beliefs, because, 'It is written.' Where do we turn now?' Then. 'Did any of this ever really happen, or was this just more mythology and legend? What are people with faith, meant to believe in now?'

Sun-Ky looked kindly on Janet. 'Reality is for each of us, to decide for ourselves. Centuries after the initial discovery by Copernicus, there's a far greater vision of reality, which needs to be further explained.'

Then. 'Currently there remain many good Christian voices, across your cultural communities. Supported by high levels of morality, sound principles, good character and fearless courage. As discussed these values remain timeless. Personal choices can have both good and bad consequences.'

Now Oats was in several minds. 'I have never seen the Holy Bible go through an examination of exploratory logic and analytical scrutiny before.'

Michael asked. 'What are you questioning, Oats?'

Oats was reflective and slow to start. 'When we create written works in present day times, there are rules introduced, so people can understand the legitimacy of what they are reading.'

Janet immediately jumped at this and questioned. 'Legitimacy?'

'Well yes Janet, in modern times, written works are usually described as either fact or fiction. It must be remembered that the Holy Bible contains both. The Bible was first printed at a time, where the only scrutiny came from the church, using the interpretations from their own collected historical works and beliefs.'

'Currently when you publish ideas, thoughts and opinions, you have to justify, verify and clarify. When the Bible was written there were none of these guidelines.'

'In its time, the Bible was a brilliant reference work of past collective beliefs. I can't ever recall a time though, where the Bible was so openly questioned for its historical accuracy before. It just comes down to whether or not, you believe that in the beginning anyone at all, knows what actually happened.'

Michael pressed on further. 'Yes Oats, but what is your point?'

'As a historical reference, the Bible is an outstanding start, to a million questions about origin and these records, form a foundation, for ongoing research. As to what happened in the beginning, well the jury is still out on that. No one really knows for certain, what took place at the point of the Origin of matter. It is just speculation.'

'And mythology?'

Oats was trying to deal sensitively with a delicate issue. 'Well it's all woven in together. You can accept what the ancients imagined, but the more we learn to question, then the more some of this belief, looks to be unsupported by natural evidence.'

'There's also another aspect worth considering. The more you teach and repeat a story, the more it can be believed and becomes accepted.'

Janet asked. 'But it is still our history, just the same.'

Oats smiled. 'Janet, no one is questioning the Bible's historical value, but as discussed I grew up with fictional super heroes, in my own time. Many children do. The Bible is wrapped and blanketed with revered acceptance. I don't believe anyone has ever questioned its authenticity before.'

Janet jumped at this too. 'Authenticity?'

'Yes, the dependability, accuracy and reliability as a record of how Origin, actually began. The Bible is sincere in its speculative delivery. However, remember what was said before. People have been asking these same questions about Origin in the universe, for many thousands of years. No one was there, at the time and no one really knows.'

Michael agreed. 'The Holy Bible's speculation on Origin is a brilliant reflection on our planets past beliefs. However mythology has been presented as a testimony of fact, without any verification to confirm its authenticity. That's why research is still so important, because an enquiring mind will always admit that there is still so much we don't know, about the universe.'

Pim saw Janet was still trying to understand why the Bishops agreed to all this.

'The empire never gave up the conceptual vision of greatness. Many among them saw the continuation of greatness, in the early times of this peaceful transition.'

'We are not the first in history on a voyage of discovery to find answers, to questions of the unknown. The Holy Bible was printed with the authority of the Roman Catholic Church at a time, where printing records of belief, was done with trusted acceptance.'

'Copernicus discovered our system had been formed differently and that the churches interpretation and assumptions on creation, were incorrect.'

Michael then began to add dates together. 'So from about A.D.1455 the Bible was published, to be widely circulated for almost ninety years until Copernicus in A.D.1543.'

'Yes and then Galileo was called to an inquisition almost ninety years later again after that, in A.D.1632. For nearly five hundred years since, the Bible has remained a reference work, on Origin.'

Oats was consumed in a moment of deep reflection. 'When I grew up I was instructed to learn the Lord's Prayer and the Apostles Creed, among many other historical, spiritual and biblical references. The first book I was ever given was a copy of the Bible. When I look back now, it is as if nothing about belief has changed, in over a thousand years. At the time of Copernicus's inquisition, the church just brushed off his conceptual vision on the movement of heavenly bodies, as another philosophical difference of opinion, which challenged their own, grounded in beliefs.'

Michael interrupted. 'We know all this Oats, what's your point here?'

'Let's go back to a time when advanced ancient societies, believed in spiritual creation. Many civilizations believed in their own version of heavenly creation and the worth, of their own interpretation of these beliefs.'

Janet interrupted. 'Oats, can we please keep this simple?'

Oats broke out into a broad laugh. 'I'm nearly there Janet.'

'When you think about it, ask yourself this. **If there ever was a 'God the Father Almighty'; a 'One True God', a supreme being** who created all heaven and Earth, why would he send his only son down to Judea to be killed, to forgive the Roman's?** The memory of the crucifixion of his only son, doesn't make any sense, except as a forgiving gesture to placate, centuries of aggression, by the Roman Empire.'

Michael conceded. 'Yes Oats, the biblical references on this point, when considered, with all other current evidence, just don't make logical sense.'

Then Sun-Ky added this. 'To suggest that the creator of Heaven and Earth, had no power, to stop his only son, from being killed by the Romans, is not logical. Because 'J.C.' did not become the 'Son of God', until about three hundred years after his death.'

'This was a Roman legend, created from A.D.325. There was no God, to protect 'J.C.' at the crucifixion, only a Roman garrison there, to kill him. Rome, not only rewrote this time in history, they were influential in creating these changes, from A.D.325?'

Now Oats was becoming increasingly frustrated. 'Pim, we understand the history a little better now, but you promised we would see universal enlightenment. It's the unexplained cosmological mysteries, which have been plaguing me for many years.'

Pim laughed. 'Of course Oats. Let's quickly pick up where we left off, with this major discovery by Copernicus.

Janet was immediately stunned. 'You can help us, with this Pim?'

Pim had been understanding and composed throughout this reexamination, of our past. 'Absolutely, yes of course I can.' After a moment they moved on to experience enlightenment, once more. Many more visions began to appear.

27
The Return of Enlightenment.

With a beaming smile, Pim began to explain. 'The reasons why Copernicus was enlightened, is because he chose research over ancient belief. From the very first sentence in the Holy Bible, Copernicus realized that God did not create Heaven and Earth. Otherwise God would have known, that the Sun was at the center, of your solar system.'

'If the very first claim, from the very first passage, in the Holy Bible is proven incorrect, then this calls into question, all other unnatural claims. Copernicus discovered that the endorsed biblical chronicles on Origin as envisioned, were not real.'

'In A.D.1632, when Galileo was charged with heresy by the church, his views on orbiting spheres, were seen as a risk, to the ancient conceptual beliefs on Origin. Galileo and others fought courageously to disclose their discoveries, only to have charges of heresy, brought against them, by the church.'

Janet, having considered all of this, appealed for insight. 'There is still something mysteriously missing and unexplained, about all of this, isn't there?'

Sun-Ky continued. 'Yes there is. So, Copernicus made an observable deduction, on planetary positioning. However, there was no logical reasoning at the time, to explain the function of universal design, its energy sources, its purpose or the extent of

Natures cosmic influences. Open discussion was blocked by the church.'

Janet appealed with humility. 'Can you please explain this simply for us?'

Sun-Ky had everyone's attention, now. 'The main reason why your planet is still trapped in this visionless chasm of divine acceptance, is because the discovery was never allowed to be properly studied or clarified. The authority of the church, believed that God, created Heaven and Earth. We need to review this now.'

As we settled, Sun-Ky continued. 'We need to correctly interpret this discovery, to understand the enlightenment you seek, before we reach Tamaryn's galaxy?'

Oats replied. 'Yes, our early science discovered a solar system, the forces of motion, gravity, and centrifugal force.'

Sun-Ky countered. 'Yes, those are the more obvious, universal forces.' Then Sun-Ky revealed some more images, to help explain this further.

Janet queried. 'So, how do we interpret, the other forces in the universe?'

'They begin at the moment of Origin, with the fundamental forces that hold all atomic and molecular structure together. From there are built the solids, liquids and gasses, forming the matter we see, throughout the universe.'

Oats was on the edge of his seat. 'Yes, so where's the illuminating connection?'

'If you want to understand the universe, then you must stop thinking parochially about history. Your ancient world has lived in this illusion of creationism, with the Earth at the center of the heavens. The reasons why Copernicus's discovery created a revolution in scientific thought, was because, cosmic reality was so completely different.'

'Consider the discoveries made by Copernicus, Newton and others, as a glimpse into your future. Look for the little piece of truth in all things. Which means we reassess the way we judge, all your parochial history, even including your own current research.'

'Consider this for a moment. Copernicus discovered that the Earth, is part of a solar based system, rather than being at the center of a creatively conceived concept, as described in your ancient biblical creeds of belief. So from Copernicus's time, absolutely everything changed.'

Janet then exclaimed. 'Yes, the sun's at the center rather than the Earth being at the center. I get that part. So what are we missing?'

Sun-Ky, with the experience of his astronomical genius, smiled warmly at her childlike innocence. 'Apart from motion, force and gravity, what purpose does your sun serve? How does your sun help the continuation of all life and existence on your planet?'

Oats suddenly exploded with excitement. 'Primary heat and light energy, motion and gravitational stability, slow rotation leading to the existence and continuation of all life forms as we know them.'

Sun-Ky intervened with this illuminating thought. 'Consider how many stars there are in the universe, Janet?'

Janet's innocence showed as she appeared challenged as Michael and Oats listened on with rousing excitement. 'I would say many, many millions, maybe billions, why?'

Sun-Ky was watching the building fascination, in all of them as he clarified. 'The central star, which supports your planet, is replicated many billions of times across countless galaxies, yet it appeared to your ancestors that every heavenly body orbited around your own planet. This is where your planet's mythology, misunderstood creation.'

Janet nodded. 'Yes, there are many billions of stars in place, however it has yet to be determined how many of these stars have planets like ours, which support life.'

Sun-Ky smiled. 'Yes, natural evolution in the cosmos, still lives on your planet with the innocence, of a parochially focused viewpoint.'

Janet queried. 'What other view, could be taken?'

'Consider that the fundamental formation of matter is not global, it is universal. Elementary atomic and molecular structure is universal. We don't exist in isolation, we exist universally. The lack of your planetary populations' cosmological experience, is not the fault of the cosmos. The Natural Force lives, as a challenge for each of us, to explore and discover.'

'Look at what the universe shares in common. Chemistry and physics are universal and so is biology. Solids, liquids and gasses, are all part of this enormous natural phenomenon. Natural Forces are spread throughout, this expanse.'

Pim felt compelled to intervene. 'You're a strange race of beings on Earth.'

If it was possible, Janet was becoming even more fascinated. 'Why, Pim?'

'You are willing to teach your children legendary folklore, held in the ancient published records of a mythical past and yet the reality of Origin, lives in front of your very eyes and you stand ready to doubt it, disbelieve and even question its existence.'

Sun-Ky laughed again and then said. 'The cosmic view would be to consider your planet as just the beginning of your quest. Think of your planet as a street address and one day you will all leave home, to discover who lives amongst the gravity fields, in the next cluster of stars.'

Pim added. 'To journey with genuine curiosity into the unknown, across the cosmos and into another nearby galaxy. Think of the next galaxy, as millions of jurisdictions with massive variations in cultural heritages, more adaptive habits, and different species with elevated and uplifting natural life experiences. It would be an enormously vast and spectacular adventure of discovery.'

Oats just blew up, with excitement. 'Of course it is true Janet, no one on Earth can say how many other inhabited planets exist. However the probability of more natural life forms across the universal expanse, is persuasively convincing, given the replication of our solar system design, energy and galaxy size.'

Oats continued. 'Consider also that our entire planetary population lives on just one of billions of addresses, in the universe. Many on Earth are still willing to believe the universe is about us, with our ancient beliefs alone and the reality is, we are not alone. Our ancients formed a conceptual belief, in their time to explain our existence and this needs revision. An observation that began, with the discoveries made by Copernicus.'

'We are discovering unfolding evidence, which is astonishingly reassuring and besides.' Oats paused for a moment as his passion built. 'I'd love to discover the other diverse life forms, across the galaxy and throughout the universe.'

Michael went to hug Oats warmly and quickly agreed. 'I'd love to come with you Oats.' The two old friends laughed enthusiastically, together.

Then Sun-Ky clarified further. 'In Copernicus's time biblical scholars believed that someone could walk on water and that a child could be born from an unfertilized egg. These entrenched unnatural beliefs, are inconsistent with Nature's universe.'

'So consider how hard it would have been, in the times of Copernicus, to challenge those beliefs, with this natural celestial reality. He'd have to convince historians that ancient beliefs, for thousands of years, came simply from cultural folklore and legend.'

Oats observed. 'It was because 'It was written'.' Then. 'To be fair, in earlier times they were just looking for answers like we are now and they found it, in creative belief.'

Sun-Ky continued. 'All these competing beliefs are why your planet is in a constant state of conflict. This is what is confining your planet to a lost past, rather than an uplifting future. You have global societies, embracing a series of ancient conceptual beliefs, while ignoring this larger, natural universal reality.'

Sun-Ky continued. 'While your planet's age can be considered as advanced in geological terms, your awareness of the natural expanse, is yet to be fully appreciated.'

Then Oats mumbled. 'This is where enlightenment became limited, in our developing renaissance period. Galileo, Newton and others, discovered Natural Forces but weren't able to complete, this greater connection. It is the survival of natural living species, due to the influence and dependability from solar light and heat energy, on an incredibly grand scale. This is the natural cosmic reality.'

Sun-Ky agreed. 'Yes, what was the defining moment of change, for you both?'

Oats just realized something for the first time. 'What Copernicus was unable to uncover, question or even debate at the time, was the real origin of life on our planet. The church had a monopoly on that. To question their authority on the origin of this belief would have been considered blasphemous and offensively profane.'

Michael laughed. 'You're in several minds again Oats?'

'Good heavens, we took the narrow parochial view. This was never just about geocentric verses heliocentric positioning, in our understanding of local astronomy.'

Janet smiled at Oats's infectious enthusiasm. 'Oats, please keep this simple.'

'Yes, yes of course.' Oats was still struggling to grasp, the greater conceptual reality. 'Alright, okay, okay.' Oats spluttered, and then. 'For many years, the discovery by Copernicus had been explained away as to whether the Earth was at the center of the heavens, or the sun was. This was seen as our enlightening revelation. The larger discovery is that we are not alone, as just one star system, in a galaxy full of them.'

'We are one, among many billions across the cosmos. This is where early belief was flawed. **God didn't create life on Earth; the early forces of Nature created life across the universe. The whole concept of Gods was founded, in ancient mythology.** For thousands of years, our planet has misunderstood this illuminating insight. Many still don't see that Nature is a force, which unites and combines with all other forces, across the universe.'

Oats then thought further on Sun-Ky's first revealing explanation. 'Remnants of the Roman Empire's greatness still exists on our planet, to the present time. In many of our churches, in our various cultural beliefs, by ancestry and descent.'

Then Oats added. 'There are many different views and beliefs held by other cultures as well. This goes to show how difficult it can be, for anyone, on our planet to change the hidden layers of historical belief, stored deep within, our past teachings.'

Sun-Ky then went on to clarify something. 'Janet, let's be clear about what we are saying and what we are not. We agree there is a higher intelligence in the universe, among different species. However, no species created the original matter in the universe.' No paternal or maternal gods ever existed, in the role of creation. Equally not all species are the same on other planets. At a more complex level, the universe is still a vast and evolving phenomenon, on a time scale beyond our measure. Over millions of your years, individual life, is quite insignificant, despite what many of us may want to believe.'

Janet was now enjoying this open discussion. Her interest was held in learning more about advanced concepts which challenged her. Rather than the repetitive tired old clichés of triteness and platitudes, given to her, as answers throughout her schooling.

Janet was brought up to believe that a male God had created Heaven and Earth. It had always intrigued and confused her as to why this male God did not have a mother. She now felt that a logical debate with credible answers on Origin, was long overdue. Gradually Janet became fascinated and more involved.

After a pause, Sun-Ky continued. 'So, just to be clear there are billions of stars, spread out over many galaxies, giving local light and heat energy throughout the universe. In your ancient past, people on Earth could only observe their own existence, at a planetary level.'

Oats looked puzzled. 'Michael, the inquisitions were protecting the embellished beliefs, created by the Roman Empire from AD325.'

'Yes, we've been over some of this before, Oats.'

Marmuron asked 'Why is this important, Oats?'

'Inquisition's were made up of groups of bodies inside the Catholic Church whose aim was to combat heresy. They began as early as the 12th century in France, to fight religious dissent, among many free thinking groups. They then expanded throughout Europe and into many other countries. During the early Renaissance period, the scope of these inquisitions grew significantly, in response to the Protestant Reformation and the Catholic Counter Reformation.'

Oats added. 'Marmuron, it was all about maintaining control, over ancient belief. Over time, inquisitions spread to Spain, Portugal, Africa, Asia and the America's including Peru and Mexico, lasting for centuries. In 1965 they were renamed the 'Congregation for the Doctrine of the Faith'. Their purpose was to defend belief in Catholicism and one of the most famous cases was around A.D.1632. Galileo was held and challenged for trying to prove, that the Sun, was at the center of our solar system.'

'For hundreds of years, these Inquisitions have been trying to hold back progress, debate and the evolution of thought, by compelling acceptance of the Roman Empire's revision of history, with the advancement of the 'O.T.G.' and 'JC' as his only son.'

Marmuron asked. 'And people still accept this today?'

'Yes, many do.' Then Oats refocused 'There's more about Universal Origin to learn here, isn't there Sun-Ky?'

Sun-Ky smiled. 'Yes, there is.'

Now Janet took the lead as she was about to have many of her questions answered. 'Sun-Ky, where does the further logic exist, in all of this?'

Oats and Michael could tell that Sun-Ky was a well informed and complex individual, whose mind was several logical layers above their own.

Sun-Ky began. 'I'm going to run through some things now, however for a more complete verification on the stages of the origin of matter in the universe, you will find Tamaryn's visions, more enlightening.'

28
Why Earth's Parochialism, isn't Logical?

'Being sexually different, is a function of reproduction, giving rise to the creation of offspring. Any image of humanity is not the source of Origin in the universe. The Origin of the universe is not male or female. It is pure mythology for any religion to believe that a god of either sex, created the universe.'

'Once you can visualize Nature as a force, across the cosmological expanse, then it follows that humanity, is a species of Nature, not the creators of Nature.'

This last statement of the obvious from Sun-Ky reverberated, amongst them and provoked a flurry of interjections and responses.

Oats watched as Janet pleaded. 'Can you please, just go over that again?'

Sun-Ky was measured as he spoke. Clearly Janet was still having some trouble accepting an original concept, which was so completely different from what she had been brought up to believe. 'Certainly Janet. Any images showing or depicting any human form, as the creator of Nature itself and all other Natural Forces, is imaginary and mythical and begins from ancient fables, stories and legends. Please remember this.'

'The human species are creatures of Nature, not the creators of it.'

As the history of our established global beliefs, created since before Roman times was finally laid bare, all the images showing creation by deities in Janet's mind, slowly began to disappear and vanish.

Janet's expression changed. 'This is so simple. Why didn't I think of it before?' Suddenly for Janet, the mystery of thousands of years of our ancient beliefs were seen as founded, in the past. 'This is what the church has been protecting, for over a thousand years.' Janet became enlightened. 'The past.'

Oats agreed. 'This is so simple when you think about it.'

Janet continued mumbling to herself in riddles and half sentences. 'It's illogical.'

Janet was a lovely, sharp individual and as Michael's soul mate, had been a source of great encouragement, for these missions. Still Janet had been rattled, through this process and kept on talking to herself, as the rest of us waited for her to rethink and reconstruct, the newfound logic she had now uncovered, from our planet's history.

In support, Sun-Ky asked. 'Why is it illogical Janet?'

'Well, ancient biblical belief, in the times of the Roman Empire, doesn't make any sense. How can you say? 'I believe in God the Father Almighty, or 'Our Father who art in Heaven.' When the Heavens weren't created by God?'

Sun-Ky smiled. **'And the reasons?'**

'Any male God would have had to have come from parents of his own. How could he possibly have been the creator of the universe, if his parents were born before he was? A male God, must have had a mother.' After mumbling to herself incoherently, Janet was now convinced beyond reasonable doubt, of the logic, hidden in these thoughts.

Oats then said. 'Janet, there's another very important part of this historical analysis. Many people who believe in the past, will challenge these views, because they can seem offensive to them. This search is about gaining a better understanding of the universe in which we all live. **None of us are against the past, we are just for the future with an open mind, asking the same questions, which began thousands of years ago.'**

'All biblical records, showing the creation of the universe by God, in human form were simply crafted from ancient folklore, legend and mythology.'

'All creeds of belief in gods, for thousands of years, came from this same age, of ancient belief in mythology.'

As Sun-Ky observed, the deconstruction of myths, he smiled in agreement.

Janet was stunned. 'Wow.'

Sun-Ky watched as her mind cleared. 'So the history of the cosmos, with human deities can't be logically supported, on a time scale, an evolutionary scale or indeed on a scale of any existence regression.'

After a moment Michael asked. 'Oats, how can it be said that Origin has been misunderstood on our planet, since the time of Copernicus?'

'Because, as Sun-Ky just pointed out, hundreds of years later, Charles Darwin came up with his own flawed parochial theories on the 'Origin of the Species' and then with his book on 'The Descent of Man'. Breeding gives a blended inheritance. **How could his single celled organism theory, create the diversity of life forms, we have on Earth?'**

Michael was still trying to clarify something in his own mind. This was fascinating to hear a rational debate on belief, in logical terms. They had discussed some of these issues before, but now our written history of belief, was being so openly questioned.

'The logic of our planets highly held history, was facing scrutiny and the science of logic and research, was now able to have its say, free from intimidation or harassment. In Copernicus's time, we would have also faced an inquisition.'

Michael could see Oats meditating. 'You're still in three minds again Oats?'

'Michael, for centuries now and from the early times of biblical records, people have believed in a paternal or fatherly deity. No one has been able to prove belief to be either right or wrong, you're either a believer, a skeptic or an atheist with some doubts.'

'So much of the debates, between different entrenched positions, have resorted to just name calling, or personal abuse, from one side or another.'

Janet seemed a little perplexed, 'I'm still wondering, was any of this, ever real?'

Everything had become, so much clearer for Oats. 'It was real for them in A.D.325. These manuscripts and stories, have been built on over the centuries, forming the basis of their biblical records.' Oats put it, in his own words now. 'You've seen numerous volumes of an encyclopedia's, collected works before?'

Janet smiled. 'Yes I grew up with one.'

'Think of the Holy Bible, as the Roman Catholic Churches earliest anthology, of ancient works. Beliefs about Origin, are stories from accumulated ancient manuscripts.'

'A collection of references, containing profound thoughts, opinions, beliefs and ideas, which came together over thousands of years and compiled from around AD325. The Bible eventually became a reference work of history, as they saw it, in one volume.'

'However, in accepting this, it is very important to note several things. The emphasis was on a revision of belief, from the beginning of time, as the gathering in Nicaea saw it. This was an assembly of the elite and scholarly; the celebrated philosophical thinkers and the most enlightened astronomical observers, of their time, supported by scribes and many others.'

'Their cultures had come from a time of acceptance, in a multiple number of pagan gods and some of this legendary folklore, was carried forward.'

'While conceptual belief, in an all-powerful 'O.T.G.' had grown from a past belief, in mythology, the paternal loving Father had to be, by definition, the most powerful creator of all time. With formidable legendary feats, surpassing all the other gods in pagan history, this for them, was the reality of their time.'

Janet smiled with some relief. 'So this became their key, to rebuilding order.'

For Michael, this answered many unresolved questions, about our past. 'We are able to ask questions, now. Unlike some in our ancient cultures, over thousands of years back on Earth, who are willing to continue to believe, what has been passed on down, since their earliest of times.'

Oats was a study of reflections. 'Without an enquiring mind which investigates, evaluates and scrutinizes all established historical beliefs, we will never find the answers. It is a lonely path we walk Michael. There are still, so many protected interests on Earth, trying to control what people think and believe and also how they react and behave.'

Michael was reflective. 'Yes, it just creates frustration for everyone in our race. A mind, deprived of a forward looking vision, will never see Nature as the force, which has been revealed to us.'

Sun-Ky then confirmed. 'You are all about to see, so much more of it.'

Then Oats acknowledged. 'Our planet has yet to understand this. It seems that some on our planet, would sooner fight with each other, over ancient belief. Rather than feel challenged, by the discovery and reality of the forces of Nature, in the universe.'

Sun-Ky added. 'When you give up the right to think and just believe, you are throwing away the wisdom to decide, with the intelligence you are given at birth, to question conceptual reality. Strong character values, are taught and learned. Honor, integrity, decency and morality are essential elements, of a childhood upbringing.'

Sun-Ky then said. 'I want you all to consider the flaws, in accepting creationism's false hopes, faith and belief.' There was a pause as Sun-Ky continued. 'Hope, faith, belief and trust in mankind's future, begins from the resilient foundations, created in childhood from parental guidance, direction and supervision.'

'Nature gave us an intellect to use. We learn nothing, without challenging our minds to critically examine everything. All religious theory, blind faith and belief. One could well ask, why were we given intellectual capacity by Nature to think with in the first place, if not to continue, to find more credible answers?'

Then Sun-Ky amazed us with another defining thought. 'Nature has existed beyond any known life span in the eternity of our species existence. Generations from now, when illumination and enlightenment, far exceeds the present, please remember this:

'Your ancients weren't entirely wrong. With Origin, we are not looking for who, we are looking for what. So the question becomes this. 'What were the circumstances which created elementary particle matter, in the first place and why?'

'Educated reasoning will continue into the future, with answers about how nuclear fusion was conceived. Then turning hydrogen into helium and giving solar energy on such a grand scale? When and how did these events take place and most importantly, the questions of why and for what purpose?

'Yes, these are the beginnings of a million questions. Can you please tell us more about your reasoning behind, **what**? That is, what are we looking for, with Origin?'

Sun-Ky began. 'The most profound, logical reflection would be to see all life as being creatures of Nature. It is important to understand, we continue to exist as a result of the creation of these forces.' Then, 'Tell me one thing that happens to all life on Earth?'

Michael was reflective. 'Well life is created and then ceases to exist, it perishes.'

'So the ancient conceptual vision of an eternal living God, doesn't make sense?'

Janet asked. 'Can you explain this a little more?'

'With Origin we are looking for the circumstances, which created Nature's primary existence and the forces that sustain all life. We are searching for an intelligence, which cannot be defined by any known life force. The ability to believe in spiritual beings with super powers, has lived in the minds of children, for hundreds of generations.'

Michael then opened up with his most compelling of concerns. 'It is the unknown in all of this, which has always fascinated us.'

Then Oats followed with. 'Millions of us have grown up looking at creation through a narrow parochial perspective. We didn't see Nature as the silent force amongst us. The Natural Force doesn't decide our moral issues or even consider whether we have been a good person or a bad one. Individuals make their own choices, for which we all take ultimate self-responsibility.'

Janet queried. 'Sun-Ky, why has this revision, been so important?'

'Janet, where we are going, the citizens look at life very differently. You are now ready to see Tamaryn's galaxy.'

Janet was puzzled. 'Will our parochialism ever give way, to a more forward-looking and uplifting view, of the universal expanse? Will humanity look back on these times as a defining moment and a turning point? Will we ever become, united, again?'

Oats laughed. 'One day, when we let the minds of our children, ask questions again they will find a way? Nature is a universal experience, not a parochial one.'

Michael replied. 'It would be wonderful, to see all of humanity united, Oats'

As Sun-Ky stood to return to his suite, they thanked him sincerely. It truly was a refreshing insight. The long journey to Tamaryn's galaxy was almost over.

Pim then summarized our research of Earth's centuries old, ancient history.

Having considered these findings, advancing social progress owes much of its cultural strength, to the creation of heavenly belief, under the Roman Empires control.' The patricians and elites created a more thoughtfully cohesive and elevated society, leading to a groundswell of transformational change, across their empire.

We also need to ask and consider, why would they do this? Considering there was little loss to them and with everything to gain. Ask if this was just another, well scripted plan, for the continuing greatness, of Rome's empire?'

'Ask if religious tolerance, was more about creating compliance and suppression, over ancient uprisings and revolt? The endorsement of love over hate, hope over fear, compassion over vilification. Were the great unwashed and the conquered barbarian hordes, willing hostages, in Rome's larger transformative plans?'

Finally. 'Let us retire now and return, to look forward to our own futures.'

29
How does Tamaryn's Society, see Natural Law?

'We woke up from a dormant state and sensed the Corillion slowing down. Visions showed us passing through the outer perimeters of Tamaryn's galaxy. It felt like ages, since we had left our own galaxy.'

Pim counselled Oats, Michael, Janet and Marmuron, to come back to the Map Room, to receive a timely briefing, on the Corillion's current position. 'Michael, we are going to see a society, which is very different from your own. Tamaryn's societies, look at life's choices, from a purely natural perspective.'

Oats was fascinated. 'Can we please see some more images?'

Pim obliged. 'Oats, for generations, many of your people have learnt to live with control, rather than, to take control. They've been taught to believe, rather than to search for answers. Many are encouraged to live in a state of dependence, rather than be independent. The universe wants us to explore, to research and to discover, not to be submissive, passive, compliant and obedient in our thoughts.'

Michael asked. 'Pim, what are the obvious differences, in these societies?'

'In many respects we share common ground, both in social advancement and preservation of communal enrichment.

Probably the greatest difference, is in provincial authority, minimal jurisdictional regulation and with a lack of personal constraints.'

We were starting to look puzzled as Oats asked. 'What does that mean, Pim?'

'They follow Nature's laws in practice and routine. The best way to consider this, is to look at the universe, in which we all live. Natural Forces embrace the peaceful, unrestrained laws, found in Nature. An evolving ecological environment, where elementary laws of the jungle, combine with a compassionate warmth, found in the forest. Humanity has seen these interactions many times before and some have learnt from it.'

Pim continued. 'The predictable and yet uncertain behavior between the species in Nature, is without fear or favor. An experience where the strong survive, communal engagement is tempered and the weak struggle and suffer. It can seem to be just as cruel, as it is to be kind, but despite the diversity within Nature, some species are food choices for others. At a more educated level, the rights and wrongs of this can be debated, controlled and guided, but nothing changes the reality of Nature's conceptual creation.'

Janet was becoming a little troubled. 'I don't quite understand Pim?'

'Oh dear, where to start?' Pim was also remembering that her son Mykron was now there and seemed temporarily perplexed. 'Janet look at the complexity of your animal kingdom and the more obvious, influencing factors. Have you ever tried to hold back the tide? Ever wondered why a volcano erupts, or considered why some species crush their kill before consuming it, while others poison their pray first, before devouring it. Why do some spiders weave traps and whales filter krill? We need to understand the simplicity and complexity, of these natural realities.'

'Consider a perspective, which sees benefits in working within this existence, rather than exhausting ineffectual effort, trying to change, what will never change.'

Janet was becoming more emotionally engaged. 'Yes but Tamaryn's people don't live by the laws of the jungle, do they?'

Pim looked kindly on her. 'Janet, look at any social order in modern day society. There are those that strike a balance between seeing life, for its possibilities and choices. In many cases their efforts are rewarded as they learn to live, within the strengths that social order can bring. These individuals are motivated to achieve, self-educate and see strength in an enduring moral fiber, of an evolving social fabric.'

'The weak, by contrast, will struggle. A misplaced sense of compassion can encourage weakness and lower individual expectations, where all of society will suffer. This is not a judgmental issue. It is simply natural law verses applied laws, depending on what kind of society, we want to see.'

'Tamaryn's ordered society is compassionate yes, however weakness or flawed failings are not encouraged, or rewarded.' There seemed to be a developing caution in the two different choices from Pim, as she reflected.

'If society panders to weak choices and indulges in failing standards of natural behavior, it may not become evident immediately. As future generations develop, with increasing tolerance of weakness, then the incomparable character and building fabric we all hope for, will be changed and society will become the poorer for it.'

'This is not a question of right verses wrong, or one way being better than another. The question for them became this. If they want to build a society that follows an evolving ecological path, it begins with a logical and elementary sequence.'

Michael remembered the four truths of self-interest, taught to Mharn as a student at his Academy of Higher Learning.

He uttered 'Self-control, self-discipline, self-reliance and self-respect.'

Pim responded. 'Yes Michael, if you want an advancing global society, which is governed to achieve greater enlightenment, then it must start with self. At the highest levels, some choose to live this life simply, within their natural surroundings.'

Pim reflected. 'Consider animal behavior in real life. A lion may be outnumbered, cornered and trapped. However if he projects and radiates strength, power and cunning, while traveling in a pack, with a hunting strategy, based on learned intelligence, then his chances of survival, will be much greater.'

'By contrast if the same lion radiates weakness, without skills to survive, his chances in life will become much more limited. Ecological evolution and Nature's Forces are at work everywhere, in the universe. It is up to our own willingness to engage with the Natural choices we face, which then decide our destiny.'

'The strong will survive. If we truly wish to engage with Nature's universe, then we need to strengthen our position, within this design, as it cannot be re-engineered or re-invented by us. Tamaryn's followers, decided over thousands of generations, to follow these natural elementary laws.' Pim smiled with some reassurance at the angst being projected by Janet. 'Of course there is love, fondness and time for forest creatures.'

Janet seemed bewildered, before Pim added this.

'The living values, which the Natural Force cherishes the most, are the character strengths, many in our humanity understand the least.'

Oats queried. 'Can you explain that a little more, Pim?'

'Peacefulness, character, serenity, privacy, tolerance, contentment and empathy. Embracing life's diverse vulnerabilities, shows in strength of resolve. When we understand the intent of Nature's forces in the cosmos; we come to appreciate the hope, wished for by many, to survive and to discover its diversity.'

Oats thought out aloud. 'And we are land bound, until we do?'

Pim reflected. 'Remember when I said previously that Nature does not have a voice, but will not be ignored? A well-established population, in a distant ancient community, many times older than our own, has found civility with graciousness in life, by binding personal choice, with Nature's laws.'

Oats was first. 'So how does an established society, find existence with compassion and justice with fairness? Within an environment of strong character values, where inspiration and enlightenment, is their hope?'

Pim laughed. 'I believe you are going to love what you see in this galaxy.' And then. 'Don't be too alarmed, by this conversation Janet.' Tamaryn had anticipated some escalating fears, prior to our recent Galaxy Exchange. Some may find this new system challenging to accept, while others will find it motivating and inspiring. Our mission objectives are to learn from this and bring back those, who need to come home early.'

Pim also added. 'In many respects Tamaryn's society lives in an abundant natural paradise, with many flora and fauna varieties, quite different from our own.'

'If you have order, harmony and tranquility in your life, then you will find these galaxy differences are a truly refreshing and inspiring encounter. Remember, Mharn's parents were so mesmerized and overwhelmed, they overstayed their visit.'

Pim paused. 'What I can say to you all is this. For all those seeking a harmonious existence, this could be their chosen mystical reality and sanctuary.'

Several visions continued. 'Civility with warming respect, is matched with an inquisitiveness from the many different life forms. Beautiful valley floors surrounded by enormous cliffs. Copious amounts of massive trees with abundant outcrops of floral ground cover, interwoven on either side of fresh mountain streams, are simply stunning.'

'Old growth forests, with many as yet undiscovered varieties of both intriguing and friendly wildlife. It is a utopia for the many, who find their way there and it is also a very hard place to leave.'

'Mharn's parents will remind you of this, which is the main reason for our journey. To help others, in the advanced party remember, there is a life to come back to.'

There was an easing of angst and torment receding from Janet's pretty face as she tried to digest what was in front of us all. Marmuron was holding Janet's hand in support. 'It appears that our thrilling journey will be full of surprises. A visionary and inclusive, ecological society, within several spectacular, planetary systems.'

We were coming to the end of our long journey and now saw the magnitude, of this building celestial mass of Tamaryn's galaxy in the foreground. It was now just a question of where we land first. Everyone had assembled in the Map Room as we watched a three dimensional image, begin to form and expand.

From the horizontal plane of rotation, as the deeper images grew, many galaxy levels developed. The images continued to rotate while adjusting to show a vertical depth.

Tamaryn's home could be found at galaxy level 1473, quadrant 3, system 476, and planet 4.

As their chartered course took them closer, carefully avoiding other solar masses, the excitement between all the passengers, rapidly grew.

Karina's friends erupted. 'Wow.', 'It's just amazing.' Then. 'Overwhelming.'

Pim confided. 'No one can see all of this, in just ten rotations of Kendagon.'

Oats was stunned by the growing expansive conceptual beauty, of this creation. 'This universe, was never an accident Michael.' As other images became clearer Pim advised that one of Tamaryn's aides, would appear through the Map Room portal soon.

All Mharn's friends were excited to see and hear everything unfolding. Marmuron left us quickly to have a word with Karina and her friends on the other side of the Map Room. She returned momentarily, seeming emotionally anxious.

Oats noticed. 'Everything okay, Marmy?'

'I was just thinking about Karina and Mharn. They love each other so desperately and yet Karina is more worried about Mharn's future opportunities, than her own pregnancy. They're so far away from each other at the moment.'

Marmuron began to wipe away tears, as a reassuring smile came from Sun-Ky. 'Don't worry Marmuron, I've arranged with Tamaryn's ship to contact us on arrival as soon as they can. Once we are close enough, we will be alerted and Mharn will be able to come here for a brief moment to reassure and comfort Karina.

'Important though to keep this between ourselves, until these plans are confirmed.'

Marmuron's face began to blossom. 'Yes, yes of course, thank you Sun-Ky.'

'There was an interruption to everyone's conversations, as a knock on a panel was sounded by one of the ship's crew. He nodded respectfully to Sun-Ky.

Sun-Ky smiled back and said. 'Thank you.'

Janet was quick to ask. 'What's happening?'

Pim whispered. 'I believe Mharn's coming on board.'

Marmuron, grabbed Janet's arm to ask. 'What was that?'

'Yes, the captain has been able to make contact with the others and we're close enough now, to make the transfer.'

Janet just erupted. 'Karina will be thrilled.'

They continued to be amazed with the unfolding events. Sun-Ky left for a short break to return later. As he left, Karina and her friends came over to see what all the excitement was about, as a vision appeared through the Map Room portal. It was Mharn.

30
Early Reunion with Mharn.

'**Mharn**'. Karina screamed out with loving warmth and complete elation. She jumped to greet him. 'How, I mean, where did you come from? Then. 'How did you get here?'

'I was told we were within range.' Then. 'I'm not really sure what's happening.' Then. 'Someone is helping me. We heard you were coming and I'm just thrilled that you are all here.'

All Mharn's friends rushed over to welcome him, with a volley of greetings.

Oats and Michael held back until the chattering slowed down. Karina was ecstatic and came over quickly with Mharn to join Michael, Oats, Janet and Marmuron.

Michael began first. 'Mharn, welcome. How is your mission going?'

Mharn seemed almost in a daze. 'So much is happening, so quickly.'

Oats then said. 'Why don't we let these two, have a moment to catch up?'

Michael agreed. 'Yes Oats, yes of course. We can all catch up later.'

World Peace in Our Time: *The Logic behind Universal Creation*

Karina and Mharn glanced lovingly at each other. Karina had some important news to share and everyone could see she needed time now with Mharn, to herself. They raced off happily, holding hands, as if they didn't have a care in the universe.

As they reached her suite, Mharn took her in his arms and hugged her, once more. 'There's so much to tell you. We are stopping over at the planet of Prisium first, so Mykron and Velia can see her family, before we go on to Tamaryn's home planet.'

Karina immediately picked up that Mharn didn't know about the pregnancy issues and dangers. Mharn was buoyed by his challenges and thrilled for his chances. Karina softened as she became caught up in hearing the news, of his mission prospects.

Once inside, Mharn was elated to have her so close to him and coming to share his excitement. His heart was filled with love and passion, as he grabbed her tenderly around her waist. Karina was adoring and smitten in return, as she now had her companion by her side once more. The tyranny of great distances between them had been broken and now they had each other, to continue sharing this adventure together.

There wasn't much more in the way of deeper conversation, as this moment of unity and passion, overcame Mharn. His hands moved, from Karina's waist, as he felt lower around her buttocks. Karina became caught up in the romance of the moment.

Mharn sealed the entry access of Karina's private suite behind them, as the passion intensified. Mharn was consumed with Karina's natural beauty, her sensitivity, warmth and charm and she seemed to encourage the building urgent needs, in his foreplay.

After his warming hands, rubbed her buttocks, Mharn turned her around and held her from behind. He pulled her closer, as his hands moved under her arms to cup, her full firm breasts. Karina's eyes closed, as she stood willingly, under the influence of this passionate display and his caressing advances.

The heightened sensitivity around her erogenous zones were rapidly stimulated with the memories, of their past sexual desires. Karina became more aroused and willing as Mharn's intentions became more evident. She was now swept up in his arms, as his exploring hands, moved around to excite her passions.

Karina was now feeling Mharn's building erection pressing between her cheeks as the moments of passion built between them and became more urgent. Nothing else in the universe seemed to matter now, that they had found each other again. Finally after removing some of her garments, Mharn felt the last of her remaining garments slip to the floor, as the burst of excitement built between them.

The lighting was dim, as they felt their way around, closer to Karina's bed. Mharn's feelings of lust and desire showed, as he quickly undressed himself, next to Karina's naked body. Karina held Mharn's erection in the palms of her hands and squeezed him with warming sensitivity as he lay her down.

His hands were everywhere now, as her shapely figure became increasingly submissive. 'Oh Mharn.' She breathed lovingly as he continued to massage the areas around her erogenous zones. After further caressing, Mharn climbed in between her as she braced for the powerful thrusting motions yet to come. As Mharn entered her, she instinctively lifted her legs to wrap them, around his waist. Her tight legs, could feel the building intensity, of Mharn's throbbing erection, pounding into her bracing frame.

Mharn moved purposefully and with clear intent, to lift Karina's moment of pleasure. As she panted with every thrust, Mharn pushed himself deeper and deeper into the warm receptive regions, of Karina's erogenous zones.

Nothing else mattered at the moment, but the sharing of love, the feeling of spontaneity and the explosion of desire, building between them.

Mharn gripped her buttocks firmly as he thrust himself with urgency as deeply as he could. Finally with a gasp from Karina, Mharn exploded deep inside her, again and again and again. As he felt this sense of release, Mharn held her firm cheeks, as they both enjoyed the thrill of this explosive climax, with a kiss. He remained deep inside her.

For a moment, as they held together, Mharn reflected on how long it seemed since they had last seen each other. Locked and entangled together, Karina held Mharn even closer, while she decided to protect the other important news, concerning them both.

For Mharn now, to caress her warm breasts and hug her limp form was a treasure, he had sorely missed in their union. He loved Karina more than simple words could express. To have her here now, sharing herself and the warmth of their union, meant everything to him.

Karina was listening to the built up excitement in his future plans, without him understanding any of the reasons, why she had come this great distance, to see him.

Mharn then breathed. 'I'm just so happy to see you.'

Karina was ecstatic 'I just found out, you were coming aboard.'

Mharn's building mission excitement continued. 'We're having a final briefing when we get to Tamaryn's planet. We're leaving Prisium soon and I don't have much time. We can catch up again, when you all get to Tamaryn's planet.'

Karina rolled over to hug him and Mharn held her tenderly. He soon became erect again and as he pressed against Karina's side, she could feel the urgency building up inside him again, to have her once more.

Mharn gazed at her. 'You are just gorgeous.' He breathed as he lay behind her willing form. She sensed the throbbing tension, building in his erection, as it stiffened almost with a mind of its own. This renewed urgency, was becoming larger in the minds of them both, as the great desire for more passion and physical pleasure emerged.

Karina leaned back over her shoulder, as she laughed wildly at Mharn's determined efforts, to have her once more.

Karina giggled. 'You don't know how much, I've missed you.'

Mharn replied. 'I love you Kari.'

Mharn reached again, to gently fondle her firming breasts, as he lay bonded behind her. His throbbing erection, with a mind of its own, was determined to have her again.

Karina smiled as she felt herself once again, becoming the object of unrestrained wanton desire. She just loved this chance to be reconnected with Mharn and as his searching hands began to massage her breasts, buttocks and all over her body, she just melted into his arms.

Mharn gasped with urgency. 'I want you.'

Karina giggled again, with boisterous anticipation. 'I know.'

Mharn now sat up on the side of the bed, with his feet hanging over the edge and motioned Karina to come to him. She climbed back onto the bed in front of him, sitting on his lap, facing him with her knees on either side. Mharn continued to massage her buttocks, as he pulled her closer to him. He gripped her bottom tighter with both hands as she sat completely exposed, to the penetrating and pulsating desire that was stiffening between them. His throbbing ambitions became too much for them both.

He lay back down, penetrating her as she moved around sensually. She continued to mount his erection. She gently positioned herself, again and again on top of him and as Nature took its course, his throbbing erection entered her deeply, over and over again.

Karina groaned with pleasure as she took control of this continuous motion to relieve her panting cravings. Mharn held her warm breasts, as she leaned down to kiss him. He now thrust himself with increasing pleasure, deeper into the receptive warmth of her erogenous zones. After some moments of shared soaring pleasure, Mharn held onto her tightly, as they gently rolled with Karina on her back again, in the center of the bed.

She stretched her arms out above her head, as Mharn began to have his way with her again. Mharn had settled himself, between her outstretched legs. The passion between them became more intense, as the urgency in his throbbing erection, continued to build.

Karina held him tighter as she wrapped and squeezed her outstretched legs around his waist in anticipation, of a greater releasing satisfaction. They wrestled as one as the writhing pleasure built between them. He thrust himself again and again, with mounting energy and determination to penetrate, deeper inside her.

There was an instinctive desire, to push himself in as deeply as he could, while he gripped her buttocks more firmly. Karina could sense the coming eruption, as Mharn squeezed her cheeks. With one final thrust he came with an explosive pulsating surge, until the urgent throbbing ceased and the power in his erection, was spent.

Mharn sighed. 'I want you with me forever Kari.'

'I love you too.' And then more softly, she whispered. 'Much more than you know.'

It was some time later when they were dressed and they joined their other friends. Mharn seemed pressed for time, as the others on the first mission were waiting for his return. There was a lot of friendly banter and cheer between them all, as though the friends were all now reconnected and there would be every chance, to catch up again.

This moment for them both, became a lasting memory, as Mharn waved goodbye and his own mission continued. Karina smiled warmly and her mind was in another place as Mharn's image, disappeared through the Map Room portal.

Janet asked. 'Did you tell him, Karina?'

Karina seemed a little confused about this. 'Not yet, but we're going to catch up again soon, when he gets his mission briefing, on Tamaryn's planet. Mharn has to return to his own ship, while this gateway portal is still open.'

Janet looked on with understanding and warmth as Karina found her voice again. 'I will find a way, to tell him soon.'

Sun-Ky soon returned and we continued to be fascinated by the prospect of seeing many different life forms, in another galaxy. Sun-Ky sounded excited. 'We now have some time to show you, their main planetary systems and their history of choices.'

31
What is Nature Trying to Teach Us?

Marmuron was increasingly excited. 'Is this a vision of their twenty three planets?'

Sun-Ky said. 'Yes, however there is a tremendous amount of background history we won't get to see this time.'

Janet seemed puzzled. 'Why not?'

As Sun-Ky spoke, the images began playing out. 'Well, because Janet we are on a return mission, with the shorter duration envoys.'

Other questions came swift and fast. 'Sun-Ky, how do we begin to understand their systems, their processes and their natural justice laws?'

Sun-Ky then began. 'From early childhood, family orientation learning is about schooling in family responsibility and societal values. No child progresses without early learning levels on self-control, self-discipline, self-reliance and self-respect.'

Janet was reflective. 'That sounds a little hard.'

'You need to consider this, in the way of preparation. It is not deliberately unfriendly. What they are teaching all children in their early training, is to learn to take self-responsibility, for their own personal choices.'

'The question always remains, what kind of personal traits do you want your children to grow up with? To be personally strong, facing intellectual challenges and being decisive. Being self-aware and confident with aspirational settings. Being methodical and aiming to achieve or, do you want weakness, reliance and idleness with an undisciplined and lawless pursuit, which lacks in basic character strengths.'

Michael smiled. 'I've heard some of this before.'

Sun-Ky responded. 'Yes, however here it becomes a fundamental choice.'

Then Janet asked. 'Why?'

'Let me tell you about a different kind of belief. If you want to understand Tamaryn's ancient society and its generational successes, then you must consider the following.'

'It begins with the question, does life have a natural purpose?'

Marmuron queried. 'Meaning?'

'It begins with Natures silent messaging, to appeal to an advanced intellect, to maintain an orderly and disciplined existence. To begin with, survival must have a sense of self-belief, to protect the existence Nature has given us. Humanity needs to create a way forward. You will have seen how life can be unruly, disruptive, and uncontrollable, among some animal classes, without any structural discipline.'

Janet queried. 'Where does this start?'

'Life must have character and a sense of honor which supports purpose. For them to integrate harmoniously, their communities must observe a moral code of ethics. It leads to the next question, of how do we respect each other, in the short time, we all have?'

Oats asked. 'Is this taught at their global youth exchanges?'

'Yes, however, preservation of moral existence must begin with self-respect and then respect for others. When you stand back and observe disintegration in social order, it is easy to see what happens without values. Those who will tolerate and endure anything and believe in no values, cause the most harm, to the unity in social conscience.'

Sun-Ky pondered. 'We're trying to understand, the depth of what helps this society survive in peace for as long, as it has. Those without moral principles, will shape a more fragile structure, which corrupts future cultural advancement.'

Janet asked. 'Where do these foundational beliefs come from?'

'The silent opportunities in Nature, can be seen everywhere? Those who don't accept some level of social cohesiveness, risk disunity, conflict, division and dissent. You can see these visions, on the planet of Isolation. The inhabitants there, don't even see this exclusion and separation, for what it really means.'

'What is it that they don't see?'

'The rejection by themselves, of the fundamental realities of Natural law.'

Sun-Ky's explanations, became an absorbing and intriguing insight. 'Old growth forests start from small beginnings. It is not so much how we start in life, it is how we finish that matters. Consider how you have grown and helped bring another life into being. Also consider, all the beneficial experiences you can show, with an uplifting influence, on your own children's future.'

'To begin in life with nothing and leave the place a little better for our being. Life is an amazing experience and children need to be prepared early, in order to understand their choices. We are here to learn, with kindness and the miracles of natural messaging.'

'Have you ever watched the mystery of children in infancy, or young bear cubs being nurtured, or a small calf in a pod of whales? Have you ever seen an elm tree as a sapling and then through the ages, going through seasons from spring to autumn?'

'The appeal in Nature, is to see the miracle of seasonal change, after decades of growth. This is what Nature is trying to tell us. A vision of where we all start in life and with the right struggle, energy and motivation, where we can be, if we try.'

'Tamaryn's many planetary populations are evolving, according to the realities of these values and perceptions. They have learnt to survive, to grow and live in peace.'

'What are the different laws of compliance in Tamaryn's galaxy, Pim?'

Pim could see Michael was puzzled. 'At a regional level on your planet there are local and cultural jurisdictions, beginning from ancient interpretations of origin. Tamaryn's different societies adapted long ago, to the irrefutable natural laws that begin with light and heat energy, including gravity and motion.'

Michael seemed puzzled. 'I'm not quite there, yet Pim.'

'Since the beginning of our time, humanity has had to work with the certainty of Natural Forces. While the issues of travel between galaxies requires increased care, these same natural laws will apply equally, across the entire universe.'

Then. 'Michael, have you ever wondered why our society has indulged, your sense of natural inquisitiveness, about your planetary history?'

Michael looked a little dumbfounded as Pim seemed to be verging onto something important. 'Well no, not really. I just believed we were finding things out.'

'I want you to consider the timeline for humanity from the period of Origin. Our time is so short and what we have been trying to prepare you for, is so momentous and profound. I'm not sure where to start.'

Oats laughed. 'The beginning, would help Pim.'

There was a giggle from Pim. 'Your first two missions were designed to help you understand us and the history of our more advanced global societies. Your last three mission were to help you understand, how much time is lost with past theories and the illusion created over historical belief.'

'Your Big Bang theory had significant flaws and Darwin's theory was also parochial with parochial findings. This history of belief, were early attempts to understand, universal design concepts.'

'These insights have gone someway to help you rebalance universal reality. We are coming to a galaxy with a history of natural development, much older than our own.'

'Pim, has their evolutionary development, been more effective than ours?'

'Yes and no. There are choices and boundaries, with social and fundamental laws. Consider what happens in a forest fire?'

Michael was now completely focused. 'I'm listening.'

'Depending on severity some things wilt and die and may never recover. However, have you noticed how Nature often picks itself up and is revitalized, regrows and is reborn, to go on living once more? It is a little like the human spirit after we fall over, we pick ourselves up and dust ourselves off and get on with life.'

'Nature doesn't choose to die unless the fire is completely devastating. Even then as damaged as this may be, there is some regrowth over time. What is Nature trying to say to us all?'

Now Sun-Ky answered. 'The living spirit is saying, never give up and never give in. The laws you make, are the self-disciplines you follow and each of us have these choices, to make in our own lives'

Oats asked. 'What happens, when we feel challenged by the elements?'

'We can yield, surrender, succumb and perish or we can struggle to survive, we can battle to live on, and stand up to the never ending encounters which bring some of us down. We are being shown everyday how to make choices in life. True some face more hardships than others, however we can use our intelligence, to be ingenious and astute.'

'Have you ever been attacked on a hot summer's day by flies, fleas and mosquitoes? In the cycle of life, we are fodder for worms, Michael. However our initial responses are to struggle and battle to live on, to fight to survive. But we have learnt to do it, with belief in ourselves and the guiding principles, of the trusted values, most of us share.'

As we continued to watch these visions of the planets in Tamaryn's galaxy and their many societies, Oats, began to smile.

We all noticed it and then Marmuron asked. 'What are you smiling at Oatsy?'

'I've seen a lot of these examples before, on our own planet Earth. Some of these visions remind me of another place, at another moment, a long time ago.'

This claim, caught most of them by surprise, as Pim asked. 'In what way Oats?'

Oats paused. 'Before Michael and I met, I use to travel overseas a lot with my parents, where I attended an international school, as a young student. I made some early friendships with other kids and some of us, have remained close, ever since.'

Michael grinned. 'Yes, I remember you telling me about it, Oats,'

Then Sun-Ky asked. 'Remind us all Oats.'

'Well, many of the villages we've seen on your images here, remind me of the communities and townships I've seen in parts of rural England, the south of France and many other places. Local and well-developed, although the vegetation is quite different, many of the behavioral customs, seem quite similar.'

Marmuron asked. 'In what way Oatsy?'

'It's in the attitude of the people towards each other. When I visited my friend in Hawaii, the tropical floral varieties were simply stunning. The people were warm, friendly, cheerful and happy, just to be alive. Everyone seemed welcoming and there existed an enormous self-respect and respect for each other. They celebrated their ancestry with song and cheer and with dance and a growing magnetism, all of its own.'

'Yes, everyone needs to work, but you don't need to own extreme wealth. You can be rich in spirit, with happiness in your life. You don't need power over others, if you have self-control and self-respect. Harmony comes to those who pursue existence, with passion in their lives and Hawaii has plenty of this.'

Oats was nursing some happy memories. 'With music in your heart, melody in your spirit and happiness in your soul, there is a gentle kindness, held in the mind of all creatures.'

'So where do you see any similarities with the planet of Isolation, Oats?'

'Oh dear, I also had a friend who came from the Middle East and he felt lucky to be able to leave and seemed happy to be alive and able to escape. Some children there, only ever know violence, torture and abuse, with little respect held by some others.'

'Consider living in an environment, where people are willing to believe the worst in each other. Rather than seeking friendship and happiness, they seem willing to find fault and criticize, often leading to violence and suffering. Hate filled rants, often divide people, rather than unite them.'

Sun-Ky found some agreement. 'Yes Oats, if you are ever fortunate enough to see the planet of Isolation, these poorer choices will become more obvious. If you look for the good in each other, then you very often find it and if you choose to criticize, find fault and condemn others, many will be the less happier, for it.'

'The early student programs run by Tamaryn's society, can see these human choices, through the minds of others and then witness the value in cultural differences. It then becomes their choice, if they want to live with the harmonious emotional benefits of a warming natural environment, or a more contentious and hostile existence. Being happy rather than sad, is such an easy choice to make. Have love in your heart, a searching wisdom in your mind of thoughts and an advancing global society as your aspirational dream. We are not too far away from this, if we all choose wisely.'

'It is a far better choice than greed and regret, anger and mistrust or memories of despairing and divisive impoverishment.'

Marmuron asked. 'Oats, what other differences, did you find in the Middle East?'

'Well, there are much fewer trees and flowers, life can be particularly harsh. The thing is, many there don't seem to realize an existence, that's any different from this, where savagery, hostility and brutality is common. Many of their homes and villages are often destroyed and the peace loving among them, are forced to flee and find shelter. It's been going on there, like this for many centuries.'

Marmuron then asked. 'Do people on Earth, see these challenges in their lives?'

Oats seemed to pause. 'My experience with people, is that many just want to be happy in life and have a fair chance, to share what life offers. When you treat someone as you would want to be treated yourself, then that brings out the best in everyone. My early school friends learnt this from each other and we remain strong friends today. We found the levels of respect you mentioned and we strived for self-improvement.'

'In a moment of peaceful reflection, we are able to appreciate the contrasts, found in Nature. The unforgiving, the resilient, the beautiful and the serene, shows the extreme differences, found in Natures presence. It truly is insightful and thought provoking.'

Janet smiled. 'Well done Oats, well said.'

Both Pim and Sun-Ky smiled at Oats, with his lengthy explanations about his personal experiences. 'Oats, this is why Tamaryn's societies, choose to send their older students on these missions. If they can begin life with a mature mind that sees the balance in cultural differences and the choices of others, this then helps their own enlightenment.'

As they continued to watch these insightful visions, one thing became perfectly clear to them all. The futility of hostility, built around historic cultural differences. Then, by contrast to consider the appealing case for generational change, in global human values.

The adjustment to personal responsibility, self-control and determination was convincing, in seeking global advancement. One choice was a way forward and the other choice, was seen as a way backwards. A way back, that led to nowhere.

The only planet they had not seen a vision of, was Tamaryn's primary planet. As they all resettled, Sun-Ky came over to help with this further illumination.

'Sun-Ky, can you help us grasp the living experience, on Tamaryn's own planet?'

Sun-Ky was thoughtful. 'Oats, I want you to revisit the experience created around your cabin in the nearby native forest areas and foothills on the Pimeron planet.'

'Yes lovely isn't it.'

Sun-Ky smiled. 'What's lovely about it?'

32
The Inspiration, in Nature's Silent Messaging?

Oats looked a little puzzled for a moment. 'Well.' Was as much as Oats could get out right away, before he seemed to relax more and then it just came to him. 'Initial impressions are of the peace and quiet. Yes there are many sounds of chirping birds and smaller scurrying animals, but you can stand there absorbed, in the middle of it all. In the forest there are no conflicting opinions over anything at all, really. There's a stimulating sense of permanent harmony and tranquility, between these living creatures. Some of the many smaller creatures, really bring a smile to your face.'

Oats laughed as he continued. 'You can watch them play together while following their routines, just fossicking around. There's the activity in rebuilding their family habitats, during the changing seasons. I often go there for my own peace of mind and the loving environment, without any real tensions. It helps me reflect, on other important things in life, in an uninterrupted ecosystem.'

Then. 'I love the way tall trees can exist for ages in the one spot while growing older.' Oats paused for a moment. 'Some trees are older than I am. They contribute to life's purpose in silence, without harming anyone, or causing pain and suffering to others.

I'm really lucky in many ways, to be able to share this living experience, just for a moment in time, without a care in the world. The forest for me is almost reclusive. Marmuron and I both enjoy the simple life there, just living off the land.'

Oats face brightened, as he remembered something else.

Michael asked. 'What is it Oats?'

'I was just thinking about the seasonal changes. It's a pleasant temperate climate, in summer, with a warm log fire in winter. We help the forest by clearing out and storing all the accumulating dead wood, which builds up from time to time. Some of the smaller critters hibernate and everything changes again in the spring and autumn periods.'

Sun-Ky said. 'It sounds like an ideal place, to go back to Oats?'

'Yes, Marmuron and I love it there. It's our home and from our cabin you can see elevated views, with many changing colors, across the valley floor. They are a joy to behold, to discover, watch and observe.'

Sun-Ky was leading now. 'How's your interaction, with others, in the forest?'

'No one is there to question you, tell you what think, how to behave or what to do. It is just peaceful and serene in the extreme.'

Given all the ancient research they had just uncovered, Sun-Ky asked. 'Does anyone coach, or try to program or lecture you to believe anything?'

Oats was getting the essence of this now. 'No one asks anything of you or criticizes your thoughts, or chastises your behavior. No one questions your views, or wants you to change your habits or challenges your beliefs. No one doubts you, or tells you how to live your life, or what to wear or how to mind your p's and q's.'

Janet and Marmuron, looked at each other and laughed.

Sun-Ky then reminded us of our recent ancient discoveries. 'Oats, there are other logical considerations, worth analyzing and considering in your forest.'

Both Michael and Oats seemed surprised, that they may have missed something. 'We're listening.'

'Over hundreds of generations of existence, there has never been anything to match humanities capacity to be brutal, attempting to dominate and control. There's no quest by other species for extreme wealth, or attempts to manipulate the thoughts of others. Your own recent history, has been kind to you both.'

'Nature does not take advantage of you, because you may be poor. There's no animosity or hatred, in the Natural Force.'

'There is a sense of freedom, where you are encouraged to think, plan and act for yourselves and yet throughout the ages, the forest has had this stable and enduring influence. In many respects this natural environment and the species within, hold an eternal peace, often craved by humanity at large. Nature is a self-perpetuating silent force, enjoying an ageless and peaceful survival, from lasting energy sources.'

'Nature has shown a way forward, for unity between cultures where the ability to debate any conceptual differences, in an environment of harmony and diversity, still exists. You will soon find out why this natural environment is worth protecting.'

'Yes, we see it already. The environment is certainly worth protecting.'

Pim asked. 'Why Oats?'

Oats seemed suddenly struck by something. 'Because we get to see that differences of opinion are tolerable and that peace of mind is found, in looking for answers with an open mind. There's nothing wrong with a reasoned debate, to find a more balanced point of view, from other more different perspectives. This has been the impact, of watching millions of years, of living with Nature.'

Marmuron questioned. 'What has Oats?'

'That differences are tolerable. That life, as a force is fascinating and that rather than be held to experiencing only one belief and one type of existence, with an open mind we get to appreciate, many forms of life. Yes, if someone is single-minded and intolerant, it becomes harder for them, to see the virtues of patience.'

Sun-Ky watched with amusement, as Oats and Michael, debated the obvious. 'Are there any other issues in the forest, about the laws of natural existence?'

'It is the application of Natures laws which allows any community, to see value in a unity of purpose and the chances for peaceful co-existence.'

Then Sun-Ky began. **'It is the Universal Natural Force, which created the original innocence of perpetuating life and without question gives an inalienable right, to this life. It is this force of Nature, in combination with the other universal forces, which creates the protection, for life's innocent existence. It is within this silent existence, we discover our protected freedoms, having an intelligence with which to think, where we learn a sense of moral courage, with which to build character on.'**

Sun-Ky then counseled. 'If you get to visit the twenty three planets in Tamaryn's inner systems, you will see many examples of the lives, we have discussed and you will form your own views, on the many fundamentals, which drive human diversity.'

'However, Tamaryn's home planet lives with this warm hearted forest atmosphere, you have experienced. This is what the villagers there, all want to protect and preserve. A cheerful place, free from any complicated anxieties and perplexing struggles, created by competing cultures, from some other societies.'

'The humble villages there, don't pry or scold. They don't judge or doubt you. There's no hostility or animosity, or feelings of being left out and isolated.'

Sun-Ky laughed. 'There is a mischief, with merriment in laughter and amusement, in bantering exchanges. The villagers are born with different sets of skills and live with a happy social disposition. Their existence is completely unspoiled, with friendships, built around their unique caring, for their Natural environment.'

Sun-Ky smiled. 'Overwhelmingly though, it is this sense of having a united cause. There is a shared empathy, for the nurturing of Nature, which holds them all together.'

'Their lifestyle is buoyed by a sense of the calm, found in Nature and each of them remains unjudged, by anyone else. It is a cherished, treasured and touching existence.'

Michael beamed at Oats. 'It sounds like, our kind of place.'

33
Begin with an Uncluttered Mind.

Janet was loving this experience and became more motivated in her questioning. 'I'm still trying to understand why, their societies have these inter planetary programs for their children?'

Sun-Ky said. 'If you went back to the societies on your planet Earth, you would see these contrasts more clearly. Imagine someone who had travelled widely. This person would have had the many experiences, like the one's Oats spoke of before.'

'With the benefit of hindsight they too, could look back with some wisdom, about the choices people have made in the past. What happens in Tamaryn's systems, is that the children share these experiences. So, the students are selected at maturity, after their preliminary training, for these interplanetary missions. To learn from historical choices, taken by others before them and observe the impacts of these choices, on society for themselves. Understanding the wide-ranging choices Nature gives us, the children get to see the impacts, of these previously made good and bad choices.'

Janet felt enthusiastically persuaded. 'I'd never considered it like that before.'

'Yes, it's the opposite of how some societies treat their children. These children have not made any bad choices so far, in their young lives. They are taught to explore optimal excellence, while witnessing the past choices of adults. You see, this way it is the children who will be able to influence their own futures.'

'Sometimes, experiencing the silent influence of natural choices early in life, helps everyone, to reconsider their future direction. These exchanges, challenge the innocent mind, to explore, to question and to empower their intellect, towards peaceful choices.'

'Self-governing of behaviors, for the innocent to learn, so they can respect the sound logic, found in an advancing social cohesion.'

As Janet continued to watch the images, she noted. 'They seem so young?'

'Probably the best way to explain this, is to localize it for yourself.'

'A young citizen with free choice, is observing the lifestyle and customs of past civilizations as a whole. Without judgment of any kind, they make a choice on how they would like to live and where they would like to spend, the rest of their life.'

Pim then said. 'Do you choose peace, freedom and constructive engagement? You see Nature doesn't compel us, to do anything. It is up to individuals to search for the type of society they want to be a part of. Parents can see their children form these views, on the importance of balance and sustainability, at a personal level.'

'Parents want their children, to see what society has become, through choices taken and boundaries crossed over time, which then helps children decide for themselves.'

Marmuron was drawn to these values. 'What a brilliant way to start a young life.'

Pim was reflective. 'Yes, we all have had many different motivations.'

'You mean these children are able to make up their own minds, at this age?'

'You must understand natural choice. Nature shows preferences, while not criticizing your decisions. Nature accepts both good and bad choices, can be made.'

Oats began mumbling to himself as Michael asked. 'What is it Oats?'

'Michael, look at the history of civil unrest on our planet, over the last say three thousand years.'

Michael questioned. 'Whose history?'

'Well most of the arguments have been over a few things. If you took away all the disputes over different beliefs, the elites concerns about money, power and control in maintenance of privilege , then the meek and mild, could truly have inherited the Earth.'

Sun-Ky smiled as he continued. 'Each of us are here, for what seems like only a short time. Do you want to help your children understand this expanse and enjoy life, or do you want to ignore the silent messaging and try to change, what can't be changed?'

As the visions continued, Janet's puzzled expression vanished. 'There's no pressure on these children to believe anything, or be forced to follow, ancient customs.'

Pim confirmed. 'It's about learning to find quality of life Janet. Remember the inventiveness of discovery. Mankind, has the ability to change and improve. To not be disrespectful, to not hurt someone else's feelings, or harm their values or damage social cohesion and destroy the hopes and dreams of others.'

'It's about finding a happy balance and developing a mature understanding of Nature and working with these, powerful silent forces. To learn, respect and appreciate, Nature's silent messaging, which we can all share.'

'The children are innocent and this is the beginning of their guiding influence in life. Nature has laws and their choices become thought-provoking, about what Nature says, by implication and by consequence.'

'Natures laws can be harsh, requiring self-protection and sometimes also be warm and sensitive, but always consistent. These children must learn character and moral judgment. Self-preservation can be a powerfully motivating influence, in wanting to live and survive. The children's parents understand, that their progenies future, must be better, than their own.'

34
The Reappearance of Tamaryn's Aide.

Sun-Ky concluded. 'When children learn to understand these laws and live within their meaning, surviving becomes so much more cheerfully pleasant and good-natured. By contrast if they choose to challenge these laws, or the peaceful ambiance of social harmony, then living on the planet of Isolation, becomes their chosen destiny. It is not Nature which will condemn them, but the embracing by them, of their own weaknesses.'

We were all still sitting in a group in the Map Room, as the Corillion continued on its course, towards the planet of Prisium. The visions coming through of the different planetary experiences, were vivid, magnificent and inspiring, as we came even closer to our destination.

Sun-Ky had just received a timely message, revealing another imminent visitor.

A vision appeared through the Map Room portal. It was Tamaryn's aide, wearing his unique ancient costume dress. The same aide we met once before, back on Kendagon. At that time, he took us to Tamaryn's mountain top hideaway, at Benlay.

As the aide's vision appeared, he formed into a mortal image and looking around questioned, 'Michael?'

Michael remembered him from the last time. 'Yes'.

'Your guests will need to separate, into different groups to protect the unborn.'

Pim jumped at this request. 'Please, what's happened with the first mission?'

'You will be arriving at an interplanetary auditorium, on our nearby planet of Prisium. The unborn need to be protected from harmful exposure, posed by the forces of renewal, coming from Foundation Forest, on our primal planet.'

Janet asked. 'Are the earlier delegates from the first mission, still there as well?'

'Yes, this is a standard precaution, for all incoming emissaries.'

After a quick consultation, Pim suggested. 'Why don't we all split up into two primary age groups? This will also help our hosts with logistics.'

Sun-Ky agreed. 'Let's land first and then plan, for any other developments.'

The aide then announced. 'Munkhan will be coming aboard soon, to enable a smooth transition, for those going on, to the primal planet.'

This brought a smile of relief for Michael, Oats, Janet and Marmuron. Munkhan, was a well-established galaxy historian. Having his help so soon, was a stroke of good fortune for them.

Finally the aide finished with this. 'It will take some time for events to unfold. We have to enter our inner planetary systems first.'

As the aide smiled and his image slowly faded away, Pim quickly counseled Karina and her friends on their chance to pack, change and get ready.

Karina readily agreed. 'We'll be back soon.' This left Oats, Michael, Janet and Marmuron alone with Pim and Sun-Ky for a moment.

As the images continued, Pim counseled. 'Remember, ours is only a short mission for the purpose of bringing home, some of the other delegates.'

Pim left us a little stunned, then Oats remembered our mission responsibilities. Oats appeared a little tentative. 'Michael, we are about to embark on a journey, into some complete unknowns. We are wanting to bring Mharn back, from a galaxy experience, we haven't even seen for ourselves yet.' Oats seemed baffled.

Michael rested his hand on Oats wrist. 'Let's take things, one step at a time.'

Oats replied. 'That's what's worrying me. All we can do is try to influence Mharn to remember his family loyalties and his future back home.'

'I don't believe it will come to that.' Then. 'This could all blow up in our faces Oats.' The two friends continued to speculate and wonder what lay in front of them.

Janet and Marmuron were sensing the thrill, of the changing cosmic visions, while Mharn's friends continued in their suites, getting ready.

Oats and Michael were completely overwhelmed, by the images of massive celestial diversity unfolding in the foreground in front of them. This vast approaching inner galactic region, was a place of enormous and immense, splendor and beauty.

Meanwhile back in Karina's suite, the anticipation was building. Her girlfriends were all chatting with building excitement. Everyone was captivated by the thrill of the unknown. Their plans, seemed to be changing, from one moment to the next.

'Karina, you must confide in Mharn about this. You may not get another chance.'

'I will Uri, when the time is right,'

'Do you want us to help you, Karina?'

Karina was left pondering. 'Mharn doesn't know the details of his own mission yet.'

A worried look from Uri. 'What are you going to do if you don't get that chance?'

Karina looked puzzled. 'I really don't know.' And then tears of solitude began to form, as though her life was suddenly becoming much more complicated than she had planned and she was beginning to feel separated and alone, with her news of joy.

Karina held out her arms, for a hug with her old friends, as she realized that these decisions weren't easy to make. Arkina and Urundayy had stood by her through thick and thin for most of her life. 'Thank you both. I'm very lucky to have such close friends.'

As the girls shared a tear and a hug, Uri asked. 'I wonder what our men are up to.'

35
Nature's Illuminating Laws, on Order and Morality.

Michael and Oats were thrilled to arrive within the inner formations of Tamaryn's galaxy. Sun-Ky came over to advise that Munkhan, would be appearing momentarily.

The researchers had to stop and think every so often, about the time and distance challenges facing them. The last time they saw Munkhan, was his visit to Oats alpine cabin, just before he joined the first mission to leave on this mission. Oats and Michael valued his vast insights on the complexities facing them, in this cosmological expanse.

The vision of their old friend Munkhan, coming through the Map Room portal, lifted their spirits enormously. His face just radiated wisdom, confidence and happiness.

Michael's face grinned. 'Munkhan, how fantastic to see you.'

Munkhan began. 'Our first mission is getting ready to leave Prisium soon, on our way to Tamaryn's primal planet. We're meeting an advanced class, of their local students, who have just completed an excursion, exploring the inner planets. It has been a self- enriching exercise, on how multiple civilizations, have evolved over time.'

Oats replied. 'Yes, we've just been briefed on it. When are you all leaving?'

Munkhan laughed. 'You want to come with us?'

Pim said. 'Yes we'd love to come with you, on our way to see Tamaryn.'

Munkhan quizzed. 'How long is your visit to Prisium, scheduled for?'

Pim responded. 'We're dividing into two groups.

'Mharn's friends are going to see Velia and Mykron for a while. We are ready to leave, almost immediately. Can you wait for us?

'Yes, it's quite possible, let's find out. I'm noticing how difficult it is to keep measure of time, as we move into different time zones. There's so many dimensions to consider.'

Janet and Marmuron came over to join them. It was a very happy reunion. Janet asked. 'What's happened to Mykron and Velia?'

'Some from our first mission are stopping over there with them. Velia is thrilled to see her family again. Her father is leaving shortly on a mission of his own, to help expand the resettlement plans for several species, on another nearby planet.'

Oats exclaimed. 'Wow.'

As a galaxy historian, Munkhan had a wealth of knowledge, on the ancient history of many civil societies, in multiple jurisdictions. 'This is why I'm here now. To help you all quickly meet, before they leave.' Oats and Michael often found themselves completely in his debt, for the deeper knowledge, which Munkhan shared with them.

Pim then confirmed. 'Sun-Ky and I will come as well. We can leave WIL's ship orbiting Prisium and take one of our transports down to the surface.'

Janet and Marmuron were thrilled to come and so Pim advised. 'The six of us will be going on to Tamaryn's planet. We are dividing by age into two smaller groups. We will all come down to Prisium and then join Tamaryn's ship, back to her planet.'

Oats asked Munkhan. 'What have you learnt so far?'

'Within their local astronomical region, there are eight star systems with twenty three habitable planets. Thirteen of these planets have large sustainable levels of evolving life forms, supporting many species.'

'There's another three central planets comprising large rainforest regions with many varieties of exotic plants. One of them is Tamaryn's own primal planet and the other two have large regional territories, with sustainable vegetation. Six more, protect a large variety of other animal classes and finally there's the one isolated planet, for those who see none of Nature's boundaries, in their lifestyle at all.'

Munkhan then added. 'This is just within their own, cosmological frontiers.'

Janet whispered to Pim. 'No one can visit this and complete their objectives and return home to our galaxy, in ten rotations of Kendagon. It's just not possible'

Pim nodded, their timing was tight and bigger plans were looking very unlikely, however they had to grab, every opportunity they could.

Sun-Ky came back over and counselled. 'We will be orbiting Prisium soon.'

Oats grinned, as this all began to sink in. 'So how do we begin, Pim?'

'Let's all go down in the one transport and later, Mharn's friends can come back on this shuttle to the Corillion, before we all have to return home. I'll go and advise them to get ready. It will be easy to shuttle between these destinations and we can make plans as we go. I'll be right back.'

Mharn's friends were advised about their longer stay on Prisium and to meet and catch up with Mykron, Velia and her family. The time had come to enter the transport to go down to the surface, Oats was eager for as much knowledge, as he could gather.

'Munkhan, what other variations are we looking for, on these different planets?'

'The fascinating aspect of being able to view, other planetary animal classes, is to understand and interpret their instinctive behaviors, for natural preservation.'

'Really.' Breathed Janet.

Oats asked. 'What instincts specifically?'

'Flock and herd habits, social behavior, civility and personality, which help hold Nature's animal classes and colonies together.'

'With an ordered structure in place, the desire to protect, stay alive and evolve, encourages higher levels of rational conformity. Without behavioral stability, elementary existence, can become chaotic.'

'Not all animal classes, show higher levels of open-mindedness.'

Janet seemed puzzled. 'How can you tell, whether they do or not?'

Munkhan laughed. 'Why, you look for it Janet.'

'With evolution, their ancient societies understood this question of order. The most important ideals learnt, were the instinctive values, contained within Nature's past.'

'Their children can see, once humanity compromises on different levels of morality, with betrayal or unfaithfulness, by violating long held character strengths, then their bond with Nature, can be temporarily lost.'

'Nature's motivation, is for an intellectually gifted advancement, which improves our character choices. We are given intelligence at birth to appreciate Nature's charismatic fascinations. The high scenic mountain areas with enduring gentleness of stability and to share the peaceful serenity.'

'Tell us how the children see choices and boundaries, on these missions.'

'If their society wants an ecologically sustainable and naturally defendable living experience, they must observe Natures rules, for appropriate behavior.'

'The question becomes this. What standards are they prepared to uphold and defend and then what boundaries are some prepared cross. If society is not prepared to support any natural boundaries or standards, then what do they hope to teach their children?'

'These determinations, decide where they live, how they live and with whom they live. They all start from an age of innocence and search for their own choices, in life. Some of these children as you will see, prefer a simple existence, with an environmental focus. Others prefer a more complex, demanding and challenging existence.'

Oats was fascinated. 'Munkhan, where did their social orders, originally begin?'

'Why on Isolation Oats. That is the reason they routinely send all their graduating children, on these missions. To help each of them understand, the choices their forefathers made in leaving and any social boundaries, which may have been crossed.'

Michael agreed. 'Yes, we saw some visions of that, earlier.'

Munkhan continued. 'You will be able to observe for yourselves their cultural differences. The steps they take, to consider life's choices. When we see them, we will find out how the children evaluate, the benefits and choices for themselves.'

Michael was still a little confused. 'Is there a greater purpose here?'

'Yes, choices and boundaries follow Natural law in the universe. It's greater than just a simple comparable observation of humanity. These sets of guiding principles are more powerful, than any parochial, planetary, family, civil or jurisdictional authority. Natural Law gives them one chance at life and they alone have to decide their own values and guiding moral principles and their own character choices.'

'All of them will want some measure of normalcy, happiness and cheer in their lives. However, it is self-discipline, self-control and some measure of restraint, which decides how well they achieve this, when they interact with others.'

'Unless they accept and believe in a defining set of character values, they will never grow to understand completely, the essence of Nature's Force. A force that has rules for a gifted and remarkable existence, but does not judge. A force that gives each of them a life to appreciate and yet, will also take it away. A force that survives as an unexplained universal influence, with an enduring silence and a focus on procreation.'

'A force, which is prepared to share a history of experiences, through the lives of all of Nature's species, encouraging each to learn and discover, from each other.'

'They do not see any right to cause harm to other animals, or injury to the defenseless. In life, vulnerability needs some measure of protection and all life teaches something about choices. They will see on the planet of Isolation, what can happen, when the living experience has been compromised.'

Munkhan continued. 'Prisium is named from ancient times for the multi-colored, floral species, covering large areas of this natural paradise in front us. It is an oasis of botanical beauty. As the transport descended, they noticed numerous distant provincial regions, covered within many ancient forests and filled with a proliferation of aged trees.'

'As you can see, these densely scattered forests have many fast flowing, clear water streams, surging down from several high mountain ranges, in the distance. The frozen glacial ice capped regions, gradually melted into seasonal, cascading waterfalls. This abundance of chilled water descended through many deep gorges and nourished the immensely complex jungle areas, of colorful flora and fauna below.'

Still further down, there were larger open clearings, where they could land.

Marmuron smiled. 'Oh, it's just so beautiful, Oatsy.' It was the sheer beauty of the multi-colored floral settings, which everyone noticed and Marmuron found, so appealing.

The visions continued. New varieties of plant life, with a stunning proliferation of rich colors, became hard to put into mere words. Hidden among the flatlands, in the dense tropical rain forest regions, were many provincial villages. Gathered below were a growing group of dignitaries, waiting for them to land.

Marmuron breathed excitedly. 'There's Mykron and Velia, with her family.' Marmuron was stunned at her own advancing ability to interpret, unravel and comprehend the highly valued, silent messaging, contained in Nature's primary force.

Their transport landed a short distance away from the larger central village. A plethora of happy faces, were there to greet them, from the first mission. Mharn had been expecting them and was overcome, as he greeted his closer friends again. There was building excitement, as he waved to the others.

36
Prisium, a Land of Botanical Treasures.

'Herron, Kendy, over here.' As they were warmly greeting each other, Pim rushed over to hug her son Mykron. You could be forgiven for thinking they had been away for an eternity. More aides, came to greet them, with initial consent and clearance routines. Karina and her girlfriends were led away to discover, their temporary accommodation.

Marmuron stood gazing in amazement, as if hypnotized by her surroundings. She saw all their species, as part of Natures force. 'I've never seen anything like this before.'

Mharn came over with his friends. He seemed completely overcome, as Kendu agreed. 'The floral coloring, is truly magnificent.'

Herron murmured. 'Nature, brings warmth to the spirit and music, to the soul.'

As the responses to these beautiful visions, of natural splendor on Prisium slowed down, Mharn asked. 'What is this force, which befriends us with its beauty and tantalizes us, with such diversity? Nature flourishes, as a calming presence across this entire planetary region. You could spend a lifetime, confounded by this endless serenity, which excites us with its seasonal changes? What do you make of it Michael?'

'We could spend a life time exploring this planet alone.' It truly was a refreshing and stunning picture of diversity, beyond anything we had ever seen before.

Oats was in characteristically good humor as he questioned. 'What impresses you the most, Mharn?'

'Oh Oats, this is a natural wonder, with an enchantment you want to explore.'

Oats agreed. 'Yes, Nature is a miraculous, phenomenon.'

Mharn was looking around. 'The people are charming, warm hearted and friendly.'

Oats asked. 'You're not ready to go back home yet Mharn, are you?

'Why we've only just arrived Oats?' Then. 'I've struggled my whole life, for a chance like this.'

There was the first hint of a revealing smile. Mharn was very much aware that history had dealt him a cruel blow, in his early childhood. He looked at Michael with great sincerity as he realized the adventure, he was now sharing, had some risks. It was a turning point for him and indeed for all of them, to be in this envious position, of exploration and adventure. That said he well understood the hidden personal costs of time loss. 'Oats, I won't let that ever happen to me, in my life.'

Prisium had the stunning charm, of a peace loving planet, with an ambience all of its own. These surroundings created an anticipation, of what was to come. Michael's group were enthusiastically welcomed, by the local authorities and those with shorter duration tasks were scheduled to stay there temporarily. Others with a more senior organizing role, would shortly leave for Tamaryn's primary planet.

There were seventy members in the larger delegation, moving on, almost immediately. It was a happy meeting of minds and Pim was absolutely delighted to catch up again with her son Mykron. He was here for many reasons, however his new companion in life Velia, was coming back home, to introduce Mykron to her family.

Velia's parents had been there to meet her and this was a happy occasion. Velia was lovely as she and Mykron were now involved, in a blossoming number of conversations, with a bubbling boisterous sound, building everywhere around them. Each of the visitors were making plans, for the opportunities to meet again, in the near future.

Those continuing on to Tamaryn's planet were absorbed in their own assignments.

Mharn was openly elated. 'I want to thank you both, for bringing Karina to me.'

Oats smiled. 'Happy to help. She has been a delightful passenger.'

Mharn's youthful exuberance glanced at the energy, coming from his friends, who were now gathering around Velia's family. 'I'll see you both again in a moment.'

Mharn left to reconnect with Karina, among a circle of friends, which grew exponentially larger. For Mharn, having Karina this close to him, on his own mission, dispelled any fears of not seeing her and alleviated many of his concerns. However something did not add up for Mharn, or seem quite right.

As Mharn came back over, Michael saw this and said. 'Let's take a walk.'

Mharn was curious. 'What, did you want to talk about?'

'Mharn, you can always come back to adventure and yet you can't always come back, to the stability in your own life, without the risk of some changes.'

Mharn laughed. 'My father asked you to remind me of this, didn't he, Michael?'

'Yes Mharn, he is naturally concerned for your wellbeing. He's very proud of your appointment and for this adventure. He remembers what happened in your life and he's thinking of Karina. She has enormous obligations, in leading her own province.'

Mharn was thoughtful. 'Thank you Michael, yes I remember my youth very well?'

Michael then added. 'Your father also advised me, for my own benefit, about lost time and the unintended consequences, of everlasting change. Your mother's message, was about not missing out on important events and changes, as they happen. You can always come back to this.'

Michael appeared to be talking in riddles. Mharn also began to wonder why such a large contingent of his old friends had come along, on what was scheduled to be an unofficial visit. Then it struck him, maybe something has happened at home. Were his parents, still in good health?'

Mharn suddenly appealed. 'Michael, my parents, are still in good health?'

Michael was reassuring. 'Yes, yes of course.'

As he stood there, Mharn felt like he had half an answer to a confusing puzzle and was becoming a little baffled. He became more mystified by the surprise visit of his oldest and closest friends. There were also other distractions, impacting on him.

And then. 'Thanks Michael, I'll keep all that in mind.' Mharn decided to have a quiet talk to his old friends, Herron and Kendu, as he remained perplexed. Everyone else seemed in highly jubilant spirits though.

Mharn found his friends and soon discovered they weren't much help either.

Kendu began. 'All of us have aspiring hopes and dreams, however sometimes things happen, moment by moment, where a dream can be lost forever.'

Mharn finally cracked. 'What the heck is going on? You're talking in the same double speak as Michael. I'm very happy to see you all, but is there something wrong at home?'

Now Herron interjected. 'There's nothing to be concerned about. Mykron and Velia are visiting her parents and our girls decided, they wanted to come too. We are only on a short visit, because Tamaryn invited Michael and Oats to see her galaxy, of combined planetary systems.'

Something still didn't quite add up for Mharn and he now believed that his father organized this mission, to remind him of lost time. 'Did you get a chance to see the many visions, of the Natural formations of Tamaryn's galaxy?'

Herron was first. 'Yes, it was graphically magnificent.'

'So everything's alright then?'

Herron saw his chance. 'The only issue, was with the Clean Beam.'

This prompted Mharn. 'Yes there was some disturbance in the Force on Tamaryn's ship as well.'

Kendu asked. 'Did anyone work out why?

Mharn hesitated and then. 'Well not really, there were a hundred of us, all in different briefings. Velia was excited about coming home, to introduce Mykron to her parents on Prisium.' Was all Mharn could figure out, right now.

Mharn's expression changed with the confusing gazes, as he watched the growing and puzzling looks, building on the faces of his closest friends.'

Mharn wasn't getting anywhere with this. He had seen Karina recently and knew that she was in good spirits. The three friends laughed, as a bevy of other delegates came over to talk to Mharn, about their plans and the moment was soon lost.

Munkhan came back over to greet Michael and Oats and smiled at Mharn's youthful enthusiasm. 'Mharn has known of the existence of primal planets from his father, Kisun-Shi, but has never actually stayed on one.'

Oats said. 'He is just overwhelmed with early excitement?'

Munkhan then asked. 'If you were standing in the vicinity, of an original life force, would you want to leave straight away?'

Oats began glancing around beneath the aged trees. 'No, thank you Munkhan.'

Then Michael asked. 'Oh, did you realize that Velia has a beautiful younger sister, who is still single?'

Munkhan's face erupted with a telling grin as Oats asked. 'You've met her then?'

Munkhan's smile broadened. 'Yes, twice now.'

Oats chuckled. 'I guess you're not ready to go back home yet, either?' It became a buoyant, cheerful and jaunting mood, as they watched many adventurers, recapturing their old friendships.

Michael asked. 'Oats, what do you make of all this, so far?'

'Sun-Ky was quite right to elevate our thinking. **The origin of the Natural Force, was gender neutral.**'

Janet came back over quickly. 'What's happening Munkhan?'

'They're just separating all the delegates, into several briefing groups. The younger guests are gathering, to stay on Velia's planet. We're facing a tight schedule and we're running out of time. We have just confirmed the numbers and have reserved places for the four of you, Pim and Sun-Ky, to come with us.'

'Brilliant.' Janet and Marmuron were also ready to go. Pim was on her way over as well.'

Mharn saw us signaling to him and came running over. 'What's up?'

Munkhan began. 'As part of the official party, we need you to come now.' Then. 'We can always come back again, but for the moment we must move on.'

They all quickly said their goodbye's, but at this stage everyone understood, they all had different schedules. Pim joined them, leaving some of the younger adventurers behind. Mharn gave Karina a hug, as he said goodbye. 'Love you.'

Mharn noticed a look of building apprehension from Karina that he took to be the farewell parting, from a loved one. However it began to worry him as if something didn't quite add up. Anyway he gave her another gentle gripping hug.

Although the rush was on for some, Mykron and Velia lived in a world of their own. Never before had Mykron been this close, to an experience of a warming natural reality. Never before had he been so openly embraced, by the woman he loved and never did he believe in his lifetime, he would have this chance, to share love again.

It was innocence at heart, it was compelling and enchanting, and it was captivating and enticing. Velia embodied everything in life, he had hoped to share, a loving experience with. A mind to engage and challenge him, a charming nature to entice him and a body of desires, to lure him.

The prospect of beginning a family, with all that life could offer him, brought out the little boy in Mykron once more. For soon he would be a parent, with a child of his own. A chance to bond, with parental affection, was at last, his to share.

37
Velia, a Maiden in Nature's Forest.

From her early childhood on Prisium, Velia had become a passionate believer in the wonders, of Nature's forests. She had discovered her own favorite places, in the large heavily wooded areas, close by her village, including many secluded secret shelters.

She made friends easily, with other forest creatures and would talk with them constantly, seeking their cherished advice. For the forest was their home too and here they felt as one. Now she would have to try and explain the wonders of these curiosities to Mykron, for it was in a deep woodland like this, that they first met, long, long ago.

It was here that Velia saw life struggling from the beginning, with every renewal in between. The cycle of life was on display everywhere, in this forest. From new seedlings, striving for source light, to fallen aged trees which couldn't last any longer. There were scurrying critters, with so many plans and now, she too had plans of her own.

Mykron, had met Velia's parents and celebrated the news of their union and now Velia wanted to steal him away and rediscover her favorite, romantic places. She loved Mykron and recently found out that she was pregnant. Well, there were so many things to talk through, like how would they spend the rest of their lives together.

Velia was still remembering, the deep valley gorge on WIL's distant primal planet of Giant Vines. It was there, that she spent ages, embracing and making passionate love to her Mykron, among the profuse displays of multiple floral ground cover varieties.

Velia recently discovered from her father, that it was through the efforts of both WIL and Tamaryn that she and Mykron, were brought back together again. It had been an enchanting opportunity for the two young lovers, separated long ago, through no fault of their own. Now she saw a chance to recreate this setting, giving them some valuable private time to themselves. As they wandered deeper into these woods, she held Mykron's hand and played with his fingers. After all this forest was her treasured place of natural solitude. A timeless place for her, which she had always loved.

Mykron asked casually. 'What tempted you here, in the beginning?'

Velia was a study of amusing expressions. 'Like us, everything around here is reproducing. The state of motherhood is built into the fundamental laws, governing Nature's existence. Love, passion, warmth and romance are an integral part of generational change. A change, many animals here, take for granted.'

'This forest has thousands of species and here we see Nature's Force, at work. I love watching Nature recreating itself, through the many different life cycles.' Velia was completely captured by this natural diversity of existence. Then a sensation, a little closer to them both. 'I can feel someone, growing inside me.'

Mykron rested his arm above the growing life form, in Velia's womb. She then rested her hand on his. Yes there was a living struggle going on inside her. A growing battle for life to evolve. A child to teach and to guide. The struggle would continue, from its first breath of fresh air, until its last gasp in life. It would be a personal struggle, to strive for acceptance and knowledge, about how to live and advance, with life's choices. It would be a chance for the two of them, to nurture, guide and teach a newborn of their very own, from infancy.'

A broad happy smile erupted between them as they began to consider the many steps, on this evolving journey together. 'I can feel something else growing near me.' Velia laughed. It was true, Mykron's wandering hands had moved to grip her near naked form. The firming buttocks of Velia's enchanting and tantalizing figure had captured his primal thoughts, amongst this haven, hidden in the warm soft grass.

While there may be privacy from the others, there was no privacy from Nature. Undaunted, the urges within Mykron grew and his desire for release, put a growing smile on Velia's adorable face. She writhed with pleasure as Mykron's advances, became more penetrating. As they lay in the soft grass, his roaming hands gently held her breasts, straying quickly all over her body. There was no turning away now, as she surrendered completely. The constant massaging of her sensitive regions and arousing vulnerabilities, became completely overwhelming. Mykron's delicate touch, knew how to excite Velia, as she rolled back over and her legs wrapped around him to hold him closer.

Mykron saw Velia as his love. She had shoulder length, pale golden blonde hair and smoldering good looks, showing off her prominent and distinctive figure. She was visually exquisite, charming and a treasure to behold. She warmed to his advances, giving him the confidence to further push, his muscular charms and have her completely.

This only helped to serve the vigorous muscular energy building within him. She moved her hands now to hold his erection, with its forming muscular urgency. His previously hidden and uncontrollable desire to have her, was now in the palm of her hands. Raw passion and high emotion soon took control, as she became completely aroused, groaning quietly with an approving hint, of increasing pleasure.

Mykron laughed with a warming smile. 'We need to practice for the next one.'

Velia laughed. 'We haven't had this one yet.' Then feeling the pleasure of the moment. 'We need to be careful though.'

After several moments she surrendered completely and the rest of their clothes peeled off. The erotic passion built between them, as she rolled over on her back, inviting his advances. Mykron climbed over to settle in between her and gently thrust himself, pushing further and deeper inside her.

She stimulated his passionate yearnings and desires, into a loving embrace.

Velia's own senses had become more erotic and sensual, as Mykron continued to press his expansive muscular needs deeper, inside her. Velia could sense his growing urgency and need to explode as every muscle, in her tense body said yes.

Her beautiful form became increasingly taut and rigid as she felt his throbbing, muscular force, pounding purposefully inside her. Her breathing became more adoring as the urgency to explode built and Velia groaned softly, with increasing pleasure.

Mykron held on for as long as he could, until his thrusting explosive release burst several times, deep inside her. The jaunting sassiness and mischievous cheek, built between them. 'What if our first child is a girl?'

Mykron laughed. 'Well we would have to keep on practicing.'

Velia laughed. 'This is only the first, of my favorite places, in our forest.'

It seemed Velia had some ambitious plans, where their love making would continue on, into a timeless future. Mykron grinned broadly 'I love you Velia, never forget that.' He had warmth in his eyes and joy in his heart, for the wonderful future in front of them.

Several moments had passed. As he stirred, his muscular erection began building again, at the thought of an endless passionate embrace between them. Velia noticed the forming muscular urgency and melted in his arms once more. They rolled around youthfully in the long grass, shielded by natural privacy. Mykron began massaging her breasts and buttocks again as she opened herself to him, once more.

'I have always loved you Mykron.' And without any encouragement he began again. He held her hips, gently rolling her over and lifting her up so she rested on her knees face down to the grass. He positioned himself behind her and gently massaged her exposed buttocks. She groaned with increasing pleasure as he began rubbing her gently around her erogenous zone.

Velia groaned more intensely. 'Ooh, I love that.'

Mykron then repositioned himself and held her buttocks firmly by pulling her tightly back towards him. Then he gently began thrusting himself again, deeper and deeper inside her. He pulled her buttocks back, by her hips towards him again. This slow motion penetration and rolling thrusting motion, built further excitement for Velia. She writhed with pleasure as the gentle, relentless pounding and thrusting motion against the soft buttocks of her beautifully formed, feminine frame, built to a climaxing crescendo.

The excitement built for Mykron too, as he held on for as long as he could, before exploding again and again, inside the deep warm recesses of her beautiful form.

'Oooooh.' Velia groaned with sensual pleasure, after his muscular expansion exploded, coming multiple times deep inside her. He held her buttocks, firmly in front of him. Their shared desires, came to a climax, as he leant down to reach forward and gently hold her warm breasts, in the palms of his hands once more.

They continued to roll around together, enjoying each other's companionship. While their moments of warm, sensitive embraces continued, Velia truly was a maiden at home, in a rainforest full of endless natural experiences.

38
Mharn's Evolving Mission, Unfolds.

Tamaryn's ship was now well on its way, to her central primal planet. The excited chattering among the delegates aboard continued. Michael and Oats had spoken to Munkhan, about the hopes and concerns, expressed by Mharn's parents.

While this truly was a great opportunity for Mharn, some fear was held, for the two young companions being separated. How does this serve Natures purpose? Karina had missed an opportunity to tell Mharn about her condition, letting him know he was going to be a father.

Karina believed she had plenty of time to tell anyone she wished and it was her news to spread. Mharn being on a mission in a nearby galaxy, seemed much less of an issue, now that she felt so much closer to him.

After some time Munkhan found Mharn, who was completely absorbed in his developing experiences. 'Hi Mharn, sorry we couldn't bring Karina with us.'

'Yes she and the others will be staying on Prisium for a little while. It was a chance to visit Velia and Mykron. I'm still puzzled as to why my other friends came, though.'

'Maybe the answers you are looking for, can be found on Prisium.' This was as far as Munkhan was prepared to go. Mharn's inquisitive nature would take over now. He was very astute, but this mystery, had the better of him so far.

As they continued towards Tamaryn's primary planet, the one person with the greatest evolving visionary sense, was Marmuron.

Her anticipation and expectations rose, with each announcement of their progress. The three dimensional visions continued, showing the natural beauty of this planetary jungle, of aged trees and enormous vines. Marmuron remained absorbed, by the stunning natural surroundings. 'This is just breathtakingly beautiful.'

Pim remembered her private conversation with WIL, just before she left on this second mission. It hadn't escaped Pim's notice that Marmuron was captivated and drawn to this place. Pim asked. 'What's going through your mind, Marmuron?'

It took a while for Marmuron to put her thoughts together. 'Well, my background as you know is from the planet of Troth, where there was great poverty, among some on the dark side and extreme privilege, held by a few on the light side.'

'Many clan kings on the privileged lighter side, took sexual favors with the low paid female help and my mother found this out, after she had tried to get work there. It appeared sincere at first when the clan king befriended her, but after he quickly had his way with her, she became pregnant. When the pregnancy was discovered, she was given provisions to leave, as long as she never came back. When she returned to the poverty of our traditional home, on the darker side of the planet, I was helped by my uncle Aiden. After my mother died I met my father for the first time, just before the convention of elders.' Marmuron paused and we waited for the next part, which appeared to be important as tears rolled down her cheeks. 'I never really new my father.'

She seemed a little distressed and Oats moved quickly to console her. Janet, Oats and Michael just listened as Marmuron was pouring her heart out, when Pim asked her. 'What visions, are you seeing now?'

'It's strange really, I feel like I know this place, almost as if I belong here.'

Pim then prompted her further. 'How would you describe your visions so far?'

'On some other planets you can fall victim, to natural threats more easily. Many of the threats here, are isolated. They are very careful to protect their people from poisons and toxic substances. There are no predatory, carnivorous animals in the wild here, or any sense of overcrowding. It's beautiful and serene, peaceful and tranquil.' Marmuron was glancing, anywhere and everywhere at the same time. 'Your independence to be free is preserved here, with high moral standards, supporting your personal life choices. It's uninhibited. I love this natural, village living simplicity.'

Oats was thrilled to see Marmuron becoming happier as he urged her to go on. 'Anything else?'

Marmuron looked on lovingly. 'You're not jesting with me Oatsy, are you?'

Oats put his arm around her. 'No, I'm really very happy for you.'

Marmuron seemed to stumble. 'I see courtesy and respect among them, in an open society, without any exploitation. No ill-treatment or hidden plans or agendas. They foster a society that inspires self-development. An intelligence gathering, which builds on itself, to seek insight and illumination.'

Marmuron's attention was interrupted as Sun-Ky called everyone together, to brief them on what was about to unfold and he seemed a little reflective. There was a larger contingent here now and so he began slowly.

'If you were to just consider Natures laws, Nature doesn't have any rules about how you live, where you live, with whom you live, how long you survive or even how moral your experiences, may have been. Just that, life is created to replace life.'

'Where we land, the decision on where you live is made by how closely you follow Natural laws. Apart from Tamaryn's primary planet, there are several other planets which follow Natural laws, completely. Here the jurisdictional authority, is one of being self-imposed. What that means is that here, the students decide with self-discipline how they would like to survive in their futures.'

A voice from the back asked. 'What are some of the guiding reasons, for this?'

Sun-Ky smiled as he continued. 'Nature needs friends and students need to decide their place, in this evolving process. Their decisions affect where they live, and on which planet.'

'Those who choose wisely, live close by and those who have little respect for Nature's laws, will live a little further out, where they can do the least harm.'

'It is important to remember that people here, do not pass judgment on each other. It all becomes a personal choice, as to their own levels of compliance and conformity.'

As Sun-Ky finished he was approached quietly by Oats, Michael and Pim. 'Sorry to interrupt but many of us are concerned about Mharn and Karina. Mharn will be heartbroken, if he doesn't find out. They are so young, Sun-Ky?'

Sun-Ky could sense the compassion in their voices. 'When you're young, you always believe, you still have plenty of time and there will always be more chances.'

Janet appealed. 'She doesn't want him to give up his mission and feel as though he has to come home early. She desperately wants him to feel success, in this mission.'

Finally Oats asked 'Sun-Ky, how is it possible for Mharn to make a balanced choice here, when he doesn't even know the options?'

Sun-Ky then remembered. 'Yes, I know Mharn battled through childhood, without his own parents. I understand all the issues of compassion, however we have an important mission of our own to complete. Leave it with me.'

They all thanked Sun-Ky for his considerations.

It was some time later Sun-Ky met Mharn, near the Clean Beam while chatting with fellow delegates. Many were curious as to how their different objectives, would evolve.

As Mharn paused, Sun-Ky found a quiet place, where more explanations began to unfold. 'After your initial orientation with your first group of students, I'm sending Munkhan back to our galaxy with some of these graduates. I want you to help here and accompany him on this mission. What we are undertaking is three dimensional. We want to understand their galaxy better and at the same time, we want them to understand ours.'

'It is a chance for their students to appreciate the cosmic expanse and at the same time understand the huge vulnerabilities in humanities, short lived experiences. It will be their first opportunity to capture the vision of the larger Natural formation. It is a remarkable learning opportunity for these older students, to see evidence of how the Natural Force endures, survives and continues to exist.'

Mharn asked. 'How long, would we be away?'

Sun-Ky smiled. 'Until we learn to manage time better. We will all live with continuing missions of shorter durations, for the time being. So when you get back I want you to prepare for a return visit, within about three rotations of Kendagon.'

'Sun-Ky, have you heard if anything has changed at home? I've had some hint that something may have changed back there, while I've been away.'

Sun-Ky was measured. 'It is a good idea that you keep an open mind and continue asking these questions of why. A searching and inquisitive mind will find the answers you seek.'

'Thank you Sun-Ky.'

'Now if you rejoin Munkhan, he will introduce you to your first group of students on landing.' Mharn left in high spirits, confident that there would be a preservation of balance in his life, with the tasks ahead.

Three envoys from Tamaryn's planet beamed aboard, to give further guidance on what to expect, when they landed. Munkhan came over quickly to counsel us. It was a brief philosophical vision of their history, as they saw it. Everyone went quiet, as they began.

'Eternal hope, is a vision which lives in the hearts of all creatures, at birth. Trust, lives in the friendship between many of Nature's species. Self-belief, grows stronger in the mind, with more thoughtful choices. Character forms, in the sharing of moral decency. Peace comes with honor, found among equals. Everlasting happiness, is found in the shared vision, of like-minded souls.'

'Love for others, is a sincere and inspirational desire, shared with Nature. Nature is a silent force, which lives in us all. A gifted mind, learns in silence to question themselves, as to why it is so. Understanding why, is the longest journey in any lifetime. A greater knowledge of all Natural Forces is found, in a cherished respect and regard for the unknown. Courage is found, in character's determination, to exist with Nature.'

We were momentarily stunned as Oats found his voice. 'You learnt all this from just observing Nature?'

There were some amusing looks. 'Why, yes.'

Then one of them said. 'The only person we have to answer to, is ourselves.'

Sun-Ky was becoming amused, as Oats became more puzzled.

One of the envoys continued. **'Oats, you are part of the natural living force. We all are. The urge to reproduce, lives within each one of us. We are the means, of evolutionary progression. Every memory you have, every feeling you sense and every thought which comes to mind, is part of the gift of existence.'**

'It is what you do with your life, which counts. Nature gives you so many choices. The simplicity of self- control, is found in making choices and not crossing boundaries.'

'Nature has given each one of us this power to choose. Every idea, embracing social harmony, comes from elevated levels of learning. This is why we send our students out on these missions, without any prejudices, preconceptions or proclivities, to make open choices for themselves, on how they choose to live their lives.'

Oats queried. 'Your society, places a great deal of faith, in these children getting their conceptual thoughts, in balance.'

Now one of the aides, answered Oats' query. 'Nature can seem indifferent to our plight, which can occasionally be wildly random, unpredictable and precarious. Equally the experience can be innocent, warm, friendly and welcoming, offering us all hope. It's a confident voice which communicates decisively, without any judgment. A force, free of any imposed coercions or constraints, other than, the choices of our own making.'

Marmuron asked. 'How did life begin, for you here?'

Another spoke with complete innocence. 'None of us really know. Nature as a force, has lived here, with an almost timeless presence.'

Oats then realized something. 'These people aren't obsessed by regulating other people's lives and telling each other what to do, or how to behave. There's no wealth building, power seeking, or control taken over other people's existence. They are just warm to each other, friendly and inspired by the Natural Forces, all around them.'

While these envoys were talking to them, the visions continued, showing many natural archways, covering multiple spacious pathways, surrounded by thick colored vines. The well-worn paths, reached a larger opening in the rainforest which spread out before them. There were light filled panoramic visions, of ancient jungles surrounding a large auditorium area for Mharn and his fellow delegates.

The floral colored beauty, blossomed and bloomed everywhere around there and was breathtaking. There was a profound depth of wisdom, to Nature's miracle here.

Munkhan came over to advise us. 'Won't be long now.'

Oats thanked Munkhan. 'Yes, yes of course.'

39
Marmuron's Moment of Illumination.

Pim was watching the building excitement. Oats couldn't wait to gain a deeper cosmic view, from Tamaryn. Marmuron was thrilled about what lay ahead.

The long voyage for Mharn was soon over, as his larger party entered a transport to go down for their first briefing, with two of the envoys. The chattering of voices quieted down, leaving only Michael, Oats, Janet and Marmuron with Pim and Sun-Ky to continue on, towards Tamaryn's Giant Forest compound.

Marmuron had been mesmerized by the cultural warmth and the natural settings so far. Janet held Marmuron's arm, as her nervous energy began to explode. They were in the final stages of transferring to Foundation Forrest, when the envoy came over and whispered to Pim. 'Tamaryn will meet your party, at her residence.'

Marmuron was thrilled. 'So she is expecting us?'

The envoy seemed hesitant for a moment. 'Yes, Tamaryn is expecting you all. She has her seven senior village elders there, who have never seen anyone from another galaxy before. They are excited by your visit and are looking forward to showing you around their village compound, of cherished, ancient gardens.'

Oats whispered to Michael. 'Maybe this is what Sun-Ky was trying to prepare us for. A cultural experience that supported their vision, of living with Nature. Yes, you could argue that it was primitive, however they were advanced, in so many other ways.'

It really was a unique gathering. There was a common vulnerability, quite evident among the villagers. It was an advanced society, founded on the simplicity, of an inspired existence. This peacefulness reminded them a little, of the settings around Oats's alpine cabin. However the many new varieties of trees, vines and floral outcrops were intriguing and the massive shaded trees they saw, were a simply stunning natural phenomenon.

On the way to Tamaryn's home, they passed over both large and smaller communal villages, beautifully set amongst the heavily forested areas. Oats quickly realized the similarities between Tamaryn's planet and that of the ancient forest, of WIL's birthplace.

The forest regions on Tamaryn's planet were massive, with many floral displays scattered throughout the undergrowth. Janet noticed a change in Marmuron, whose early times were in a baron environment, on the darker side on her former planet of Troth.

WIL had warned Pim to expect a rapid process of enlightenment, to overtake Marmuron, once she came back to the ancestral villages on Tamaryn's ancient forest planet. Janet could see Marmuron struggling, with many rapid visions, as the transport landed. Marmuron became even more excited as they entered the perimeter of the private village, adjoining Tamaryn's birthplace.

'Tamaryn's residence is just over there.' Hidden amongst a narrow hillside jungle clearing, was the loveliest free flowing waterfall, cascading down a steep rocky outcrop, only a short distance away. A picturesque ancient stone residence, merged and blended perfectly, with these beautiful natural surroundings.

Oats was moved. 'It's like a vast and prolific botanical garden.'

They couldn't wait to see her now, as Marmuron sped up with Janet close behind. Rather than being lavish and pretentious, Tamaryn's lodge was inspiringly crafted, to blend in with these surroundings. Tamaryn smiled and waved to us, from her wide sheltered veranda.

Marmuron was just thrilled to be here and excited for the coming discoveries, but held her bubbling enthusiasm closely. The seven elders, smiled thoughtfully. Tamaryn's aides were everywhere now, in this magnificent ancient natural forest.

Tamaryn's home was positioned well above ground, hidden within a forest of massive aged trees. Colorful undergrowth, was in the shade and broken intermittently, by warming beams of flickering source light.

They walked through the door, into a picturesque meeting room. After the initial greetings, everyone sat around an elaborately carved, old wooden benchtop table. Oats was hoping to learn more about their ancient societies. Marmuron couldn't hold back any longer as she pleaded with the elders. 'How did your society evolve?'

After a moment one of the elders replied. **'The history of our evolution shows, a most powerful and ageless balance of peace, love and serenity with Nature. There's a warmth of companionship in sharing and this ancient spirit within us all, gives eternal hope. The choice for an advanced global society, is ours if we choose. The parochialism on Isolation will not change, without this wisdom of insight.'**

Marmuron suddenly erupted with. 'This setting, feels so natural.'

Surprisingly though as we settled, the elders were eager to learn about the history of civilizations, on our own home planets.

'Yes of course.' Oats agreed. Then he recounted, while Pim showed past visions of our Earth's global cultural history.

It then became evident, each of them could read our thoughts, about life on our planet as one of the elders asked. 'Nature's messaging, is not well understood there yet?'

Oats went first. 'We have some questions, which have few answers.'

The logical order, of evolutionary origins in creation.

Oats cautiously asked Tamaryn. 'If I may, how did you know, that no God of any kind, created the universe?' Oats held back tears, as he appealed for more answers.

'Apart from the historic visions we saw, this is about the logic of evolution, Oats?'

This prompted Oats. 'Yes, it began for us almost five hundred years ago, with some observations from a man named Nicolaus Copernicus and enlightenment has been hampered, ever since then. We just want to understand why.'

Then Tamaryn began. **'Just for one moment, put everything you have ever learnt, out of your mind and consider this. I want you to go back in time, before solar systems first formed and galaxies evolved. A time before observable forces impacted on the mass of visible matter in the universe. To an age in time, of the creation of elementary atomic particle matter, for classification and by grouping.'**

'There's a fundamental relationship between the forces, which holds elementary particle matter together. These essential building blocks, must have formed first.'

'Nature itself, began as a force much later and well before the appearance of all human species, whether mortal or immortal. The functions humans perform, the air we breathe, the energy we consume, all came as a result of earlier beginnings of natural elementary evolution. It is illogical to believe that the order of evolution, puts any human form, before the architecture, of all these other earlier origins.'

A moment passed before Oats completely erupted. His mind for him had now found the definitive answer. 'Yes, yes of course, it is so simple, when you think about it.'

Janet quipped back quickly with a laugh and a smile. 'What is so simple, Oats?'

Oats was in good humor. 'This confirms what we heard from Sun-Ky. We were trying to resolve the part of the riddle, about who or what, created Heaven and Earth in the beginning, correct?'

Janet answered hesitantly. 'Yes?'

'The question always comes back to what came first, at the time of Origin?'

Janet looked at Oats in a state of almost complete confusion. 'Yes?'

'Janet, almost 99% of the mass of the human body is made up of six elements: oxygen, carbon, hydrogen, nitrogen, calcium, and phosphorus. Only about 0.85% is composed of another five elements: potassium, sulfur, sodium, chlorine, and magnesium. All eleven are necessary for life. The remaining elements are trace elements, of which more than a dozen, are thought, on the basis of sound evidence, to be necessary for life.' Oats was grinning broadly and obviously, very pleased with himself.

Janet smiled warmly and laughed. 'You said this was going to be simple, Oats?'

Dear old Oats was lovely to watch, when he had found the logical answer, to an ancient and historically, unresolvable, problematic issue.

'Janet, before we have the origin of life in the universe, in any form, we have the origin of matter. No animal class of any description, could have created Heaven and Earth, before elementary matter itself, was first created. **That's NO creation occurred,**

by any human form, before the formation of matter itself, in the universe. Elementary matter came, before any animal class evolved. Take a moment to think about that.'

Everyone in the room was smiling at the simple logic, in Oats enlightened reasoning. Michael was first. 'Yes Oats, you are right in the order of things.'

Janet was still mulling over the simplicity of the stated fundamental logic as well. Michael looked kindly on the love of his life, as Janet tried to grapple, with the logic of evolutionary order.

Michael smiled in agreement with Oats' stated logic. **'Ancient Biblical records, tried to interpret the creation of Heaven and Earth by 'God', early in the first chapter of Genesis. Although we can state that this model is logically incorrect, these early ideas, formed the classic speculative belief, on creation in ancient times.'**

'The origin of the universe will be better understood in our future, when further research, discovers how elementary matter, in this expansive universal vacuum, first evolved. So we need to understand, what the circumstances were which enabled particle matter to form by class and by type into gasses, liquids and solids in the first place.'

Oats smiled. 'Yes, as researchers we are not looking for the 'God particle', we're searching for what were the circumstances which created particle matter in the first place? **There could not have been any human form, at the origin of elementary matter.'**

After a fleeting and puzzled look Janet asked. 'Okay, so where do we go from here?'

Oats then responded. 'Back to the present if we may. How do we answer the broader questions, we have all been seeking answers to?'

One of the elders smiled at them. Then each of the seven village elders took it in turn to describe the meaning of Nature and so, one by one they began.

Creation: 'Ask yourself, what created this evolution of matter in the first place, which asks nothing in return. An energy force which allows you to be born free, without instruction, guidance or judgement of any kind. An immensely powerful force which gives life, without any conditions to manipulate, influence or try to take advantage of this innocence. All built within a vast and complex, cosmological design.'

Universal Forces: 'What universal force, creates natural laws and gives energy to life? What is the origin, in the distribution of particle matter, which allows life to exist?'

Eternal Life: 'What essential power was it, which created natural laws enabling early life to exist, reproduce and proliferate giving opportunity to future generations?'

Oats looked at Michael a little gob smacked, as another elder continued.

Nature: 'A combination of cosmic forces, which determines our time and place of existence, with an immense variety of living species, in our planetary systems alone. After thousands of generations, we are still mystified, in trying to find real answers.'

Belief: 'No Natural Force is telling us what to do, or what to think or even how to behave. The Natural Force gives, peace without judgement and serenity without cause?'

Discriminating intelligence: 'An instinctive force, which allows you to analyze, to think and to plan for yourself? We are emboldened to believe in ourselves, observe the natural choices around us and use perceptive wisdom, for our own good judgement?'

Enlightenment: 'What cosmic origin, provides multiple species with food choices, intelligence to learn and to grow, with emotions to survive through this process?'

After a moment Oats laughed. 'You all sound just like us, with more questions than answers.' The elders laughed and joined in the merriment of the yet to be discovered and the many remaining cosmic unknowns. Michael and Janet smiled as well. These were many of the same thoughts, which had motivated them, in their missions.

Tamaryn asked Marmuron. 'What is appealing to your senses, Marmuron?'

Marmuron began with some emerging thoughts, in her mind of forming visions. She was describing what she felt, which just came out from nowhere.

'We never had any of this on our planet, we were too far away from an energy source. Nature teaches us to have courage, endurance and perseverance in the wild. In the forest we learn character, integrity, spirit and shared family values. That we may grow tall with lasting tolerance, patience and good character. In your community we see cheerfulness, merriment and contentment, in the lives of your villagers. From them we learn of support, in times of need, with communal strength and tranquility. With this learning, villagers see optimism, enthusiasm and a building of life long, self-confidence.'

'In life, there is purpose, in the nurturing of Nature and to this end we see serenity. Our children's future character strength, is found in the decency, which has evolved in the history of communal warmth, left behind.'

As Marmuron's mind cleared, Sun-Ky then met with several other elders outside, to plan the beginning of the greater transition objectives, towards the new conference duties.

40
The Frontiers of Enlightenment.

Tamaryn was very hospitable, as we began to walk around her village, she began to reflect. 'You are seeing the ancient forests, of our family's home, Marmuron.'

Tamaryn gazed at Oats and smiled. 'Oats, you recently asked about how our civilization began, many thousands of generations ago?'

Oats relaxed a little. 'Yes, I heard you followed natural law, in your systems.'

'Yes, striving to understand Nature's vision, might be a better interpretation?'

'Sorry Tamaryn, I still don't quite understand, how your society has adapted?'

'If impediments to social unity are never resolved, nothing will ever change.' Freedom of thought, forms the foundation of an inspired vision. Courage is a storm, weathered by a lifetime of strength, in good character.'

Janet was inspired by the visions she was seeing, however she remained confused by an earlier conversation from the long voyage, on the way here. Tamaryn was reading her mind and asked. 'And your question is, Janet?'

As they walked, Janet could see many social groups, working happily together 'Just admiring the surroundings.'

Immediately Oats found inspiration, as he began to speculate about the visions confronting him. 'Janet, you asked for answers as to the why, in all of this?'

'Yes, Oats, yes I did.'

'It's complicated Janet, but I believe Nature has an enormous number of elementary components, built into an emotional and compassionate spirit, within this force.'

Janet was stunned. 'What?'

'Consider, our vast vulnerabilities as a race and our given senses. We are nothing, compared to these massive forces controlling matter, in the universe. Socrates, Aristotle and Plato among others debated this philosophical reasoning, within creation.'

'It was the caring nature found within humanity, which led the persecuted to believe in a loving Spirit. Copernicus discovered the architecture of our solar system. Newton, Galileo and others have further explained, the working design, contained within some of these forces.'

Michael laughed. 'Oats, you're rambling again.'

'Michael, ask yourself this, why would any grand lifeless force, create a universe on this scale with these creatures in existence, unless there was caring, in the makeup of the Natural Force. All the evidence we have seen, points to a gifted silence, within Nature's origins.'

Janet asked. 'Gifted silence Oats? Wait a minute, you make the Natural force out to be planned, almost as if life itself evolved, in an orderly and structured way?'

'In some ways it did Janet. It most certainly did.'

Now Janet was confused. 'But how, I don't understand?'

'Consider the simplicity of humanity alone and ask why.'

Janet was intrigued. 'Why what, in particular?'

Oats progressed carefully. 'Why is it, there are times of fertility with humanity?'

This turned to confusion for Janet. 'What do you mean?'

'Well, children don't experience any feeling for fertility, because it is not their time and adults in old age, no longer retain productive fertility, because it is beyond their time.'

'Why does Nature grant the excitement to reproduce, during times of fertility, by age?'

'What are you getting at Oats?'

'As a race, we don't even understand the driving urges, behind the enthusiasms and dynamisms, created within ourselves from Nature yet.'

Michael began to wonder. 'Here we are looking outward, when some of the answers can be found within.'

Oats laughed. 'Fascinating, isn't it Michael?'

It was then that Tamaryn began to further engage with us. 'You are trying to interpret the fundamental and dynamic forces of life, held within Nature. These rudimentary urges, live within all animal species to replicate life. Enhanced intelligence was given to humanity to help understand and interpret nurturing, which helps with population control and balance.'

Then Pim thought back to an earlier time, long ago, when her son Mykron first established the four truths of self-interest, as the first clan king on Candon. Pim felt this might help. 'The reason why Tamaryn's societies have followed these rules, is because they are essential laws found for survival in Nature. Self-control, self-discipline, self-reliance and self-respect.'

Tamaryn could see some of us were still baffled, so she began to enlighten us.'

'From the earliest formations of existence, it is Nature's time to be acknowledged and heard, with caring messages of peaceful co-existence, to be revealed and observed.'

'The reality of Nature as a living force is undeniable, as the evidence of existence is irrefutable. Understanding the cradle of Natures origins and the magnitude of our cosmic diversity, still remains to be discovered.'

Then each of the elders reflected. 'Throughout our history, we have believed there maybe another answer to this perpetual, eternal and timeless conundrum about Origin. We believe, the forces want our given intelligence, to uncover these answers. Nature's wisdom, with other natural forces, comes to us in peace and harmony, without any question or explanation. We are being asked to question, reflect, resolve and discover.'

Then another elder. 'There is no intimidation or requirement for empathy, mercy or clemency, or any compulsion to accept, or even acknowledge this force.'

One more voice spoke up. 'Nature's presence comes without any obligation to believe. There is no intimidation from Nature, to accept or agree, to any diverse spiritual or sacred opinions, attitudes, beliefs or judgments.' Then they continued.

'Considered character values. The reality of diversity in Nature's species, comes without stipulations, reservations or conditions, destiny or fortunes. Nature's messaging is subtle. There is no criticism or condemnation, denigration or blame for any preconceived failings, in any creatures.'

'Perpetuation of generations. The depth and generational presence of enduring fertility, comes with a quite inclusive and intentionally deliberate plan, in the evolution and reproduction of the species. There is an affection for diversity and an intelligence for emotive sharing, among animal species.'

'Mortality of life. Nature, shares experiences, without any reason or explanation for its presence. While fundamental, to our very survival and existence, all the reasons underlying natural and physical laws, are yet to be fully understood.'

'Nature shares a history, with many other powerful celestial forces of energy, motion and gravity, from the earliest of times and clearly predates early existence.'

'Is there a purpose? Nature asks that we exist and be charmed by the diversity of all living things. That we consider Nature, as an all-inclusive cosmological presence, rather than an early planetary, evolutionary conceptual vision.'

Tamaryn then asked. 'Oats, do you believe Nature, has a purpose?'

'I can think of one. Every hope begins with a dream. Peace on Earth, has been an enduring dream, for many generations over thousands of years now. Many pray for the serenity, which would bring harmony and a cease-fire, which brings reconciliation. We are hungry for the insight, which brings illumination, to the soul and yet, the promise of a peaceful existence, still seems to elude and confound so many.'

Then one of the elders said. 'There is absolutely nothing wrong with having faith and belief in the warmth and fellowship of our humanity. It is entirely possible, for a race of beings to enjoy each other's friendship, in complete social harmony.'

Another elder added. 'As a race we have choices, for the diverse paths we follow. It is up to each one of us, to pursue decency of character, with Nature's fellow creature's and observe the innocence in others and receive, respect in return.'

Oats felt inspired. 'If humanity was able to take a step back and find peace on Earth, it would lift the hopes and dreams of many. Over past centuries, we have lost this vision of unity, in a path forward? One day, when we look for it again, peace will come.'

Another elder agreed. 'Nature's complexity in the wild is not easy to judge. We all begin life with an open mind at birth. Each of us has one lasting chance, to discover, to build, to create and to engage with Nature. In the age of the universe, individual life can seem like, such a fleeting and transient experience.'

Another elder asked. **'What instinct is it within Nature, which gives us the desire to share love, the innocence as children to**

seek wisdom, the struggle with determination to survive, the courage with hope to find freedom, the warmth in our hearts to be happy and the strength of character, hidden in the depth of our spirits, to endure?'

Then Michael said. **'Understanding the depth of Nature's true innocence may give us all a sense of peace, if we just look for it. Life is so easy, if we choose good character over bad. Nature gives us this virtuous choice, to learn and the path is ours to follow, from there on, if we choose.'**

41
Questions for the Future.

Oats found his voice again. 'It is really peaceful here.' Oats paused as his sense of elation built and then said 'It is just lovely.'

Michael asked. 'Oats, let's show Tamaryn, our list of unresolved questions?'

Oats had finally found someone, who may be able to help him. He seemed emotional as he began. 'Tamaryn, I have been carrying this list with me for a long time. Could you please consider this list for a moment and maybe, we could discuss some of it?'

'Why of course Oats?'

Oats carefully pulled out his list of unanswered questions, looking for illumination and then showed it to Tamaryn.

Twenty outstanding questions, throughout time.

The Universe of particle matter

1) What are the origins, of elementary particle matter and molecular structures?
2) How was this matter itself first created, in our weightless universal expanse?
3) How did matter form, from atoms, creating planets, stars and galaxies?

4) Why do we have a central solar mass, generating heat and light energy?
5) One structured, orderly galaxy could be an accident, but hundreds of them?
6) How do we explain, the rotating, geometric symmetry of matter, in motion?
7) Why do planets move with consistency and stability around primary energy sources?
8) Why do star systems, seem to move as a stable mass, around in galaxy formation?
9) The time line; how long has the universe been in existence? No estimates.
10) How big in dimension and proportion, is the universal expanse?

Natural Forces.

11) When, where and how, did life start in the universe?
12) How long has Nature existed, as a force in the universe?
13) There are four observable fundamental forces or interactions that form the basis of known interactions in Nature. What other forces in Nature are there besides weak nuclear, strong nuclear, gravity and electromagnetism?
14) How did billions of examples of solar heat and light energy begin, evolve and advance to form star systems?
15) Not who, but what is the architect, of this orderly, all-encompassing expanse?

Looking beyond our own parochial vision, of planetary history.

16) Where did life on Earth come from, in the beginning and how did we get there?

17) How did the age of Dinosaurs begin over 200 million years ago? How did all life and cultural diversity develop, by geographic region, on our planet?
18) How extensive is the evolution of intelligent life, in the universe?
19) Why is it, that humanity has only several thousand years of memory and recorded history of evolution, on our own planet?
20) Why do we not question our recorded history, for omissions and accuracy?

Oats continued. 'Some of these questions have been asked in different forms on our planet, for many thousands of years.'

Tamaryn was kindhearted. 'It is a thought provoking list, Oats. When you next see WIL, he will begin to answer some of these questions for you. However, he will not ask you to believe anything, he will want you to think and reflect, with your own natural intelligence. You were given this skill, of insightful reasoning, at birth.' Then. 'When you come back, we can continue with further revelations.'

Oats was stunned. 'You know already, what our future plans are?'

'Yes, your objectives will also be explained by WIL, the next time you see him.'

Oats looked bewildered as Tamaryn laughed. 'Unearthing Nature's motivations, has become, an adventure of discovery, for us all, Oats.'

Janet asked Tamaryn. 'What is it that Nature wants?'

'It is the reproductive reliability and continuity of all life. Nature, as a force drives this struggle to survive. All classes and animal life varieties, are part of this process.'

Janet became curious. 'To what end, Tamaryn? I mean where does this all lead?'

'In your future, a better understanding of Origin, will reveal itself, when we finally come to appreciate, the true magnificence of this enormous expanse.'

Janet's innocence, then showed. 'Reveal itself, Tamaryn?'

'Yes Janet, Nature has the illuminating characteristics of a design, for the endless reproduction of all life forms. For the reasons already discussed, Nature is striving to reproduce, in the battle to give balance, for many species to exist.'

Oats was measured. 'Life has also created a contest of ideas, a philosophical encounter, for humanity to elevate our minds and broaden our horizons. A quest, to discover what society we can become. A challenge to be a better civilization than we are.'

Oats paused as his sense of elation built. 'To uncover the missing pieces, to the greatest puzzle ever known and then work out how and why, it was all put together, in the beginning.' Oats continued to be amazed by his surroundings.

Tamaryn then went on to explain. 'Here, we have many who work for a gentle and kinder existence. Every child born here, is given self-improvement as a first step. We teach the children these four truths, before they are sent on these missions, to look at other planetary social experiments and then let them decide for themselves.

'It is when citizens choose to break with Natures laws, they can move to another planet with an existence which is more to their choosing. Finally there is the planet of Isolation, with few rules, where Nature is almost ignored and existence can appear heartless, for those who have little respect, for Natures primary laws.'

Janet asked. 'How does this help to ensure, civil discipline?'

'Several issues to consider. In early education and training our focus has been on self-development. Order must begin, with discipline, restraint, control and respect.'

'Tamaryn, can you please describe, your highest ambitions?'

'There are important settings in land care. Imbalances can create extinction and as a race we have to ask, if that is what we want. Or do we want to take control of our weaknesses, to maintain natural balances?'

'The reason our society places such a high value on the four truths of self-interest, is to help maintain balance. You see, it is our experience that Nature knows how to stimulate the reproduction of the species, but not how to control this expansion and growth.'

'When one species has mastered dominance, without self-control or self-discipline, then many Natural imbalances can occur. This is why Nature needs friends and nurturing, to help maintain the balances required, for peaceful co-existence. When a race chooses to care for the natural environmental, then population growth, can be controlled, to maintain this balance.'

42
Nature's Four Truths of Self-Interest.

Marmuron asked. 'Tamaryn, why do you believe in the four truths of Self-interest?'

Tamaryn smiled. 'Just for a moment imagine a happier world with a more harmonious existence, where as a species humanity all got along together.'

Then. 'Nature in its innocence motivates reproduction of the species, without any sense of self-discipline. It is our acquired sense of self-discipline on many levels, which takes control with an enthusiasm to create essential character. This enriches us all to evolve and progress, giving our people, an advanced global society

Tamaryn then said. 'When our children go on these missions to see evolution with little regard for self-discipline, this then becomes clear to them. We send instructive tours to many different planets, as a means of instilling, inspired personal choices. After all, a peace loving mind, will not evolve, unless citizens understand from an early age, what the alternative choices are.'

Tamaryn then amazed us, 'I realize on this first mission, your time is short. When you return, would you like to see this first-hand, for yourselves?'

Oats jumped at this. 'Why yes, we would love to come back.' Oats had one last question that couldn't wait. 'And your view of balance, in universal creation?'

'As we discussed last time, the source of what happened in the universe at origin remains an unknown for us all. However the question for our humanity becomes this. Do we wish to help a natural balance, in the rebirth of all living plants and animals or do we take no action, allowing the buildup of natural stresses to occur? These stresses may not show up for many generations, however without 'The four truths of self-interest', we may lose what we have and social order, will become the worse off, for our poor choices.'

'So this is why your children are motivated to learn, from past choices in society?

'Fundamentally yes, to see what past choices have been made and the consequences on the environment from poor social choices, through hesitation or lack of resolve.'

Tamaryn paused as she reflected on the four truths of self-interest, remembering that an individual, can also be kind and generous, of spirit and in character.

'In a universe of unknowns, cosmological insight will not fully reveal itself, unless we explore natural intelligence, with an unimpeded view and a completely open mind.'

Marmuron asked. 'Can you please simplify that for me?

'There is no need to apologize, if we never make mistakes and there is no need for forgiveness, if mistakes are never made. The boundaries of our frontiers, are an opportunity for future discovery. As long as we choose to remain a united global society, the evolution of enlightenment, will continue, between us all, equally as a race.'

Tamaryn persisted. 'Do we want to support the Natural Force, in a balanced expansion, throughout the universe? Or do we ignore this silent force and damage the future direction of sustainability, consuming resources which destroys botanical life. Resources which have been given to us all, unrestricted, to pass on to future generations?'

Oats was in several minds again as he mumbled. 'I don't believe many in our age, even understand these questions. We can learn from this grand design in evolution, or follow another chosen destiny and ignore sustainability, altogether.'

Now Oats was almost beside himself with excitement. 'The last time we met, you were able to help us with one of the greatest mysteries on our planet, the origins of spiritual belief. Can you help us improve our understanding, of the forces in the universe?

'This will become more evident, when you all come back next time. What Nature is trying to share, are the same concepts passed on down, for thousands of generations, and throughout the ages. In your ancient times, some of these messages were philosophically documented and well understood, by those who wanted to listen.'

Then Michael's enthusiasm overtook him. 'Listen to what in particular?'

'Many of the spiritual references from your ancients, became a quest of their own for the advancement of human knowledge. However their understanding of the universe, its formation and the origin of the species, was unknown to them, at the time. '

Oats asked. 'And the most important messages?'

'The most important of these, were the values in the defense of courage and character, with every high moral purpose. Enlightenment will not succeed, without the advancement of decency, held deep within the morality, of the human spirit.'

As Tamaryn paused, she had everyone's attention now. **'It is this spirit which lives on, for an eternity in the generations to follow. It is decency of spirit, which protects honor and respect for others. It is within this sense of dignity, we can find our own character and our own sense of self-respect.'**

'But how did all these choices, with their boundaries, first become self-evident?'

'Enlightenment is easily found by those with an open mind who look for it.' Then Tamaryn paused for a moment as she said. 'Some of our students who have recently come from a planetary mission, will be escorted back, for a brief visit to your galaxy. Why not ask them, what they have discovered?'

Oats stayed focused. 'Can you please clarify this larger, Natural concept for us?'

'It is Nature's qualities, which are revered and admired among equals, for the benefit of the masses. This is the important natural message, which the universal force identifies with. A harmonious message of peaceful co-existence, to be safeguarded and defended for eternity. For no species will advance for long, over all others, without this illuminating clarification, of self-enlightenment.'

Several moments passed and Oats seemed to become increasingly more puzzled. 'Tamaryn forgive me, but you can see this elevated cosmological existence and yet you choose to live in this enormous planetary natural forest, with many of your followers?'

Tamaryn smiled warmly on Oats. 'And you are asking me why?'

'Well, yes if I may? What puzzles me is that these children, for many generations have also seen the progressive choices made, by other communities in jurisdictions on other planets. Yet they choose to return here, to live out their lives in relative simplicity. Is it a rejection of evolutionary advancement, or something else?'

'One of the greatest triumphs, in any life, during a moment of reflection, is to be able to find and live with, your own peace of mind.'

Now Janet struggled for answers. 'Yes, but the villagers here seem so warm and happy, comforted with a gentle simplicity, in life.'

Tamaryn smiled warmly on Janet. 'And you are still puzzled by this? **Have you ever been judged or misinterpreted by another, who may have misunderstood something you may have said. Has any action you've ever taken, been seen or taken the wrong way. Nature does not judge our people here and they, do not judge each other.'**

Finally it was now Marmuron who began to see her connection with her past origins in this treasured natural botanical sanctuary. She began to gush with tears. She couldn't contain her enthusiasm any longer, as she grappled with the universal cosmic vision building inside her. 'Can you please share, the secrets of their inspiring cheerfulness?'

43
Visions of Natural Serenity.

'Remember the mastery of this natural creative design. Nature does not find guilt among them, rebuke, chastise or punish them. The most important feelings, are found in the innocence of their binding love, for the simplicity, of this kindhearted existence.'

Janet was emotionally moved as well, as she watched the friendliness with freedom and the industry, of natural preservation on display. 'They seem so happy and content within the enchantment, of this natural wonderland?'

Tamaryn smiled at Janet. 'You can't see it yet, can you?'

Tears formed in Janet's eyes, as we all looked on. 'I'm beginning to understand.' It was as though we had never seen anything quite like this before in our lives. A race of people, who were free to make choices of their own and governed by self-discipline. Yet as villagers, they were drawn to this life of shared happiness in a mutually beneficial existence, where no one judged them and each played their own part.'

Oats smiled unreservedly as he observed a community working together, with a rising sense of desire to belong. 'They seem unimpeded and happy, just to play a useful role in a united communal society.' Then he whispered. 'It really does grow on you.'

'This kindhearted friendship for each other and indeed, for all other species is held warmly and caringly by these villagers. This has become their choice, to live simply and share charitably, a natural life within a multitude of species, of flora and fauna.'

It became increasingly hard not to see the collective beauty of what they all shared. 'These environmental surroundings provided the most balanced of ecological ambiances. Without stress or anxiety of any kind, they find a harmonious tranquility with serenity, in the company and companionship of Nature's melodious, chirping sounds.'

We all felt inspired as Oats said. 'These surely are, vital lessons from Nature.'

Tamaryn smiled. 'Try to understand the meanings behind what you see, the values and silent messaging, among all of these species, the musical sounds and the happy chatter. What you have seen so far, is that Nature is a guidance for how each of us can choose to live and survive if we want to accept peace.'

'Don't look at natural existence as having a purpose over one life time. Look at the purpose of evolution over millions of generations. **You just need a visionary explanation for it. Consider some human weaknesses in learning. The willingness to believe without question, the rush to judgment and condemnation of others, without cause.**'

'Alternatively, contemplate a life with purpose and a motivated willingness, to alter direction. Consider the vastness of universal existence, in its own lifetime and not just in your own.' Tamaryn changed direction. 'I'm going to share some thoughts with you all that may seem hard to understand.'

'Why is it perpetually possible for love and happiness to multiply between the sexes? How can feelings of love, passion, tenderness, fondness and emotional strength, live and survive, over thousands of generations, among us?'

'That love, beyond the life of a flower, can bloom forever. Where a hug of warmth and happiness, can bring peaceful thoughts, between mankind. Then there's the greatest of all loves, the rebirth of life, uniting families together, which can last a lifetime.'

'The Natural Force instills a sense of moral principles. You can recognize it in the silence, which is only broken by the enthusiasm, of other life forms around us. Nature gives us many gifts, beginning with the intelligence, to understand it.'

As we walked back, Janet appealed. 'Please tell us about the other gifts?'

'Everything you think and feel, throughout the ages, can be seen in our natural surroundings. Kindness, friendliness and consideration are matched with self-respect, happiness, romance and character. The courage of self-taught convictions, live within each choice we make. These are not just words with feelings, but a way of life for us.'

'No one starts out in life, wanting to make poor choices. That is why we send our children on these inter planetary excursions to help them see and understand existence, with a vision for their own future. Nature teaches you guidance, in self-preservation.'

Tamaryn seemed saddened by the willingness of humanity to often make weak choices. **'Respect for natural laws, provides the closest perceptive insight, into our cosmic expanse.'**

'Natural laws are the ultimate authoritative perspective. We exist within this influence, for all living species to survive, Natural forces need to be respected, as they were originally designed.'

'In Nature's unspoken limitations, we get to reflect on many things, except the silence of our own lost time, where our time can seem endless.'

'There are no limitations, in taking personal choices, but there are consequences in crossing over Nature's boundaries. This is the benefit of given intelligence to choose wisely and to make the right choices.'

Back at Tamaryn's Cottage

Once back in Tamaryn's charming residence, it was a brilliant opportunity to discover more, about her motivations and her plans.

Tamaryn could read our thoughts and was a few steps ahead of us, as she questioned. 'In the vastness of your documented history, doesn't it puzzle you, that the time line of your own recorded history, is so relatively short?'

Michael instantly agreed. 'Absolutely, yes.'

Oats's mind was working overtime, trying to interpret the visionary concepts hidden in this last remark. Oats began challenging our current beliefs. 'Even if it was the case that we evolved from a more primitive species, where is the memory of it? Why do we all look so different from each other by geographic region? How is it possible in an ecological environment and history spanning millions of years that mankind doesn't even have an authoritative memory, going back more than say five to eight thousand years.'

Oats persisted with his unanswered questions. 'Why has the memory, of our recorded history been measured in just thousands of years, to achieve our current level of advancement? Why is it the case that in some primitive cultures, there has been almost no level of advancement at all?'

44
Natures Illuminating Vulnerabilities.

Then Tamaryn said. 'Oats, look at evolution over a longer historical period. A time frame, of say five thousand generations from a galaxy perspective. Consider how we might preserve species on other planets, where for hundreds of your generations, Nature could have existed, until over population becomes an issue again.

'Look at why humanity tries to preserve species, on your own planet. Then consider how civilizations at a galaxy level, will try to help nurture this Natural Force.'

Oats was puzzled. 'That's a lot to think about, in one vision.'

While all Janet could say was 'Wow.'

Tamaryn looked kindly on Oats. Then, in a more revealing explanation she began again. 'On your own planet, past civilizations have tried to help preserve and protect endangered species, facing some threat of extinction. So at a planetary level you know many will comprehend, the desire for the preservation of life, for many different species.'

Oats moved forward in his seat as Tamaryn waited for us to reflect on her thoughts.

'Look more closely at how Natural evolution is logically arranged in an orderly way on your planet. By climate and by class. Just for a moment I want you to advance your thoughts, to see things from a galaxy perspective as we do. Then look back at all the protected species on your planet and ask how life, could really have begun and if a greater influence, may have helped preserve the Natural Force, in your earlier times.'

Tamaryn sensed Michael's illumination building. 'Michael, try to see your global ecological, conservation and environmental issues, from a galaxy perspective.'

Michael's face lit up as something began to twig. 'Our planet could have been conceived as an animal and biological sanctuary, if we were to reconsider ourselves, as being part of a galaxy wide, evolutionary preservation, of life forms.'

Oats realized something. 'Tamaryn, if I may, your inner planetary systems, appear to have many of the fundamental foundations, we have on Earth.'

Tamaryn laughed with a knowing smile. 'And your question is Oats?'

'What happened on the planet of Isolation and what caused many to move away?'

'Nature's animal classes, are stimulated to procreate and reproduce. However reproduction without the wisdom of any control, is where we see our part in being able to help, support and nurture Nature. The challenges faced, can be enormous, however population stresses, come down to a question of numbers, Oats?'

Oats was still putting two and two together. 'We have most of this on just one planet. Multiple cultural histories with multiple backgrounds and an extraordinary variety of species. Almost as though our planet is a combination, on a much smaller scale of many other systems.'

Tamaryn smiled. 'Over thousands of generations, we have come to understand the importance of nurturing Nature. Without cultivation, fostering and encouragement, life in all its forms, can face many threats. We have learnt by helping Nature, we will all eventually come closer, to answering your larger questions of what happened in the beginning and why. **We are not independent of each other, we are co-reliant and co-dependent, on each other.** Replication of the species has taught us that.' Then. 'The only faith we should foster and believe in, is our capacity to find civility among ourselves.'

Janet smiled at Oats as she asked. 'Are you in two minds again Oats?'

Oats was reflective. 'If humanity wants to regain peaceful enlightenment, all our cultures will need to unite and build for it. **The future won't be found, in past mythology**. While we remain divided, it is our children who will be deprived of an advancing cosmic vision, and it is our children who will suffer. We are training them to believe in the past, rather than helping to unify them, to explore ways, of finding their future.'

It was then, that Oats found the words he'd been looking for. **'We need to create an advanced global society, if we want to live in one.'**

Then. 'Think about it Michael, in a larger dynamic, you could say that our whole planet began in this way. It answers so many questions, about how advanced civilizations have helped Nature, in the universe. Nature as a force can stimulate breeding, but can't control over population. Considering how diverse, our natural mix is, isn't it possible?'

'Yes Oats, the origin of life on Earth, makes more sense this way, rather than the single celled organism debate. People back on Earth, haven't even considered this yet.'

'Why would they, our people don't even realize, that Nature is a universal force?'

After a pause Tamaryn added. 'Oats, I understand you doubt the hypothesized theory on your planet's natural origins, from a single celled organism. It is reasonable to believe that breeding creates a blended inheritance. How then can one cell on Earth, create millions of quite diverse and dissimilar species and life forms over time?'

Oats jumped at this. 'Yes, this is the puzzle, which has been baffling us as well.'

Tamaryn smiled. 'The answers to this debate, will soon become clearer.'

Tamaryn then looked with warmth and sincerity at us all. 'I want you to place yourselves, in the minds of earlier civilizations, much more ancient, than your own. From the beginning of creation, Nature's design has been, to share the gift of life, with the structure and intention of continued reproduction, throughout the ages. The species are almost countless and can vary from one system to the next. The time line of natural experience for species, is miniscule for some and an eternity by comparison for others. This miraculous phenomenon of Nature as a force, is a mystifying spectacle and a cherished adventure, for us all, to behold.'

'Simply thrilling, isn't it?' Shouted Oats

Janet asked. 'Tamaryn, if I may, what is it you find most intriguing about Nature?'

'In encouraging circumstances, responsible parenting will achieve Nature's wishes. In the attempts to reproduce, there's a passion for the moment, which unites the sexes. Yet at the same time, there is a ferocity in life, between some animal classes. This leads one to consider the logical role, of intellectual governance, between the species.'

As we listened to Tamaryn's elders continue to describe how much they loved the ancient forest, which covered most of their planet, we began to see it as well. Every harmonious noise, from the scurrying sound of smaller critters, to the flocking sounds of birds. It was easy to see why Mharn's parents, lost track of time here.'

This thought suddenly occurred to Oats and Michael, while reminded by Tamaryn. 'The Shi's loved their times here.'

Tamaryn noticed their sudden awareness of this reality, which brought them back to their purpose, on this mission. Tamaryn smiled as she continued. 'In the early stages of our plans, to return Galactic Council Conferences to our galaxy, both WIL and I were aware of the many perils, which can be faced by others, for the first time.'

'This is why Sun-Ky was appointed to take charge and administer the processes of this exchange.'

Then. 'As you know he has arranged for some of our student graduates to make a return visit with Munkhan, to your galaxy compound on Kendagon.'

'A perfect example of Nature at work, is to see the developing innocence in the union between Mharn and Karina. That is why Mharn will also be returning on this mission.'

Beaming smiles grew on the faces of Janet and Marmuron who were thrilled for Karina and so Tamaryn felt compelled, to issue this vital warning. 'As advanced as we may be, there are still many essential risks, in these intergalactic missions. This is why I am asking you now, to keep these plans entirely to yourselves and not reveal a word of this to Karina, or any of her friends.

'One of our great weaknesses, is to know something and reveal it before it is safe to do so. Can I have your assurance on this confidential surprise? Karina would be heartbroken, if something were to go wrong.'

Oats and Michael quickly nodded in agreement, however Janet and Marmuron found it hard to keep this secret and were slow to decide.

'Tamaryn, she is pregnant and desperate to hear news about Mharn.'

Tamaryn was sympathetic with a kindhearted and compassionate response showing her wealth of wisdom and maturity. 'Sometimes delayed news, can be good news.'

Janet sensed there were still many reasons to be cautious, about safety and security of intergalactic travel, even by this advanced society. With some reservations, they both agreed to Tamaryn's modest request. With mature understanding they responded, 'Yes'.

Then Tamaryn paused to give another considered response. 'If I may add one more vision for you all to consider. As I said when you next talk to WIL, he will answer some of the deeper questions, about the true origin of natural life forces, on your planet.' Tamaryn then paused. 'Our people are not taught to believe, they are taught to question and to debate, to discuss, to rationalize and to resolve, these unknown mysteries for themselves. Watch for the gifted illumination, in his answers and consider, this unresolved mystery for yourselves.'

45
Long Voyage Home for Karina.

Oats and Michael glanced at each other. They felt closer to resolving this huge enigma? They couldn't wait to catch up with WIL again and help resolve this never-ending puzzle.

The minds of Michael and Oats were motivated and heartened by Tamaryn's last remarks. They were now bursting with enthusiasm, in anticipation of a revealing explanation from WIL, about the true origin of life on Earth.

They thanked Tamaryn and her elders for spending their precious time. Soon they were returning to Prisium, to pick up Karina and her friends.

On arrival, Janet and Marmuron found Mharn's friends, while Michael and Oats met with other delegates, who were scheduled to return home early. As they boarded the shuttle to rejoin the Corillion, it was a buoyant mood with many happy memories to share. As the long voyage home began, Oats and Michael met in the Map Room once more.

Michael asked. 'What's on your mind Oats?'

Oats face, was a study of many complex thoughts. 'She was sharing her reflections about Origin and the existence of Natural creation over thousands of generations. It's all there Michael. **Nature has a vision for harmonious existence, if we all just look for this illumination and listen.**'

'Life has been a precious experience of discovery for us. Tamaryn looks at life and existence from a much deeper, cosmological perspective.'

Janet and Marmuron quickly came in, after chatting with Karina. They were concerned for her well-being. Janet, was almost breathless. 'Michael, why all the rush? We seem to be racing to leave and get back home?'

'We are Janet and it's all quite deliberate.'

Janet was upset. 'It has been difficult, listening to Karina being consoled by her friends over leaving Mharn behind.' Then Janet began to get more anxious for Karina. 'We've only recently arrived here. Karina believed she was going to see Mharn again. We've only been in this galaxy, for a little more than one rotation, of Prisium?'

Michael tried to console her. 'We all feel rushed Janet, after the conversation with Sun-Ky, it was decided that coming home this quickly, was in everyone's best interests.'

Janet was hoping for more insight. 'We didn't hear, all of this before.'

'As Tamaryn said, Munkhan is bringing back ten students, from one of their graduating classes, to observe our galaxy. Apparently there are hundreds of these exploratory missions, being planned, across both galaxies, into the future.'

The faces of Janet and Marmuron, were a little more relieved.'

Oats then explained the importance of these events. 'Inter galactic travel is still very new to us and Sun-Ky felt it important, that we learn to manage the experiences of time loss, better. None of us will achieve anything, if we get this part of these early missions wrong. Mharn's parent's experience here, was important, for all of us to share.'

Michael continued. 'So, these early objectives of time management, are for both galaxy's, to become comfortable. Also for assimilation and early interaction. Once everyone's confidence has advanced, then many more missions, can take place. We know this is hard on Karina, however our patience on this, will be rewarded.'

Marmuron pleaded. 'Michael, she is desperate for any good news.'

Oats and Michael glanced at each other and then. 'Alright, ask them all to come in for a moment.' Janet and Marmuron left quickly, to get the others.

Oats reacted. 'Michael, we can't reveal this yet, we gave our word.'

'Yes, I know, but we can still try, to put her mind at ease.'

Within moments Karina and her friends came back down, to the Map Room. Karina had been openly crying and was trying to conceal her reddening cheeks. 'Michael, you know something more, of Mharn's movements?'

'Yes Karina, please come on in, all of you. As you know we have a number of delegates with us also returning from short duration missions. This transfer of people between galaxies, is just the beginning of many future back and forth missions, to come. We know Mharn is safe and well and he also took part in a short duration mission and we are just waiting, on more complete details, as to when he will return.'

Karina began to smile as Michael continued. 'There's nothing to be concerned about at the moment and when we have further advice, on his exact movements, they will let us know, as soon as they can. Try to keep positive and be cheerful. This is a tremendous honor for Mharn. We know he misses you and he is playing an important part, in these early transfers.'

Karina began to smile openly. 'Thank you Michael, thank you.'

The mood among all her friends became a little more buoyant, as Karina appeared to cheer up. Herron agreed. 'Yes, thankyou Michael. See Karina we told you there was nothing to be worried about.' With more spreading good cheer and building confidence, they left with a wave and returned to their suites.

After a moment Oats, Marmuron and Janet looked at Michael with some amusement as he said. 'She just needed some cheering up, that's all.'

Janet still found it difficult trying to keep her news about Mharn's early return, to herself, however she and Marmuron came to understand, all the inherent risks involved.

Oats and Michael both lounged in the Map Room on the way back, watching more visions of Tamaryn's beautiful native landscapes. Oats couldn't get to sleep and he became more excited, as his vision for Earth's global unity, began to take hold. Oats' passionate nature can be like that, as he continued to chatter on and get more excited. 'Tamaryn said that WIL can help us with these answers Michael. No one will tell you what to believe, we must discover these answers for ourselves. Thrilling isn't it.'

It was much later for them now and time to get some rest. Finally Michael threw a pillow at Oats. 'Awe please belt up Oats. I'm trying to get some sleep.'

46
The Universe of Silent Forces.

Planet of Pimeron, System of Kindred Spirits.

It was some time later and Pim came in to remind us all, we were nearly home and we would have some time to ourselves, before going onto a more formal reception, on the planet of Kendagon, where Mharn's parents lived.

Once back, Karina and her friends left to return to their own provinces on their nearby planet of Candon. We would all meet later, on Kendagon. It seemed fairly hectic, however Pim was well prepared.

To Oats great surprise, after the enormous distances they had covered, his alpine cabin hadn't changed a bit. It was just great to be home. The natural outlook from Oats back veranda, was still beautiful and scenic with a building mild breeze, blowing gently across the valley floor below.

Oats and Michael found their favorite lounge chairs on the back deck and took pleasure in the beautiful natural distant views, out to the foothills beyond.

The friends settled and listened to a variety of forest birds, humming their chirping sounds of cheer and happiness. They also noticed some playful woodland creatures chasing each other around, in the foreground. While nearby, heavenly bodies slowly changed positions, as they rotated with shading colors, in the evening sky.

It was a natural wonderland in these alpine regions, around Oats cabin. A heavenly paradise, of pleasure and blissful harmony. Just one of many locations in the cosmos, where natural forces played out, their timeless existence. Oats remarked. 'Intriguing jungle rainforests, captivating botanical colors and some massive trees, housing a variety of creatures. Here it truly is, a world at peace, in our time.'

In the flurry of building visions it occurred to Oats to question. 'Anyone asked Pim, how long we've been away?'

Janet laughed. 'Pim said, as she left, it was about ten rotations of Kendagon'. Our girls were relieved to be home as well and we were feeling much more confident, about managing time. Time travel had now become a discipline, to be mastered.

'Brilliant.' Agreed Oats

Michael noticed Oats, stewing away on something. 'What's on your mind, Oats?'

'The strongest bonds we can all share, are unity. To be inspired by purpose and intent, in sincerity and direction, while living in harmony with some humor.'

'Are you thinking about our home planet again, Oats?'

'Yes, the great undoing of any society is to have a closed mind, with restricted debates. To shut down discussion and not even acknowledge, other points of view. It just damages chances for global social order, to progress.'

'Is this about our past history, revealed recently by Sun-Ky?'

'Yes, it's so simple when you think about it. A divided community cannot flourish in the same way a united one can. Community division, has its consequences.'

'Yes, in Tamaryn's community, they are all working together.'

Oats was still moved by his recent experiences. 'It's more than that, Michael.'

'So talk to me, Oats?'

'The opportunities to go back and see more of Tamaryn's many planetary societies, will surely come soon.'

'Part of me is thrilled for our future chances and another part, feels a little overwhelmed. You were right to bring this up, about losing Pim, as our mentor.'

As they struggled for meaningful answers, Oats rechecked the time. They had been back for a while now and Mharn's parents, would be eager to know how the mission went.

Janet came out with Marmuron, to join them on the back deck. Janet seemed puzzled about something and asked. 'I don't understand Oats, why are all the forces silent?' Janet seemed to struggle. 'How should people look at this universal existence, when Natural Forces, don't even have a voice?'

'With all the advances humanity has made, we need to consider ourselves as citizens of the universe. Not just as local, regional, cultural or sectarian survivors of the past.'

'Oats, what's this got to do with Janet's question, about the silence, of the forces?'

'Take your minds back through our history, to the great discoveries again. Gravity in space, appears as a silent force. Motion and stability, also appear as silent forces as well. Heat and light energy, also appear to be silent.'

Janet jumped in. 'And Nature?'

'Apart from the noises, coming from the myriad of creatures, Nature itself and the miracle of life's existence, survives through the ages, as a silent force as well. This is where all of our senses, will help us in our future, if we change the way we teach and train the next generation of children. There's so much to observe and learn, yet we train our children to believe in different cultural histories based on mythology, rather than challenging children to question, current life experiences and learn from them.'

'So, what's your point, Oats?'

'Well, how are future generations ever going to capture this reality, of universal silent forces, if they are just programmed to learn and believe in the cultural teachings and history of sectarian conflicts, in our past? While history is important, we can't change the past, however we can learn from it and help, change their future.'

There was an interrupting sound and Janet jumped. 'It's Pim and she's on her way back here.' Pim arrived more quickly than they had expected and there were many plans afoot. They walked as they talked and were soon on their way. Pim advised that Karina, Herron, Urundayy, Arkina and Kendy would soon arrive at the Shi's place and it was time for them to leave as well.

Pim had also been briefed on other plans. 'Michael, it appears I'm going to be making some periodic visits to Tamaryn's galaxy after all.' This was great news for Pim. However Oats and Michael felt they would lose the close contact, built up over the last six missions. Pim noticed Michael feeling downhearted, at the thought of her leaving their team. Our two researchers had become so dependent on Pim's insightful guidance.

Pim smiled warmly. 'You're sweet Michael, I'm going to miss some of our missions as well. However I'll still be going on a periodic basis.'

Oats mind, became a little clouded, as he searched for more reassuring answers. 'Pim do we have any news yet, on what will happen, with future missions?'

'No, not yet Oats, but WIL may be able to clear this up for you both, soon.'

Then Pim caught us all completely by surprise with this next observation. 'Munkhan should arrive soon and he has found a close and deeper friendship, with Velia's sister.'

We all smiled and grinned with happiness for Munkhan. Oats said. 'Good for him.'

Pim also advised. 'We'll see them all soon enough, over on Kendagon. Mharn will be with him and helping the ten students, go through their normal clearances.'

Janet with building excitement said. 'Wow, so Mharn will be coming there as well. This will be thrilling news for Karina.'

They were quickly on our way, shuttling between planets, while becoming more use to these faster changes, between interplanetary transfers.

47
A Welcome Surprise for Karina.

Planet of Kendagon, System of Kindred Spirits.

Mharn's mother San, greeted them, as they walked into the elaborate private lounge of the extensive upper floor suite, in the Kendagon Great Hall. Janet and Marmuron left with San to see Karina in her suite, where she was chatting with her close friends.

From the enormous central rooms in the Shi's home, Oats and Michael walked out onto the sprawling marbled, terrace balcony with Mharn's father, Kisun-Shi.

Shi began. 'Has anything changed, did you get to see Mharn recently?'

Oats and I laughed, as Oats began. 'Yes and thanks to you we have learnt so much more about planning, for the measuring of time loss.'

Shi asked. 'So what did you discover?'

Oats smiled. 'Tamaryn asked if we'd like to come back.'

Shi laughed. 'And of course you said, yes?'

Oats smiled. 'It would be our greatest adventure yet.'

Michael asked Shi. 'What was your experience like, on the inhabited planets?'

'On Tamaryn's planet, society is motivated to bring out the best in each other. Her people have a genuine understanding of community warmth. They are insightful, charming, self-disciplined and helpful, where everyone contributes. They had a true sense of what it was like to embrace, a unified living experience. They were the most respectful, self-confident and likeable souls, who melded into the flora and fauna, around them.'

Oats agreed. 'It is so easy to lose yourself there and get caught up in the illusion of a heavenly paradise. Shi, what was your experience on the planet of Isolation?'

'Many there have grown up with harsh and brutal experiences and are prepared to believe, the worst in others, rather than looking with kindness for the best in each other. Instead of embracing character strengths and strong community spirit, life for them becomes divisively complicated. Importantly though, the student programs, see all this.'

For a moment, as Shi struggled for more words, they could understand how he became so lost with his own experiences, during his time there, long ago.

Oats then queried. 'Shi, did you get to see, all their twenty three planets?'

'That was the part of our undoing I'm afraid. You know what it is like. Even on one planet, many people could spend a lifetime and not see it all. We went to many of the others and got caught up, in all their different time changes and cultural differences.'

Shi reflected again. 'Tamaryn said to me on arrival, that the only way forward, is self-enlightenment. Nature gives us, a brief and insightful chance, to find out our own part in this greater evolutionary progression and as individuals we don't ever seem to have enough time. That is the first law of self- enlightenment.'

'Did she say what the other laws were?'

'The laws came with a study of celestial understanding. Without learning discipline, character and self-control, we can find our lifetime experiences, are squandered. There are so many qualities, including patience, which are held and strengthened, by opposing the easier and poorer choices, found in personal weakness.'

Oats remembered. 'Yes, the analysis of virtues over vices, was scrutinized by Aristotle, one of our planet's ancient philosophers'

Shi realized how easy it was to come away with life changing experiences and asked. 'Was there one impression which stood out for you both?'

After thinking long and hard for a moment Oats began. 'There were many, however the most enlightening experience for me, was from Sun-Ky, on our voyage there.'

Shi seemed a little puzzled and amazed. 'Really, why Oats?'

'The logical analysis, of our planets real origins. In our ancient times, a new idea brought transformational peace, giving eternal hope to replace social tension and unrest. A vision for divine intervention from a Heavenly Father, for the persecuted who feared love had been lost to them. A path pursued by patricians, to further Roman greatness.

Many still hope for the dreams of these times, of mythical visions and of this greatness.'

Shi understood. 'Yes, there are some mountains to climb there, Oats. **Peace will only be found with global unity.** Origin in the universe is a fascinating and compelling study and may take us several more generations, to find the deeper answers, we all seek.'

Pim came over to alert us. 'Mharn is coming through now, with the students from Tamaryn's galaxy. They may need our help.'

Shi was thrilled. 'Do the others know yet?'

Pim smiled. 'I don't believe so, but we'd better hurry.'

There's a vulnerability, which endures, at the very heart of Natures presence and it is found in the innocent and virtuous purity, of helplessness. In youth, this vulnerability and purity is born, with the creation of each new generation. The beginning of life, is a treasure to behold and so these were the fears with Karina, who stood looking abandoned and a little alone. She had many things running through her warm and sensitive thoughts, as any expectant mother, may well do.

Mharn's mother San, was in Karina's suite watching on when she was made aware her son Mharn, had now arrived home and she rested her hands beside her cheeks as she whispered. 'Mharn.' San then moved quickly to counsel Karina and share the good news. Karina immediately noticed San's radiant smile, bursting with happiness.

The room, full of excited and chattering voices in Karina's suite came to a silent halt as Karina jumped up with bursting elation. She made her way out into the larger elaborate private lounge area. Her eyes were searching everywhere at once, for Mharn.

Karina gasped, as she screamed in delight. '**Mharn.**' Her face, exploded with rich emotional warmth, as she saw Mharn smiling at her with loving confidence. He boldly lit up her eyes, as he carried all her hopes and dreams. As their faces met, he moved swiftly to be supportive, standing by her side. They were lovely together and she glimmered with delight, at seeing him once more.

In the flood of greetings and excitement, Mharn spoke first. 'You look lovely.'

Karina had gushing tears of happiness. 'I can't believe your here.'

Mharn watched on devotedly. 'Michael once told me about his union of marriage to Janet and said, that for him the celebration itself was a uniting moment in life, with two spirits coming together. Then he said something which has stuck with me, for all time. **'Being united, is a celebration for the moment. It is the honeymoon of companionship, which lasts forever.'**

Karina's cheeks reddened, on hearing these beautiful words of lasting devotion from Mharn. 'Do you really believe that Mharn, about companionship lasting forever?'

A rapidly developing blissful smile, erupted between them. Mharn looked lovingly at the innocence, in her newfound sense of building motherhood and the burgeoning expressions of tenderness, coming from Karina. He smiled with great warmth on her pretty face as he asked. 'Was there something else, you wanted to tell me?'

Karina was momentarily stunned. 'You know, don't you?' He smiled again as she challenged. 'But how?' Karina's tears, began flowing uncontrollably. 'I was looking for the right chance to.' Karina seemed to stumble and stutter as she finished. 'To, tell you.'

Mharn unraveled her loving response. 'On our way back, Munkhan wanted to call in and see Velia's sister again. I had a chance to talk to Velia more closely about her own experience with the Clean Beam on our ship. Everything just fell into place after that. Why, didn't you tell me?'

'Well, well.' Karina began to blubber again and then. 'Your mission was so important to you, an, an,' and then. 'I didn't want to spoil.' Karina continued to whimper uncontrollably as he held and hugged her closely. Mharn interrupted her tears of elation, by holding his finger gently upright, to his lips for her to stop crying.

'Don't say another word.' He searched the tears of happiness, running down her reddened cheeks, as he rescued some long strands of hair, which had fallen down and began covering her pretty face. Mharn whispered quietly. 'Remember how we grew up together, and became close friends. We are living this honeymoon of companionship.'

Mharn rested the palm of his hand, on her tummy and said. 'This is our future. A long time ago, your father began delegating responsibilities in your province, to some of the head clansmen. You don't have to take all of this, on your own shoulders. I can help you as well and we can always go back there, making periodic trips to visit the others. You'll see, it'll all work out.'

They stood hugging and embracing, as one. Karina didn't feel alone anymore. The others just watched the building and loving emotion, coming from the feelings of warmth and tenderness, between them both.

Karina asked. 'When will we get the chance, to go back again?'

It was all she could get out, as Mharn embraced her warmly, in his arms. Again he stroked some falling strands of hair, from the forehead of her pretty face. The gentle breeze softened. 'Any time you want, is the right time for us.'

Their very close friends, Arkina, Uri, Herron and Kendu came closer, to share the warmth, of their support and friendship.

Mharn seemed puzzled, as he put past conversations together and chuckled. 'You all knew, didn't you?' There was an exchange of glancing looks, between them and then, an explosion of laughter, as Mharn now put all this together. 'That's what all the quizzing was about, on our mission.' The laughter broke out, into a loud and boisterous banter.

Karina whimpered. 'It's not their fault, I wanted to tell you myself when the time was right. You're not mad at me, are you?'

Mharn continued to hug her gently. 'I could never be mad at you.' And he gave her another warm hug, as all their friends continued to joke and chat with each other.

Then Mharn suddenly remembered. 'I have ten students from Tamaryn's galaxy, coming through now and they will be over here shortly.'

Mharn's father Shi, was now near the large transfer disc, welcoming Munkhan and the students, as they arrived, one after the other. The numbers in this stately lounge area increased, with aides getting refreshments and the ten students, were all warmly greeted. It was their chance to meet and greet, while coming to understand their own, precious time preservation issues.

48
Revelations from Munkhan.

Oats, Michael, Marmuron and Janet, had been waiting, near the side lounges, until things settled and everyone was introduced. The ten students looked a similar age to Mharn and his friends. A nervous quiet moment developed, as no one knew what to say first, until Munkhan stepped in and began slowly.

'We are very fortunate to have the honor of helping our young friends here, see natural existence from a different perspective. It is only a short stay, as they too want to keep measure of time. They will be going back in about three rotations of Kendagon.'

Munkhan asked. 'Mharn, could I ask you and your friends to accompany our guests, on a walking tour around these premises and we'll all meet back here shortly?'

'Why yes, yes of course.' And as they all left the chattering sound in the lounge area quietened down. Oats and Michael took this opportunity to catch up with Munkhan.

As they walked back out onto the expansive marbled terrace, Michael asked Munkhan. 'Tell us about some of the experiences, you've had, on the way back?'

Munkhan queried. 'The students?'

'Yes, what did they learn from their mission, to the other planets in their systems?'

'Fundamentally it was magnificent, quite inspiring really. I'm recommending to WIL, that we begin a similar program here. For every challenge there was an answer.'

Oats quickly asked. 'Can you give us some examples?'

'Well yes, yes of course. During their initiation and briefing induction, the students all found out, that they came from different backgrounds. The more I quizzed them, the easier it became. Some of their responses were.'

'Everyone makes mistakes, but why make the same ones, in the next generation. All of us have different futures, we want to pursue.' Then. 'Oh and there's no Prison planet.'

Oats interjected. 'Just a moment, we were advised there was a planet of Isolation.'

'Yes Oats, but it's not what you think. It is an address for those who have little respect for Natures laws. Some don't even have respect, for each other and then others who have little respect, for any communal laws at all.'

'It might surprise you to know, that this planet contains many of their original settlements. Thousands of generations ago it became a choice for many to stay or leave. We saw glimpses, of what it is like now.'

Michael added. 'Yes, we saw some visions, on the way to Tamaryn's galaxy. Sometimes hard, brutal and challenging, where Nature was seen as a resource rather than as a mentor. Forests have been cleared and water has been polluted. Respect for the environment, has been in decline there, for many generations.'

Oats asked. 'Yes, but what about the people, who are still there?'

'They are there, because they want to be and no one judges them, for their choices.'

Oats persisted. 'Yes, we heard about that, but what did the students see?'

'Well one of the first observations, was that there was little in the way of unity.'

Janet asked. 'Why aren't they united?'

'Well most of them have many different, competing personal interests. Their planet lives with a self-imposed, self-governing, staged regression.'

Janet was still looking for answers. 'Which means?'

'Well some students saw their society, as going backwards. It depends on how much they deviated from accepted natural behavior and what they considered as normal.'

Now Michael became more curious. 'Yes but, how does it work?'

'There are three stages if you like, of corrective settlements. Stage one is assisted behavioral recovery and stage two involves some restrictions.'

'And stage three?'

'You don't want to go there. It is an unregulated system for those who aren't willing to follow any civil law. It's like the ancient laws of the jungle, everyone for themselves.'

'How do their recovery laws work?'

Munkhan was heartened. 'Nature has rules. In their societies there are no half measures. You either have a moral direction, or you don't. These are the personal choices we all face. Children are shown character and integrity choices, including self-respect. These are learned choices, for an advanced global society. For them, to participate it is important to follow the traditions of guidance, found in early parental supervision.'

'It becomes a question of can you assimilate, with a community or not. This choice is yours. You can live within the confines of a cherished garden, or an area made desolate through the lack of any care, consideration or respect for others. Students see these life force rules, being played out in front of their eyes and they can decide.'

'Anyone who chooses to ignore the elementary characteristics of Nature, its values and the peaceful benefits, lives on this planet of Isolation.'

'Once again, they live without criticism. It becomes a choice for their children to adopt customary behavior or reject it. Think of it as if travelling on your own planet. Do you want to live in a barren desert or a botanical garden? It's a nurturing approach, which sees a like-minded unity, in a communal society of friendship.'

Oats muttered. 'And what of the alternatives, found there?'

Munkhan continued. 'There are other differences as well, including a combative approach, which confronts others, personal interests.'

Oats laughed. 'It seems like an easy choice to make. What did the students think?'

'This was the clear value found in this kind of self-educational revelation of choices. What was being questioned by each of them, were the tried and tested experiences over thousands of generations. Some choices do work and some don't.'

Michael smiled. 'There's a hint of conceptual vision here?'

'It's about survival. Civility is here for a reason and one day we will discover more of those reasons. However, if these children are to get there, in the generations to come, then they must learn how to survive. It's about learning how to live in peace together, giving future generations hope, while leaving the place behind, in a better shape than they found it. What is the point of having children, if there isn't this guidance?'

'The guiding aim, is to help nurture children to succeed, by watching carefully, listening to Natures messages and learning from each other, without, jumping to conclusions or engaging in petty, contentious disputes over trifling differences.'

'It seems so simple, when seeing the consequences of these choices.'

Munkhan smiled. 'Enough of Isolation's problems.'

Janet said. 'Yes, by contrast Tamaryn's home, was like a paradise.'

Munkhan added. 'That's where the students go next, when they get back. Tamaryn wants to see how the program is working, for future adaptions, revisions and changes.'

Oats smiled with a happy euphoria. 'It's, just wonderful there?'

Munkhan was also cheery. 'Yes I would love to go and see it, sometime.'

Munkhan then acknowledged. 'A pity about losing Pim.'

Michael was reflective. 'Yes, our affection is held in her youthful innocence, her warmth of character and her love of Nature. We may never find anyone else, like her.'

Our catchup with Munkhan paused, as Pim came outside to join us. Pim was in a happy mood about something. Maybe we would all discover that later.

Munkhan asked. 'Pim, what was Tamaryn's home like?'

Pim collected her thoughts as we kept chatting. 'It is truly a visionary paradise they share, Munkhan.'

Munkhan was becoming more fascinated. 'So how was your experience?'

'Have you ever stood in the grounds of a picturesque natural forest and tried to understand, why is it so? It is almost impossible to give this transient feeling of mystical silence and eternal serenity, a voice to unlock the secrets of universal existence?

'A natural influence that has endured in virtual silence, since before the time of mankind's own existence. There are many melodious sounds, within Nature's calming influence, but over a lifetime ask yourself, how well have any of us ever listened?'

Then Michael said. 'Individual existence has such a fleeting presence, in the history of time. One moment you're part of it and the next moment, you become a memory. Why are we here? What is our purpose? And what is the point of it all? We live, we love, we hope and we pass on. It all seems so hard to fathom and yet there it is? Along the way we have the chance to capture the natural beauty of existence, in so many other life forms. All of us have this one chance, to make a difference for ourselves.'

Michael asked. 'What difference, can one life matter, Pim?'

'Remember this truth. When loved ones leave us, the physical close experiences may become lost forever. However, it is also true that many kind memories from the past, live on, in the hearts of others. The loved ones left behind, are comforted and cheered on, with the fondness of these memories, from earlier times.'

Pim was then a little more reflective. 'Yes, Nature doesn't have a voice, but Nature will speak, to those of us who will listen. Peace can always be found, in a searching soul.'

Pim then said. 'We better move back inside, the students are coming back soon.'

We all agreed. 'Yes, why yes of course.'

49
Student Program to be Trialed in our Galaxy.

Back inside the students from Tamaryn's galaxy, were engaged in a discussion with Mharn and his friends, about the many experiences, in their outer regions.

Then Mharn quizzed. 'What is Nature like, on all your other planets?'

Each student took it in turn, to give their enthusiastic responses. 'Nature has given us many experiences, to reflect on. In our rain forests, carbon absorption from trees, gives us a path to survival. Ancient trees, teach us resilience, strength and stamina. Trees get caught in the sun and rain and yet do not complain.'

'Playful forest animals, teach us all, a good-natured temperament. Newly born offspring, demonstrate, a love for creative innocence. Parenthood has shown us a path to cheerfulness. Diversity of life, gives us a vision, into Nature's soul. With evolution, we have seen, an abundance of peaceful living experiences.'

'Our mountain high panoramas, reveal a stunning landscape of inspirational peace and calm, beauty and independence, living within self-sufficiency.'

'Again more contrasts with wilderness on the open plains, giving a diverse concept of cruelty and ferocity in the wild, exposing a brutality in natural existence of survival. Reproduction, shows the existence of tender hearted gentleness, to savagery in the wild. Freedom has become a choice, matched against survival, in a contest of wills.'

Another said. 'Morality and decency in Nature, is a behavioral characteristic, measured by the rights and wrongs, among our many choices.'

Then. 'Obscurity from the ocean depths, gives a myriad of other presences, yet to be interpreted and discovered. Water is our connection with Nature's universe.'

Another of the students then spoke up. 'You will see and judge for yourselves, whether some planets, have made the right decisions. Do they enjoy air and water quality, bonding of human companionships, with a shared social temperament?'

Janet asked. 'How did you discover all these natural laws? Is there a path for the survival of all these species and are there any impediments, to their existence?'

'Why that is the point of the mission, in the first place.'

Then another student spoke. 'The debates over choices and boundaries, within our societies, has always been about observing and conforming to natural law.'

'Some of the earlier laws discovered, are the easier ones to observe. While the more subtle and essential, harmonious laws for survival and existence, are discovered.'

'This is why inspiration and motivating global leadership, is so important for our planetary populations. Governance for the entire ecological system, which cannot speak for itself, lays at the feet of the sensible, the wise and the astute in decision making.'

Janet reflected. 'You all look so young and you have discovered this already?'

It was then that Marmuron shared a vision, she had discovered from her travels. 'Peace among us all, can be found, when searching with a receptive mind.'

There came a moment of silence, as the excited students tried to listen to Munkhan, talking to Michael and Oats. Munkhan asked. 'Oats, have you been given your next mission objectives?'

Pim then advised. 'WIL is coming here soon and we hope to find that out.'

Munkhan quietly reflected on this and the enthusiasm for adventure which was living in us all, as he said. 'I can't wait to get back there.'

Our shared smiles, grew into a laugh of eager anticipation, for our future travels.

One of the students became fascinated with Oats background. 'What was it like for you, at my age Oats?'

Oats was immediately caught off guard, having come from Earth. 'Well, Michael and I were students together.'

'Yes, but what brought you here?'

Oats' expression eased with some humor as he relayed once again the early exchanges in the science lab, all those years ago and Michael's long held dream of living with eternity, while discovering the greater cosmos. As Oats finished the students all seemed absorbed and fascinated. 'What was it like, meeting Tamaryn?'

'She is absolutely magnificent.'

The students became even more engaged as Janet quickly asked. 'What is it that makes you all, so openly cheery?'

All the students displayed a resiliently cheerful, buoyant and happy character. It was then that their leader spoke up. **'Nature gives the life we lead, just one chance and while age and time slowly takes these chances away, we are here now, for this time and for this moment and we will never have this chance, to be this young again.'**

Janet gasped. 'Wow that sounds so positively inspiring.'

The young student continued. 'We have learnt to seize every moment and every opportunity to be young at heart. To be free and to enjoy with impulsive spontaneity a liberated intellect, while watching Nature's influence, regenerating all around us.'

'Our life gives us one chance. We don't have your ability to continually renew Oats. So for us there remains one chance to exist and to be alive, so we always remember this ancient folklore. **'It doesn't matter how old you are, or what remains, of your time, we will never have this chance, to feel this young again.'**

Janet became captivated, at the wisdom, coming from one so young.

The attention for us all was quickly distracted, by the vision of WIL's arrival, which formed near the corner of their ornately decorated, private lounge. There was a great and muted respect, for his presence. WIL was greeted warmly by everyone there.

The excitement calmed, as WIL opened up and began to speak. 'We have some important news for you all. Given the enormous tasks facing Tamaryn's counselors, she has asked for our help, on an ongoing basis.'

50
Discovering, World Peace in Our Time.

WIL led the excited crowd out from the massive internal rooms in the Shi's suite, onto the expansive marbled, terraced balcony. The happy chattering between the guests continued, as everyone followed. Michael was about twenty steps ahead of the others and alone with WIL. Michael glanced toward the heavens and remained in awe, of the sheer size of this universal expanse and the unknown destinations, yet to be discovered.

WIL began, with this illuminating proposition. 'Intergalactic travel, adds another dimension to exploration, for our ancient societies, Michael. There are opportunities, in your future to explore, between our two galaxies. We need a mission commander, on an ongoing basis, to make frequent return trips, to all the outer lying systems, in both galaxies, if you feel you are up to this challenge?'

Michael's face was ecstatic. 'Good heavens, Wow.'

WIL wore, an amused and aging grin, as he watched the pure exhilaration, building on Michael's jubilant face. This was Michael's enduring, passionate and lifelong dream, coming true. To explore the many millions of star systems. Michael was clearly overcome, as he wondered how dear old Oats would react, when hearing of this great news. Janet and Marmuron, would also be thrilled. WIL smiled. 'Everything all right Michael?'

All Michael could repeat was. 'Oh Wow.' Michael just couldn't believe his luck with this opportunity. Of course WIL saw this reaction coming.

WIL remembered Michael's earlier dream, at the time when they first met. A fond and hopeful dream which coincided with WIL's plans for further galaxy explorations. Michael mumbled. 'I think Oats is going to have to sit down WIL, to hear this news.'

Michael also remembered the earlier caution from Pim. She had agreed to replace her son Mykron, as the mediator on the Council of First Kings on Kendagon. However, with these new responsibilities came many chances for Pim to visit both Velia and Mykron, on Prisium? This left an opening for another mentor to give Michael and Oats, the close counsel, of a galaxy historian, which would be needed on their future missions.

WIL also knew Munkhan had a growing passionate romance with Velia's sister on Prisium. Munkhan was secretly hoping for a chance to return and follow his own dreams. His recent mission, to Tamaryn's galaxy, had only been brief. WIL paused and could see all the adventurous aspirations, unfolding in front of him, coming together.

WIL waited with some amusement, for the others to catch up. On hearing of our new mission quests, Oats just exploded with enthusiasm. 'How absolutely fantastic.'

WIL was in good humor as he continued. 'Tamaryn has a great depth of understanding, on the evolution of Natural Forces. She, more than anyone else, will be able to help you unlock, the secrets of the stars and find answers to your many questions, which lie beyond the limits, of our own frontiers.'

Oats leapt at this thought. 'To uncover the missing pieces, to the greatest puzzles ever known and then discover how it all came together, from the beginning and why.'

Michael was almost speechless, as he agreed. 'Yes, Oats.'

There was an eruption of enthusiasm and cheering support for the adventures ahead, while Pim was trying to conceal her own excitement. Pim had known from the beginning of this mission, her plans were changing. It would begin a massive program of increasing exploratory quests, which had taken a generation to plan and Oats and Michael, could now see themselves becoming a growing part, of these evolving plans.

WIL's mood, remained jovial as he had planned much of this from the beginning. WIL then confided. 'Michael, both you and Oats will need a new mentor, an experienced galaxy historian, who may be motivated to join you now?'

Oats and Michael immediately glanced at their old friend Munkhan, who would be a tremendous help, with interpretive skills and the wisdom of cosmic understanding.

WIL laughed as he asked. 'Would you like to return to Prisium, Munkhan?'

Munkhan's face erupted with enthusiasm. 'Yes WIL, please, if I could.'

Oats found his voice, for their old friend, as tears of joy built on his face. 'It wouldn't be the same, without you Munkhan.'

Michael then added his own warmth and sincerity. For him it was an answer to a prayer. 'We would love to have you come with us, Munkhan.'

Munkhan was in high spirits. 'Thank you both, I would be thrilled to join you.'

Then Oats said. 'Michael, this is an answer, to the dreams we've always hoped for.'

Munkhan moved closer to Michael and Oats. The three friends erupted with hilarity and jubilation, gripping each other's arms warmly.

Janet had been watching these unfolding events and wasn't going to be left out as Marmuron giggled. 'Don't forget us, Oatsy. We're coming too.'

Oats had spent most of his life, chasing this dream of exploration and research and stretched his arms out, to hug his adored Marmuron, she was thrilled. Janet immediately came over and hugged Michael. Janet could remember their first meeting back on Earth, when she and Michael shared the same fascination, of discovering a life beyond. This richness of romance and adventure, had bonded with them, into their present research.

It was a wonderfully happy moment to be given this new chance, of many future encounters. WIL was increasingly amused at us all, jesting with each other and said. 'Michael, I want you to help Mharn with our student guests and show them some of our outer, local planetary settlements.'

Mharn, couldn't wait to go back and visit Tamaryn's galaxy again, as he looked fondly on Karina and asked warmly. 'Are we going?'

Karina understood the depth of this question, as she nodded and laughed. 'Yes.'

With Mharn now by her side and the chance to learn so much more, with his mission still to be completed, Karina melted lovingly into his arms. 'Remember, we're on our honeymoon of companionship, which lasts together and forever.'

Then WIL said. 'Michael, your next mission, leaves in two rotations of Kendagon.'

Michael's face lit up again. 'Thank you WIL, thank you.'

WIL then paused momentarily, as another purpose needed further explanation. Everyone remained in a state of quiet excitement. **'If populations only ever increase, then over population, will become a weakness for a planets Natural forces?'** Then WIL added. **'Advanced societies only colonize new planets, to give renewal and balance to Nature's evolution of the species, on a grander scale.'**

WIL continued **'The answers to the discovery of Nature's creation, are in front of us, not behind us. You have only seen planetary evolution, from a parochial vision. I ask you to consider** this process from a much larger perspective, on a galaxy wide scale. Then you will begin to understand creation better, from the beginning.'

Janet asked. 'How can you tell if a planet has been through a process of renewal?

'Look for signs of order, in the animal kingdoms on the planet, where natural evolution by species, seems to have been orderly. Look for the distribution of animal classes and flora and fauna varieties, where Nature enjoys uncharacteristic harmony. Also consider how well, the multiple types of species have been united and separated, populated and integrated, in an assembled and methodical way, by climate and by environment.' Then after a moment WIL said. **'Also consider if the class and number of species, looks like a galaxy wide sanctuary, for Nature's creatures, own protection.'**

This prompted an innocent observation from Marmuron. 'A collection of galaxy wide species, relocated onto other planet's over time, to rescue them from extinction.'

Oats mumbled. **'Good heavens, we've been looking at this, all wrong. We are not alone in the universe, we are representative of Nature's millions of species throughout the galaxy. Could this be the answer, which has eluded and confounded us, since the beginning of our time? There's no reason for racial hostility, any more. We live in an outer lying system, which is a sanctuary, for millions of our galaxies species.'**

Michael was stunned. 'I just couldn't believe this when it was suggested on our first mission, but it all makes sense now. **'Good Heavens, we are a global zoological sanctuary, for millions of Natures species, all protected on one planet, over time.** Just consider the well-ordered propagation of the classes of species. A vast planetary natural reserve, helped by a higher intelligence, as a refuge. At home, we have been far too focused on mythology, legends and fairytales in our ancient thinking?'

Then. 'Not just one single celled organism, but many species originating from our galaxy. There was a protective nurturing intelligence, of millions of species over time, by a higher intelligence, to support Nature's existence? This answers so many questions.'

'There are classes of species by water and by land mass, where the diversity, is remarkable. **Heat and light energy, doesn't just support our system, it supports many millions of other systems, throughout the universe.' This is the silent insightful messaging, no one is paying attention to. Why is it not possible, to just enjoy Nature's peaceful co-existence, like the creatures, in our forest regions? We need to revitalize, move on and restore global unity.'**

Janet was amazed. **'A living sanctuary on a global scale, who would have believed it?** This could also explain evidence of earlier intelligence on our planet. All the forests, oceans and jungle areas? I've never even considered this, as a possibility before. This is just so real, when you think about it. This is illuminating. If we were allowed to think for ourselves, we would have already worked this out by now. Then Janet breathed. **'Wow!'**

We are not alone, we are illustrative and representative of all life, across our galaxy?'

WIL continued. **'The battle to protect and preserve Nature's innocence, has been an eternal struggle, for us all.** Without renewal, Nature would cease to exist, as a cosmic force. This silent force, stimulates and inspires the reproduction of the species. In this endeavor, Nature faces many challenges, like meteor strikes, volcanic eruptions, fires, floods, droughts, famine and land clearing. We need to inspire others to help us, in this quest. Peaceful progress and harmony, is our larger mission quest.'

WIL sighed. **'There's an inherent and innocent beauty in Nature's universal struggle to survive. In understanding the hopes and dreams of this evolving process, we see the depth of Nature's, ultimate predicament and dilemma. Nature often**

reaches a turning point, throughout the ages, with stress levels, following reproductive surges.'

Then Michael asked. 'WIL, what is it, you and Tamaryn are searching for?'

WIL smiled. 'Michael, we are going back in time, to the beginning of time, itself. We are looking for the greatest of all primary intelligences, the creative origins, of particle matter itself. As all life is composed from elementary particles, this process began long before Nature, in any life form as we know it, ever began to exist.'

Oats reflected. **'Many at home are still asking if there is life on other planets and now we are searching for an origin, far greater than our own. It begins with the creation of particle matter and from there, a million other questions follow.'**

There were smiles everywhere as WIL announced. 'Michael, we wish to expand our student programs. Until our students understand more, about our greater cosmological reality, we would like to learn from Tamaryn's missions, in her larger planetary systems.'

'We want to establish, an energized intergalactic educational academy, for student graduates, where Mharn and his friends could help. Understanding the history of Natures impact on cultural evolution, with improving social unity, is part of this plan. Two rotations of Kendagon doesn't leave you all, much time.'

It was, an enormously happy moment for everyone, as WIL's aging image vanished, with a smile and a wave. The ten students felt inspired with the camaraderie, being displayed by the multitude of happy faces, all around them.

Their young lives were filled with optimism and hope, as they heard of WIL's plans and the new found team, including Munkhan. They felt enthusiastic about going back to visit the sage Tamaryn, an astute and visionary oracle in their own galaxy.

For them, she understood the silent intellect, hidden within the diversity of living species. That with Nature, none reigns supreme and that all life has a purpose. As to this greater purpose? Another of the many unknowns, which remains to be discovered.

Pim was delighted for her future chances, to see Velia and Mykron again and she couldn't wait to return there. Pim formed into a physical being, as Michael went to give her a hug, for all the friendship, she had shown and for the loving person which she was.

Michael was moved. 'Pim, there will always be a place for you, in our hearts.'

Pim smiled. 'I'll never be far away and we can always connect, in the Map Room.'

Oats and Marmuron came closer, with Janet as they all bonded for a last time. Marmuron was in tears now and it was catching as Pim said. 'You have been through so much, in your short life and recent experiences, Marmuron.'

Through her tearful reflections, Marmuron said. 'Yes, when I discovered my blood line, went all the way back to Tamaryn, it was just a humbling moment for me.'

Pim replied. 'You really must be looking forward, to going back there.' Then. 'Each new discovery, will be an inspiring and enlightening, moment for us all.'

Munkhan gripped Oats and Michael's hands again firmly, as they celebrated and rejoiced, at their good fortune. A future filled with exploration and adventure. 'This is without question, a magnificent and amazing moment, in our lifetimes.'

Pim smiled with cheerful happiness, as her physical form began to morph into an image once more and slowly fade away. Pim gave us a parting wave. 'Bye for now. See you all again soon.' The adventurers could now enjoy contact with Pim, anytime they wanted, through the portals, in the Map Room.

Janet united their heartfelt feelings, as she replied tearfully. 'It's been a lovely and enchanting experience Pim. Please remember us in your thoughts and keep in touch.' Pim's fading image, erupted with warmhearted happiness, as her vision then vanished.

There were a myriad of happy smiling faces. Oats and Michael now had Munkhan, their old friend, who was a brilliant galaxy historian, to help them. Janet and Marmuron were thrilled to return, to see the remarkably gifted oracle Tamaryn once more, with the ten student graduates. Mharn and Karina stood as one, in a loving embrace as they celebrated their many future joyful plans, together.

Oats noticed Marmuron was a little overcome. 'Everything okay Marmy?'

Marmuron's mind was a reflection of many happy thoughts, as she smiled back. She loved her companionship with Oatsy and had become great friends with Janet as she said. 'Thank you all very much. I just never would have believed, that this was all possible, unless I was here to experience it.'

Janet looked on caringly and came back fondly. 'You are most welcome.'

Oats was giving his lovely Marmuron a hug, as Janet cuddled up next to Michael. There were many great loves here. A building and warming excitement, for all their future voyages and adventures together, was coming from both girls.

Michael sensed Janet was in deep thought and asked, 'What's on your mind?'

Janet began to summarize her feelings. 'What a happy world our planet, could be?'

Janet had everyone's attention now as Oats asked. 'What do you mean, Janet?'

Janet was moved, both in the spirit of warmth and with a heart, full of compassion. 'To have a companion in life, to be near you and friends around, who can cheer you. This is worth something. There's no need for others to question or doubt you. We all come from different backgrounds. This is about finding a way to live together. Being influenced by leaders with character, who can find lasting peace. The heavens are a beautiful place to explore and it all begins, from our homes. Nature has shown us how a peaceful world could be a happier place, because peace comes with silence.'

Oats agreed. 'You are right Janet. One of the great truisms, we can all learn from with these universal forces, is silence itself. Nature doesn't have opinions, chastise or judge its species. There's a warmth of spirit, held in this idealistic ambience, over time. There's so much we can learn from Nature, if we just learn to listen. We can learn to be happy and we can learn about, warm hearted family values. We can learn to be friends and we can learn the essence of a peaceful co-existence, with a **world at peace**,'

A moment passed and Oats then quickly remembered the opportunity granted by WIL and exploded with excitement. 'No one has ever had this chance before, Michael!'

Michael, sensing the cheerfully optimistic mood, growing between them, clutched Oats' arms, at their continuing good fortune. It was hard to believe that all their hopes were now coming true. To explore life, between galaxies. Michael just radiated positive energy, while grinning happily, with this final remark. 'All our dreams of discovery, are in front of us Oats.'

The End

This series will be continued in

'Exploring the Living Forces, in Nature's Universe.'

References

I. Origins of Manuscripts, Compiled in the Holy Bible.

Origins of biblical history, shows the scriptures, date back to before the birth of Christ.

Some early historical biblical origins.

The Old Testament is from the original Hebrew Bible, the sacred scriptures of the Jewish faith, written at different times, between about 1200 BC., and 165 BC. The New Testament books were written by Christians, in the first century AD.

The Bible is the holy scripture of the Christian religion, purporting to tell the history of the Earth from its earliest creation, to the spread of Christianity in the first century A.D.

Both the Old Testament and the New Testament have undergone changes over the centuries, including the publication of the King James Bible in 1611 and the addition of several books, which were discovered later.

Old Testament

The Old Testament is the first section of the Bible, covering the creation of the Earth through Noah and the flood, Moses and more, finishing with the Jews being expelled to Babylon.

So the Bible's Old Testament is similar to the Hebrew Bible, which has origins in the ancient religion of Judaism. The exact beginnings of the Jewish religion are unknown, but the first known mention of Israel, is an Egyptian inscription from the 13th century B.C.

The earliest known mention of the Jewish god Yahweh, is in an inscription relating to the King of Moab, in the 9th century B.C. It is speculated that Yahweh was possibly adapted from the mountain god Yhw, in ancient Seir or Edom

Hezekiah

It was during the reign of Hezekiah of Judah in the 8th century B.C. that historians believe what would become the Old Testament began to take form, the result of royal scribes, recording royal history and heroic legends.

During the reign of Josiah in the 6th century B.C., the books of Deuteronomy and Judges were compiled and added. The final form of the Hebrew Bible developed over the next 200 years when Judah, was swallowed up by the expanding Persian Empire.

Septuagint

Following conquest by Alexander the Great, the Hebrew Bible was translated into Greek in the 3rd century B.C. Known as the Septuagint, this Greek translation was initiated at the request of King Ptolemy of Egypt to be included in the library of Alexandria.

The Septuagint was the version of the Bible used by early Christians in Rome.

The Book of Daniel was written during this period and included in the Septuagint at the last moment, though the text itself claims to have been written sometime around 586 B.C.

New Testament

The New Testament tells the story of the life of Jesus and the early days of Christianity, most notably Paul's efforts to spread Jesus' teaching. It collects 27 books, all originally written in Greek.

The sections of the New Testament concerning Jesus are called the Gospels and were written about 40 years after the earliest written Christian materials, the letters of Paul, known as the Epistles.

Paul's letters were distributed by churches, sometime around 50 A.D., possibly just before Paul's death. Scribes copied the letters and kept them in circulation. As circulation continued, the letters were collected into books.

Some in the church, inspired by Paul, began to write and circulate their own letters, and so historians believe that some books of the New Testament attributed to Paul were in fact written, by disciples and followers.

As Paul's words were circulated, an oral tradition began in churches telling stories about Jesus, including teachings and accounts of post-resurrection appearances. Sections of the New Testament attributed to Paul, talk about Jesus with a first-hand feeling, but Paul never knew Jesus except in visions he had and the Gospels were not yet written, at the time of Paul's letters.

The Gospels

The oral traditions within the church formed the substance of the Gospels, the earliest book of which is Mark, written around 70 A.D., 40 years after the death of Jesus.

It is theorized there may have been an original document of sayings by Jesus known as the Q source, which was adapted into the narratives of the Gospels. All four Gospels were published anonymously, but historians believe that the books were given the name of Jesus' disciples, to provide direct links to Jesus to lend them greater authority.

Matthew and Luke were next in the chronology. Both used Mark as a reference, but Matthew is considered to have another separate source, known as the M source, as it contains some different material from Mark. Both books also stress the proof of Jesus' divinity, more than Mark did.

The Book of John, written around 100 A.D., was the final of the four and has a reputation for hostility to Jesus' Jewish contemporaries. All four books cover the life of Jesus with many similarities, but sometimes contradictions in their portrayals. Each is considered to have its own political and religious agenda linked to authorship.

For instance, the books of Matthew and Luke present different accounts of Jesus' birth, and all contradict each other, about the resurrection.

Book of Revelation

The Book of Revelation is the final book of the Bible, an example of apocalyptic literature that predicts a final celestial war through prophecy. Authorship is ascribed to John, but little else is known about the writer.

According to the text, it was written around 95 A.D. on an island off the coast of Turkey. Some scholars believe it is less a prophecy and more a response to the Roman destruction of the Great Temple and Jerusalem.

This text is still used by Evangelical Christians, to interpret current events in expectation of the End Times, and elements of it find frequent use in popular entertainment.

Biblical Canon

Surviving documents from the 4th century show that different councils within the church released lists to guide how various Christian texts, should be treated.

The earliest known attempt to create a canon in the same respect as the New Testament was in 2nd century Rome by Marcion, a Turkish businessman and church leader.

Marcion's work focused on the Gospel of Luke and the letters of Paul. Disapproving of the effort, the Roman church expelled Marcion. Second-century Syrian writer Tatian, attempted to create a canon by weaving the four gospels together as the Diatessaron.

The Muratorian Canon, which is believed to date to 200 A.D., is the earliest compilation of canonical texts resembling the New Testament.

It was not until the 5th century that all the different Christian churches came to a basic agreement on Biblical canon.

The books that eventually were considered canon, reflect the times they were embraced as much the times of the events they portray.

During the Protestant Reformation in the 16th century, books not originally written in Hebrew but Greek, such as Judith and Maccabees, were excluded from the Old Testament. These are known as the Apocrypha and are still included in the Catholic Bible.

Gnostic Gospels

Additional Biblical texts have been discovered, such as the Gospel of Mary, which was part of the larger Berlin Gnostic Codex, found in Egypt in 1896.

Fifty further unused Biblical texts were discovered in Nag Hammadi in Egypt in 1945, known as the Gnostic Gospels.

Among the Gnostic Gospels, were the Gospel of Thomas—which purports to be previously hidden sayings by Jesus, presented in collaboration with his twin brother—and The Gospel of Philip, which implies a marriage between Jesus and Mary Magdalene. The original texts are believed to date back to around 120 A.D.

The Book of Judas was found in Egypt in the 1970s. Dated to around 280 A.D., it is believed by some to contain secret conversations, between Jesus and his betrayer Judas.

These have never become part of the official Biblical canon, but stem from the same traditions and can be read as alternative views of the same stories and lessons. These texts are taken as indications of the diversity, of early Christianity.

King James Bible

The King James Bible is possibly the most widely known edition of the Bible, though in England it is known as the "Authorized Version."

First printed in 1611, this edition of the Bible was commissioned in 1604 by King James I after feeling political pressure from Puritans and Calvinists, demanding church reform and calling for a complete restructuring of church hierarchy.

In response, James called for a conference at Hampton Court Palace, during which it was suggested to him that there should be a new translation of the Bible since versions commissioned by earlier monarchs, were felt to be corrupt.

King James eventually agreed and decreed the new translation should speak in contemporary language, using common, recognizable terms. James' purpose was to unite the warring religious factions through a uniform holy text.

This version of the Bible was not altered for 250 years and is credited as one of the biggest influences on the English language, alongside the works of Shakespeare.

The King James Bible introduced a multitude of words and phrases now common in the English language, including "eye for an eye," "bottomless pit," "two-edged sword," "God forbid," "scapegoat" and "turned the world upside down," among many others.

The King James Bible of 1604, remains the most popular translation in history.

II. The History of Religious Inquisitions

The Roman Empire has endured, for well over a thousand years and from AD325, the influence of the Roman Catholic Church, has only grown.

The first medieval episcopal inquisition, was established in the year 1184 by Pope Lucius III, for the purpose of doing away with dissent, building in the south of France. These Inquisitions became a powerful force for authority, set up within the Catholic Church to root out and punish heresy and they continue to the present day.

Inquisitions became famous for the persecution and oppression of ideas which deviated from the churches orthodox preaching and teachings. The 'Supreme Sacred Congregation' of the Roman and Universal Inquisitions, still exists today, though the name has changed to the 'Congregation for the Doctrine of the Faith.'

So why is all of this, so important now?

Rather than looking forward with a clear vision in a far sighted search for knowledge, biblical scholars have chosen to refer back to the history of mythology and legendary belief, while challenging the essential discoveries of Nicolaus Copernicus.

Since ancient times, humanity, has remained locked in this past, rather than forging ahead with an open mind, willing to explore the unknown discoveries of the future.

If biblical records truly are a fair record, reflecting actual history from the reality of a living and loving eternal God, then why is it necessary to have centuries of enforcement, exacting penalties over questions of faith, in this truth?

What is wrong with asking questions about our Natural reality, discovered by Copernicus? Why has it been necessary for the church to hold inquisitions for nine centuries to enforce spiritual obedience? If the claims in the Bible are correct, then why is there the need for centuries of oppressive compliance, to maintain this belief?

If there is nothing to hide, nothing to fear and no reason for concern from a loving God who created heaven and Earth in the first place as claimed, what is wrong with a civilized and open discussion, which tries to interpret and understand further research on topics of historical origins?

Why do we punish, discipline and reprimand those, for any discussion on new evidence, uncovering the universal expanse or, what lies beyond our frontiers?

It seems that the masses among humanity are being programed and controlled to think, act and behave in a compliant way to enforce a conforming obedience. This instructive guidance, is from just one of twenty major religious orders, on our planet.

We celebrate and explore new discoveries in transport, telecommunications, travel and medical breakthroughs just to name a few, while the church protects instruction of ancient mythology? Is the church there, to just protect this history of fables, imagery and mythology or to control the masses?

Yes, these are some of many questions which remain, as to why it is so?

Voltaire

'To learn who rules over you, simply find out who you are not allowed to criticize.'

Voltaire - (François-Marie Arouet, 21st November 1694 - 30th May 1778), known by his non de plume. Voltaire: was a French enlightenment writer, historian, and philosopher, famous for his wit and his criticism of Christianity - especially the Roman Catholic Church - as well as his advocacy for Freedom of speech, freedom of religion, and the separation between church and state.

Voltaire was a prolific writer, who was one of the first authors to become renowned and internationally commercially successful. He was an outspoken advocate for civil liberties and was at constant risk from the strict censorship laws of the Catholic French monarchy. He satirized intolerance of religious dogma, and the French institutions of his day. Voltaire was imprisoned in the Bastille from 16th May 1717 to 15th April 1718 in a windowless cell with ten-foot-thick walls.

Since before the times of Voltaire, intellectual enlightenment has been blocked by the protective driving forces, of Catholic Church inquisitions. While lifting the soul and spirits of humanity, religious instruction has held back the tide, of advancing progressive thought. This continued devotion to an ancient concept of mythology, needs to be reconsidered, for the future of our planet and our children.

Many ancient philosophers were prepared to accept that existence, was the result of creation by deities. If this was so, then why do we need a church bureaucracy to control the course of this belief, for over nine centuries to the present day? Apart from mythical images, where is there any hard evidence that a God in human form, actually exists or created anything? This is what the church has been protecting and hiding since AD325. The mythology and the legends from the past.

For those with an open mind, there remains a future to discover. It's a struggle against the endless wars of cruelty, persecution and oppression. It's a battle all humanity must win to find peace, where co-existence with harmony is no longer just a dream. We need to listen to Nature's silent messaging, which sustains life with enduring calm and peaceful happiness. Yes, we want our human race to be happy again. It is not too late or too much to hope for, is it?

Has humanity taken some wrong turns according to our long records of written history? Yes, maybe we have, however it is never too late for us to uncover these past myths, discover a visionary new way forward and for all of us, to recover from the mind control, which has kept many of us, still living in the past.

Our race needs a global transition, to a more peacefully united and harmonious co-existence, between all creatures and cultures. Global peace is within our reach, if we all take a step back and then move forward, together.

III. What Else was discovered from Galileo's Time?

1. In the beginning, if God the Father Almighty, created Heaven and Earth, he would have known that the sun was at the center of our solar system and not have to be informed of this, by Nicolaus Copernicus in 1543?
2) The underlying truth about orbiting spheres, exposed by Copernicus in 1543, faced suppression and concealment by the church.
3) That all historical texts, parchments and early literature from tales in fables, folklore, legend and myth implying contact with God including any words attributed to Abraham, Moses and all other prophets, prior to 1543, emanated from times when the Earth was thought to be, at the center of the Heavens.'
4) Then it follows that the existence of many ancient Gods and Goddesses prior to 1543, began from earlier created and entrenched beliefs, in myths, legends and folklore.

5) Further, that these ancient beliefs, taught throughout history to children in Galileo's time, are still being taught hundreds of years later, to our own children today.
6) That heaven and hell are parochial examples of emotive and idealistic make-believe. An imaginative concept, conceived in the minds of ancients to help control the behavior and influence the choices of the regional provincial villagers, in their time.
7) That belief in Galileo's time, did not understand the weightlessness and size of orbiting spheres, around a central solar mass. Further, that inquisitions were set up to suppress any changes in discoveries, in order to protect ancient biblical belief.
8) This was the extent to which control over enlightenment was prepared to go, in order to protect the ancient vision of the Roman Empires, 'One True God'.

IV. The Lasting Influences of the Roman Empire.

Some important times in Earth's history, to help us understand the present.

I. **Jesus of Nazareth - c. 1 BC – c. AD 26/28** ~ the recording of the birth and death of Jesus Christ under Roman rule and the early embracing of ethical choices for Christian moral values.

II. **AD 325** ~ Under Constantine 1, the Roman Empire advanced the creation of early Christian theological doctrine, through the Council of Nicaea. This was the first effort to reach unity of beliefs and consensus through an assembly, representing all of Christendom. The main achievements were the settlement of the relationship between the Son of God and God the Father. The formation of the Nicene Creed and establishing the uniform observance, of the date of Easter.

III. **AD 381** ~ the first Council of Constantinople added to the creed of belief to give in part the following. 'We believe in one God, the Father Almighty, Maker of Heaven and Earth, and of all things visible and invisible.' This idealistic concept of belief, held, that the Earth was at the center of the Heavens.

IV. **Muhammad - AD 570 - AD 632** ~ Known as the 'Holy Prophet' to Muslims, almost all of whom consider him to be the final prophet of God. The Quran formed the basis of Islamic religious belief.

V. **The First printed Bible - AD c. 1450** ~ The Gutenberg Bible was the first major book using mass-produced moveable metal type, printed in Europe. Widely praised for its high aesthetic and artistic qualities, the book written in Latin has an iconic status.

VI. **The greatness of the Roman Empire, still lives with many of us today.**

V. True insanity of war and persecution, over the centuries.

Lands confiscated, by the Roman Empire.

I. 'Were never won, jurisdictional authority was imposed and enforced.'

II. 'Control over occupied civilian populations, placed restraints on their liberty.'

III. 'Imperial wealth was not built, it was seized, taxed, embezzled and stolen.'
IV. 'Citizens who were free born, suffered from cruelty, persecution and slavery.'
V. 'While religious doctrine and feats of progressive change can be touted, the tyranny of repression, across the captured empire, lasted for centuries.'
VI. 'What has been memorized and often repeated, is the Empires greatness'
VII. 'What has been forgotten and almost ignored, is the road to this greatness.'
VIII. 'It is now time, to recall the origins of this greatness and move on.'
IX. 'To observe the universal greatness, in the millions of systems before us.'
X. 'And witness the silence and true splendor, held within the Natural force.'

VI. Mythologies and Legends, in the Search for Truth.

Humanities gift in life, has been our naturally given intelligence to engage with an enquiring mind. To be curious about the many unknowns and to unlock further enlightenment. To advance the study of science as there is still so much more to discover, outside of Earth's parochial existence. Since the beginning of recorded history, our race has struggled to understand and interpret the depth of Nature's origins on our planet. Our ancient records, have tried to explain Earth's natural reality, with myth and legend from our earliest of times.

World Peace in Our Time: *The Logic behind Universal Creation*

I. The Holy Bible records a belief in the birth of Eve, from Adam's rib.
II. In A.D.325 scholars in Roman times believed that the Earth was at the center of the Heavens.
III. In A.D. 1492 many believed that Columbus would sail over the edge of our planet, in his efforts to find the new world.
IV. In A.D. 1543 Nicolaus Copernicus found that the Sun was at the center of our solar system of planets.
V. In A.D.1632 Galileo Galilei faced a religious inquisition and held by the church for agreeing that the Sun is at the center of our system of planets.
VI. In A.D. 1856 Charles Darwin theorized that more than a million species on Earth originated from a single celled organism, about 3.5 billion years ago. Consider this thought, that a cell from one species, can create more than a million other different species over time including all the varieties of dinosaurs, trees, grasses, all animal classes and sea creatures. Really?

So, in the last five hundred years, humanity has discovered that the Earth in not flat and that our world is not at the center of our local planetary astronomical region.

While the history of our ancient beliefs cannot be changed, they form an integral part of our multiple cultural heritages, becoming a useful stepping stone, into the future of an advancing age for the inquiring mind and the scientific community.

There are still so many critical questions looking for answers and they are not found by delving into past edicts, proclamations and empirical decrees. Ancient empires used their authority to mold the thinking of their citizens to create order and civility.

The Roman patrician, senatorial and equestrian classes, guided the plebeians on laws to obey and what to believe. Created belief has stifled genuine illumination, for more than a thousand years. Enlightenment with innocent curiosity, will help advance our understanding of Natures universal forces. Our planets undiscovered last frontier, remains a revelation to behold and has engaged the most gifted minds among us.

In 325A.D. Rome wanted transformational change, to unite their empire away from an ancient history, built around many cultural pagan gods. The patricians believed that to unify their empire, change began with a new idea. Their vision was to adopt a more agreeable universal reality, as they perceived it, in their time.

For the Roman Empire, the ambition was to create 'Peace in Their Time'. This new vision would preserve Rome's greatness by being forgiven for their long history of brutality, wars and conflicts. This peace would be brought about by establishing guidelines, giving compassionate harmony between the plebeians with belief in a 'One True God'. This would be administered by the bishops, following creeds of belief.

In the last seventeen hundred years human knowledge has advanced considerably, motivated by great minds like Copernicus and Darwin. However civilization still lives with many ancient beliefs, leaving humanity with many ongoing global conflicts. For thousands of years, philosophers have been searching for answers to, 'Why it is so?'

From our ancient times, religious doctrines, have played an important part in the global civilization of humanity as a species. While many human endeavors in the sciences, communications, finance and travel have advanced over time; humanities interpretation of our origins, has become stalled and frozen in time, by acceptance of the many entrenched ancient beliefs. These concepts remain buried in our past.

World Peace in Our Time: *The Logic behind Universal Creation*

Since before the times of Nicolaus Copernicus, inquisitions have driven inquiring minds into hiding. **But not anymore.** Now is the time to speak up, as evidence from recent research has uncovered new credible answers to -

1) The Origin of the Species, on Earth and are we alone in the universe?
2) Why do we have millions of species, on a safely positioned planetary body, within a sheltered orbiting distance from solar energy? Yes why is it so?
3) The logical inconsistencies, hidden inside our early, 'History of Belief'.
4) Global enlightenment, giving a united future, for all of our children.
5) And, can we all take a small step back, to become an 'Advanced Global Society'
6) And most importantly the why, in all of this?

'World Peace in our Time' re-examines the logic of our history, which uncovers a slightly different view of our origin, than those held in many of our parochial records.

This logical evidence is compelling and is critical, to mankind's understanding of our universe. If world peace on Earth is ever to be found, then a global effort is needed to go beyond the many myths and legends from our past which have caused division among our ancient cultures. Ask, why our children are taught and trained to believe, from an early age, rather than being taught to question and research for answers to solve our many remaining cosmological unknowns?

The quest for global peace can only be found, by correctly interpreting insightful answers, from our planets cultural and historical past. Everyone has this choice. To live in the past, or discover the reality of the past, the realism of the present and then take a leap into the future. One day, humanity may well go beyond parochial thinking and our children will be able to learn and to question, once more.

There will be those among us who love Nature. The innocence and the fascinations of changing seasons, changing colors and changing tides. There's an inbuilt enjoyment in watching the evolution of all living things. Welcome, to the future of enlightenment.

VII. Please Consider the Following Logic, for a Moment.

From the records in the Holy Bible, 'It is written' that at the time of Jesus's 'Last Supper' the Roman authorities did not know who Jesus was. Yet these records were altered in A.D.325. At that time it was also claimed that Jesus's mother Mary was a virgin at the time of Jesus's birth and so Jesus became the 'Son of the One True God'. From this high position, Jesus then forgave Rome, for all of their past sins against humanity.'

'Yes, but what is your point?'

'Think about it. If the Roman Empire did not know who Jesus was at the time of his 'Last Supper', how could they possibly know in A.D.325 that at the time of Jesus's birth, his mother Mary, was a virgin? It does not make logical sense, unless you accept that this whole revision of his existence as the 'Son of God' was to forgive the Roman Empire. **'Forgive them Father for they know not what they do.'** This became part of Rome's quest for transformational change, to continue Rome's greatness, into a more peace loving and compassionate empire, offering hope to the many from A.D.325.'

'Yes but.'

'Look, just for a moment consider the evidence. In A.D.325, how could the First Council of Nicaea know that a woman 325 years earlier, had conceived a child through unnatural circumstances? Our thinking minds on this have been shut down by the institutionalized programing of belief, over fifteen hundred years 'Because it is written'.

'The elementary science of reproduction, has taught us that Nature's existing laws relating to the birth of progeny, never alter. Nature's process is ageless and timeless. This fabled and imaginary observation held by the Council at Nicaea in A.D.325 was founded, purely to advance Rome's orchestrated vision, to forgive the Roman Empire's vast history, of brutality and abuse. Just think this all through for a moment.'

And after a moment the logic began to set in and Nature's thinking mind, began to reason for itself again.

'Can we please, just go over all of that again?'

VIII. Some Challenges to Aspects of Religious History.

1. Nicolaus Copernicus (1473 – 1543)

Copernicus was a Renaissance mathematician and astronomer who formulated a model of the universe - that placed the sun, rather than the Earth at the center. The publication of this model in his book 'De revolutionibus orbium coelestium' (On the Revolutions of the Celestial Spheres) just before his death in 1543 is considered a major event in the history of science. It triggered the Copernican Revolution, making an important contribution to scientific research.

The Copernican Revolution redefined elementary and fundamental aspects of history with an analytical and logical evolution of thought. The impact of this discovery formed the basis of our research, to reveal the differences between many of our ancient mythical beliefs and the burning desire for an evolving wisdom, with an understanding and insight, for global peace and unity.

2. Galileo Galilei (1564 – 1642)

Was an Italian natural researcher and astronomer. Galileo is a central Renaissance figure in the transition from natural philosophy to modern science in the conversion to a scientific revolution. Galileo, is considered the father of modern science, he made major contributions to the fields of physics, astronomy, cosmology, mathematics and philosophy.

By 1615 Galileo's writings on heliocentrism had been submitted to the Roman Inquisition, and his efforts to interpret the Bible were seen as a violation of the Council of Trent. Attacks on the ideas of Copernicus had reached a head, and Galileo went to Rome to defend himself and Copernican theory. In 1616, an Inquisitorial commission unanimously declared heliocentrism to be "foolish and absurd in philosophy".

At the time, the church believed the Aristotelian geocentric view, that the Earth was at the center of the universe and that all heavenly bodies, revolved around the Earth, despite the use of Copernican theories, to reform the calendar in 1582.

So to be clear, up until the times of Copernicus, the church of the 'One True God' had believed that the Earth was at the center of the universe. The ancient views on the positioning of heavenly bodies, had come from Aristotle (384B.C.-322B.C.). Galileo defended heliocentric views, placing the sun at the center of our heavens.

Galileo was summoned to Rome in A.D.1632 to appear before a Roman Inquisition, a judicial procedure established by the papacy. Galileo was found "vehemently suspect of heresy" though never formally charged, relieving him from facing corporal punishment. Further, of having held the opinions that the Sun lies motionless at the center of the universe. That the Earth is not at its center and that one may hold and defend an opinion as probable after it has been declared contrary to Holy Scripture. He was required to 'abjure, curse and detest' those opinions.

He was sentenced to formal imprisonment at the pleasure of the Inquisition. On the following day, this was commuted to house arrest, which he remained under, for the rest of his life. His offending Dialogue was banned; and in an action not announced at the trial, publication of any of his works was forbidden, including any he might write in the future.

3. Isaac Newton (1642 – 1727)

An English physicist and mathematician (described in his own day as a 'natural philosopher') who is widely recognized as one of the most influential scientists of all time and as a key figure in the scientific revolution. His book 'Philosophiae Naturalis Principia Mathematica' ("Mathematical Principles of Natural Philosophy"), first published in 1687, laid the foundations for classical mechanics. Newton also made seminal contributions to optics and shares credit with Gottfried Leibniz, for the invention of calculus.

4. Charles Darwin (1809 -1882)

Was an English Naturalist who published his theory of evolution in 1859 – speculating how Mankind evolved from cellular life forms. At the time, his research and publication led to bitter controversy, but his greatest contribution was to begin the exchange of ideas and debates away from a history of belief, in ancient creationism.

Best known for his contributions to the science of evolution. His proposition that all species in life have descended over time from common ancestors is widely accepted, and considered a foundational concept in science. Published in 'On the Origin of the Species' circa 1858. A theory to establish evolutionary descent as the dominant explanation for the diversification of life on Earth and in Nature. Then in 1871 he examined human evolution and sexual selection in 'The Descent of Man' a theory to establish the evolution from primates to quadrupeds and bipeds.

At the present time ~ The Origin of the universe, in cultural societies still remains an almost timeless struggle, over competing versions of parochial theory and belief. To this day, the early Roman empires influence, still lives on with many.

IX. The Origin of the Species, in the Universe.

Ever been curious to know how the origin of matter, began in the universe, since the beginning? This has been a researcher's quest, since the earliest of ancient times. Science, is getting closer to resolving, this remarkable enigma.

To begin with, the logic so far, is fascinating. Almost 99% of the mass of the human body is made up of six elements: oxygen, carbon, hydrogen, nitrogen, calcium and phosphorus.

Only about 0.85% is composed of, another five elements: These are potassium, sulfur, sodium, chlorine and magnesium. All eleven are necessary for life. The remaining elements are trace elements only, of which more than a dozen are thought, on the basis of good evidence, to be necessary for life.

All of the mass, of the trace elements put together, (less than ten grams for a human body) do not add up to the body mass of magnesium, the least common of the eleven, non-trace elements. So, we need to reconsider past history and ancient concepts.

World Peace in Our Time: *The Logic behind Universal Creation*

1. Humanity and all of our past images, going back to the earliest of origins, are composed, from this elementary particle matter.
2. Humanity is just one species of Nature, not the creators of this living force. So, on a time scale, Nature's origins, came long before human species evolved, as a life form in our universe. It then follows that any human image, came after the creation of elementary matter, not before it. This logic, is breathtakingly obvious.
3. So, we need to go back beyond 2,000 years ago and beyond all past cultures, before the formation of our planet. Before galaxies evolved and star systems were formed. Even before the often referenced, 'Big Bang Theory' and before elementary matter itself, was created.
4. All the way back in time, to the beginning of time, where we need answers to two fundamental questions, in the first of many millions of questions which follow.
5. Firstly; the immense and seemingly endless, universal vacuous and empty expanse. How did this massive vacuum develop and evolve, in the first place?
6. Secondly; the origins of elementary particle matter, which helped fill a small part of this great void. Under what circumstances did elementary matter first form?
7. In evaluating the origins of particle matter, the issue is a question of what, not who. There were no life forms, no air to breathe, and no water to drink and no life forms of any description, in existence.
8. The contents of the universe is composed of elementary particles which evolved, in their own time of origin. From this time, solids, liquids and gasses began to form long before animal classes, mineral compositions and flora and

fauna classes began. Forces of gravity, could not act on matter until matter itself actually formed. It is impossible for a human God like figure, to have created life, in the beginning, if one follows this logical path and time line.

9. It is not a question of a male or female deity motivations or mandates, in the earliest stages, of origin. As you can see from the above, human forms, came much later and are composed, from elementary particle matter.
10. So the question, becomes a question of what. That is, what were the circumstances and events, which created elementary particle matter in the first place? Giving us gasses, liquids and solids, evolving into classes of minerals, vegetables and life forms, throughout the universe?
11. From here, there are a million other questions, but for now, there were definitely no God particles, in the earliest formations of matter, in the universe. The searching and gifted minds among us, must come to understand this. In the beginning, the evidence is clear, Nature as a life force in any form, did not exist.

Howard Dimond

CPSIA information can be obtained
at www.ICGtesting.com
Printed in the USA
BVHW090231170922
647223BV00011B/837